Sponsored by **IBM**

Planning for Student Services:

Best Practices for the 21st Century

Edited by

Martha Beede and Darlene Burnett

PUBLISHED BY
Society for College and University Planning
ANN ARBOR, MICHIGAN

 Society for College and University Planning
Ann Arbor, MI 48104

ISBN 0-9601608-9-2

Contents

Foreword   **v**

Acknowledgments   **vii**

PART 1   Creating a Student-Centered Environment

INTRODUCTION: The Compelling Case for Change   **3**
Martha Beede and Darlene Burnett

1   Student Service Trends and Best Practices   **5**
Martha Beede

2   Trends in Support Services for Distance Learners   **13**
Barbara Krauth

PART 2   Redesign as the Change Agent

3   The Reengineering of Enrollment Services: Four Departments Become One   **21**
Regina Kleinman

4   Reengineering Student Administrative Services   **29**
Madge Lewis

5   Project Delta: Planning a New Student Services Model   **37**
Frank B. Campanella and Rita R. Owens

6   The Evolution of Enrollment Services   **47**
Linda M. Anderson and William F. Elliott

7   Transforming With a Learner-Based Redesign   **55**
Karen Hayward, Keith A. Pedersen, and Floyd Visser

8   Reengineering Admission Services   **65**
Robert Bontrager

PART 3 Technology as the Change Agent

9 From In-line to Online:
Transforming Student Services   **73**
Darlene Burnett and Christian Pantel

10 Student Services: A Broad View   **79**
David E. Hollowell

11 Project 2000: A Web-Based
Student Planning System   **87**
Gary L. Kramer and Erlend D. Peterson

12 Virtual Access to Student Information   **97**
Mark McConahay

13 Enhancing Transfer Student Services
Through the Web   **107**
Michael E. McCauley

14 Student Development Model as
the Core to Student Success   **113**
Buddy Ramos and Dick Vallandingham

15 Student Services × 13:
A Consortial Approach   **119**
Vicky Seehusen

PART 4 Planning for Success: Key Considerations for Successful Transformation

16 Customer-Based Transformation   **127**
Stephen W. Klenk

17 Change Management   **133**
Earl H. Potter III

Index   **141**

Foreword

∎ ∎ ∎ ∎

How important are student services to a higher education institution? They are, in a word, essential. Student services, from admissions and enrollment to financial aid and advising, reflect the importance an institution places on its customers—the students. Those services even extend to the community as a whole, anyone who comes into contact with the institution. Whether the experience is expedient and pleasant or drawn out and difficult has a direct impact on the student's—or the public's—perception.

Like every other area of higher education, student services is undergoing a transformation due to external trends and limitations of the traditional student services model. Institutional planners, senior administrators, and student service professionals may see this transformation as a great opportunity or great threat. The authors of this book see great opportunity.

They provide insight into the rationale behind, and the processes for, adapting a student-centered environment for student services. In each chapter, experts and administrators, all IBM Best Practice partners, explain the particular challenges their institutions faced and the methods they employed, using process redesign and technology, to make change happen. It is a practical guide—a collection of how-to stories and case studies that reaffirms the importance of cross-disciplinary teamwork and communication.

The Society for College and University Planning (SCUP) is an umbrella organization well suited to publish a book about integrated planning. SCUP members span multiple planning disciplines—from academic, information technology, and facilities planning to fiscal and resource allocation—and share the philosophy that cross-boundary planning is integral to the health and vitality of higher education.

As it is unwise to look at one's field of study or profession in a vacuum, relevant trends and transformation will initially be discussed in a broad context to link what is happening in student services to the driving forces of change.

This book is meant to help planners, administrators, and student service professionals gain a better understanding of the changes emerging in student services and demonstrate how innovative leaders are responding to these challenges successfully. No single approach will work for every institution, and outcomes are never guaranteed. To succeed, an institution must create a workable plan and then designate the resources to make it happen. More important, every group that will be affected by the change, from administrators to faculty to students and even to the community at large, has to be considered and consulted. Their impressions and reactions will guide the process.

As you embark on your journey into the 21st century, I hope this book will be a valuable resource for your planning efforts by giving you real, grassroots—but forward-thinking—examples of how to adapt your current environment to these changing requirements.

David Bellamy
Practice Executive
PeopleSoft Student Solutions

Acknowledgments

■ ■ ■ ■

The editors would like to thank the IBM Best Practice Partners who have contributed to this book as well as those partners who have participated in the forum over the years. Their innovative ideas, ability to look toward the future, and courage to take the road less traveled have been an inspiration. It has been an honor and has been personally and professionally rewarding to have had the opportunity to work so closely with them. The editors would also like to thank SCUP, particularly Sharon Morioka for her patience and perseverance, for making this book possible. Finally, the editors would like to thank Dave Bellamy, Kris Hafner, Steve Klenk, Danuta McCall, Elaine Pelaia, and Steve Provost, who demonstrated the benefits of a cross-functional work team and laid the groundwork for the IBM Best Practices work in 1996.

The Society for College and University Planning wishes to acknowledge the contributions of the following people in the preparation of this publication: Reviewers Peter Balbert, Trinity University, and Mark Oromaner, Hudson County Community College; Publications Advisory Committee liaison Deborah Allen Carey, Town of Amesbury, Massachusetts; designer Lori Young, Les Cheneaux Design; production artist Marc Johns; and proofreader Sandy Cyrus.

Part 1:

Creating a Student-Centered Environment

Introduction

*Martha Beede and
Darlene Burnett*

The Compelling Case for Change

Trends in student services today are being driven by changing demographics, the advent of the information age, and globalization. The model for higher education, a model that has remained relatively stable for more than a century and that we have grown accustomed to, is being challenged and forced to adapt to this rapidly changing environment. As a result, dramatic changes are occurring in how we deliver student services to meet the requirements of today's learner.

The traditional model for student services is organized by function, with each department focusing on a specific student service area—admissions, financial aid, registration, billing, and advising. These areas, which are required to manage students' nonacademic interactions with an institution, are often referred to as functional silos because they are not integrated. In the traditional model, students often go from one office to another, frequently waiting in line to get answers to questions or complete a form.

Martha Beede, senior consultant for IBM Global Education, assists higher education institutions in improving service and efficiency through organizational, process, and technology changes. She specializes in helping institutions redesign their student service operations to meet the demands of today's environment. She holds a master's from Northeastern University and a bachelor's from the University of Vermont.

Darlene Burnett is senior consultant with IBM Education Consulting & Services. During the past 10 years, she has helped colleges and universities solve problems and implement technology and services in administrative and academic computing. She has a bachelor's in business administration from Pittsburg State University and an MBA in organizational behavior from the University of Missouri.

Changing demographics have challenged the traditional model, with the number of nontraditional student populations increasing dramatically over the past 10 years. Enrollment projections from the National Center for Education Statistics (NCES 1995) indicated that by 1998 the number of students on college campuses who were 35 and over would surpass those in the 18- to 19-year-old population—the group that most campuses have traditionally viewed as their core clientele (Green 1996). Therefore, the demand for services any time and any place has evolved so these students can balance their professional and personal responsibilities with their academic pursuits.

An additional challenge is that traditional-age students have grown up with technology in a fast and responsive world and are comfortable with self-service options that allow them to have a world of information, literally, at their fingertips. Their skills and expectations are different from those who have not grown up with the Web, e-mail, and voice mail. As technology continues to advance at a rapid rate students will demand services that meet their lifestyle needs and expectations for service delivery.

Higher education institutions face yet another challenge—an increasingly competitive market for students—as institutions, governments, and businesses introduce options such as virtual universities, corporate universities, mass customization of programs, and distance education.

The traditional model also presents challenges to senior administrators in their decision-making processes. They often experience delays and significant backlogs when they request administrative data, and they cannot easily retrieve information because it is fragmented in multiple places across various systems. Additionally, the functional silos often have different reporting lines that prevent institutions from providing seamless, integrated services or a common vision.

Institutions are also under increasing financial pressure. Administrative costs continue to soar, with tuition outpacing families' and students' ability to pay. Since 1975, administration in higher education grew at more than three times the rate of student enrollment (Heller and Eng 1996). Nationally, the annual cost of attending one year at a private university rose from 29 percent of median family income to almost 48 percent on average over the past 20 years. During the same period, the cost of attending one year at a public university rose from 13 percent to 16 percent of median family income, while public two-year college costs annual cost remained at between 9 percent and 10 percent. When adjusted for inflation, median family income rose almost 10 percent, public university costs rose 34 percent, and private university costs rose 88 percent (Marks 1996). Institutions are recognizing that this trend is not sustainable and have responded by initiating redesign projects to streamline administrative services and reduce costs.

As institutions began to respond to pressures of changing demographics, declining enrollments, increased administrative costs, decreased funding, and increased competition for students, they took a closer look at their infrastructures and recognized that their organizations were expensive and not student-centric. The models in place had evolved because of the increasing complexity of administrative requirements and the inherent limitations of technology that was available at the time systems were implemented. The advent of newer technologies began addressing some of these problems by allowing students to make routine transactions through touch-tone telephones, automatic teller machines, kiosks, and, ultimately, the Web.

There is now a shift in the delivery of student services from the traditional model to a more integrated model. This book will present the student service trends that have resulted from these external and internal pressures and will provide examples of how innovative institutions have addressed these challenges as they move into the 21st century.

REFERENCES

Green, Kenneth C. 1996. The Changing Profile of Undergraduate Business Students. *Journal of Career Planning and Employment* (Spring): 21–26.

Heller, K., and L. Eng. 1996. Why College Costs So Much, Pushing Man out of the Market. *Philadelphia Inquirer*, 31 March.

1

Martha Beede

Student Service Trends and Best Practices

IBM Best Practices Study

The IBM Best Practice Partner group was created in 1996, when the IBM Education Consulting Team experienced an increasing number of requests for assistance in redesigning student services. To better understand the issues, trends, and best practice models for student services, we surveyed professional associations and conducted peer surveys. Through this process, we identified the projects that were the most innovative in improving student services through technology, process, or organizational changes. We asked the institutions identified to submit abstracts and selected 15 projects that met our best practice criteria. During a think tank–type session with those institutions, we established a collaborative vision for student services in the 21st century.

That first session has evolved into an open forum that has grown more than tenfold. The forum is specifically designed to encourage dialogue and sharing among best practice partners and provide them with the opportunity to present best practice projects and host discussions on emerging student service areas. The partners continue to meet after the open session to share the progress they have made on their campuses and the lessons they have learned. They also spend time looking at models outside the field of higher education because, to quote Ralph Waldo Emerson, "The field cannot be seen well from within the field." These best

practice models from outside the industry spur partners to think creatively and to continue to look to the future.

When the group first met, the projects its members were undertaking were just beginning, so the outcomes of the new approaches to student service delivery were unknown. These institutions have now demonstrated success by fully implementing many of their innovative services, hosting hundreds of site visits annually, and achieving successful and measurable outcomes of their work. The group members and their projects have become a great resource for each other and for other institutions traveling down the path to improving student services. This book presents some of the projects of the IBM Best Practice Partners. Information on all of the IBM Best Practice Partners, the Best Practice Study, and the Innovation in Student Services Forum is available at www.ibm.com/solutions/education/highered/students.

Each institution seems to have addressed the challenges in a different way. However, upon closer examination, these transformation projects tend to fall into two categories: those that have used technology as the change agent and those that have used redesign efforts as the change agent. There isn't just one way to transform your student service operations. Each of the approaches discussed in this book has been equally successful, and you will find pieces that may apply directly to your institution. It is also important to recognize that your institution may require additional approaches depending on its specific needs.

Redesign as a Change Agent

A variety of approaches have been advocated to address the pressures higher education faces today, including quality initiatives, cost-cutting measures, process improvement, and reengineering. However, many of these efforts have failed because they have not

Martha Beede, senior consultant for IBM Global Education, assists higher education institutions in improving service and efficiency through organizational, process, and technology changes. She specializes in helping institutions redesign their student service operations to meet the demands of today's environment. She holds a master's from Northeastern University and a bachelor's from the University of Vermont.

fundamentally changed the way they do business. Redesign projects are most often driven by institutions that know they will have to make fundamental changes to remain competitive and viable in the changing higher education marketplace. They understand the implications this type of project will have on the people, process, and technology within their organization and give these projects the high priority and support they need to be successful. The following direction statements exemplify this philosophy:

> Boston College seeks to be recognized as the best managed university in the nation by adopting twenty-first century network computing as the means to deliver prompt, personal services and information to all constituents in a do-it-yourself manner every day and all day and by deploying a highly productive, broadly skilled cadre of employees.
>
> Boston College
> Project Delta

> Recognizing the many challenges that confront Babson College as we strive to achieve our educational mission, we are now committing ourselves, over the next twenty-four months, to a major re-engineering project whose purpose is to reduce, streamline, and simplify the administrative operations of the institution, freeing students, parents, employers, faculty and staff from the bureaucracy and paperwork so that they may devote more of their time and resources to learning and teaching. To this end, we envision a workplace which focuses upon the delivery of high quality services to our customers through the efforts of cross-functional, self-directed teams, and responsive, easy-to-use information systems and technologies.
>
> Babson College

> Carnegie Mellon will lead educational institutions by building on its tradition of innovation, and transcending disciplinary boundaries to meet the changing needs of society.
>
> Carnegie Mellon University

To help you learn from their examples and, thus, achieve your goals, we will discuss why certain projects have been successful. The first lesson to remember is that redesign projects are not easy. You will read in the following case studies that these projects, while very successful, required significant planning work and had significant implications. Fundamentally, key change management considerations were included in their planning processes. These include the following:

- Strong case for change
- Strong executive sponsorship and leadership
- Clear vision and goals
- Skill development and training
- Collaboration and communication across departments
- Customer input
- Human resource and cultural considerations
- A well-articulated plan

Institutional transformation must address how people will work together and deliver services in the new model they are designing. It must also address how to integrate these changes in a positive way into the thinking and behavior of each and every member of the institutional community. As you will see in the case studies, resistance to change is one of the greatest obstacles for redesign efforts to overcome. Key factors and planning considerations for redesign are addressed in the section on redesign as a change agent and in chapters 16 and 17.

The Southern Alberta Institute of Technology (SAIT) (see chapter 7) paid close attention to the critical success factors it established for its redesign. It exemplified the "walk the talk" concept of leadership and commitment. For example, the vice president of administration, the project's executive sponsor, was active at all levels of the project, participating in key campus meetings and work sessions and giving up his executive assistant to support the redesign team's effort. In addition, the team members were dedicated 60 percent of the time to the effort and included cross-functional participants. A full communication strategy that was put in place included campus meetings, town meetings, and newsletters, allowing two-way communication and ongoing participation among the stakeholders. Customer input was solicited in a number of ways, including surveys, focus groups, and ongoing meetings throughout the redesign. The team did not lose sight of its goal of creating a student-centered environment. Members actively worked to ensure that they met the critical success factors they had laid out in their planning process. However, even with all of these factors in place, they still met unexpected challenges and needed to adapt their process to the institution's specific needs. This is another fundamental lesson of redesign: you need to stay in tune with your team and stakeholders and adapt what you are doing to the change management considerations that emerge in your project.

Technology as a Change Agent

Information technology is another means to effect change in your organization. However, technology should always be viewed as an enabler, not as a solution. It is important to note that introducing technology without rethinking processes, understanding customer needs, and considering organizational implications is unlikely to be successful. Institutions that have used technology successfully in their projects have focused on ensuring that they meet customer needs. They are *not* delivering technology for technology's sake.

Colorado Electronic Community College (see chapter 15) undertook a collaborative effort to bring 13 community colleges together and to capitalize on technology. CCCOnline was developed as a result of students' increased need for additional learning and student service opportunities at a distance. CCCOnline was the driving force for change in the community college system in Colorado. The process of developing this service and understanding the needs that were driving it forced the individual colleges to think differently about what services they offer and when they offer them. The schools worked collaboratively to better understand workforce development needs, unbalanced learning options for rural and urban students, and the lack of appropriate support services, and to modify their types of offerings.

The advent of the Web and the changes that it brought in terms of start-up time, costs of application development, and quick return on investment have aided this process. They have also made it more critical to understand user needs because customers use the new Web applications directly. The elements of successful user-centered Web design as well as specific best practice projects at Northern Territory University and the University of Minnesota are discussed in chapter 9. The University of Minnesota is a classic example of driving significant changes through technology. The Student 2000 project, when fully implemented, will replace its administrative systems, redesign its processes, and provide a Web front end. Some schools create Web sites that continue to segregate processes and mimic the physical separations existing on campus, causing students who are entering the Web site to go to multiple locations on the site just as they do among buildings. This requires the student to understand the institution's organization to navigate around the site until all processes are complete. While this is certainly more efficient than running around campus, it assumes students know where they need to go for information and that they have the patience to track down each piece. Additionally, processes may be inconsistent from office to office, again leaving the student confused and overwhelmed with too much information to navigate through. The University of Minnesota, with student input, determined what the student really needs and designed a student-centered system. For example, a student who needs to enroll logs on and goes through an enrollment/registration process that, in turn, generates an enrollment statement. The statement gives students their class schedule, class locations, class maps, books required, parking locations, bill amounts, and other valuable information.

That single enrollment transaction initiates a logical sequence of choices for the student to progress through as needed.

Emerging Student Services Trends

The student service trends that are emerging for the 21st century are consistent whether you plan for redesign or technology to enable change. Ultimately, they are all so closely linked that you need to consider how people, process, and technology are structured within your new student service delivery model. The following design principles are consistent whether you choose redesign or technology as the agent for transformation:

- Student-centered vision
- Redesigned services
- One-stop service center
- Cross-functional teams
- Self-service objectives
- Web-enabled services
- Systemic change
- Replacement of student information systems

Student-Centered Vision

It is not unusual for a group hearing the best practice presentation for the first time or formulating the scope of its student service project to have an intense reaction when asked to identify its key "customer." The customer concept is still relatively new to higher education and can challenge current views of education. By and large, the frequency of this reaction and the level of discomfort has diminished over the past few years as most individuals understand that institutions do indeed deliver a service (education), that it is paid for, and that there are expected outcomes; in other words, they understand that the customer concept is relevant.

One of the fundamental rules in planning for and delivering high-quality service is the importance of talking to your customer, in this case the student, and you will see this reiterated throughout the book. This is significant because it demonstrates that not only are all best practice partners comfortable with this terminology, but it has become an integral part of their cultural norm to view students as customers.

In chapter 13, Ball State University describes how it talked to its customer as part of its planning process. The university recognized that, with declining enrollments in the undergraduate population and a decrease in the high school graduate pool, it should focus more efforts on transfer students. The university analyzed this population and saw that by increasing the number of transfer students who demonstrated academic achievement it could possibly stabilize enrollments and enhance retention. Ball State then focused on how to serve this population by providing comprehensive, accurate transfer course information in a timely manner. One of the efforts that Ball State has undertaken to improve student services through the Web is the Automated Course Transfer System, which has greatly enhanced service in this area. The university now supports 30,000 course equivalents and in two years increased its transfer population from 400 to 700 students.

Redesigned Services

Institutions are using a student-centered approach to redesign processes across traditional student service boundaries. To do this, organizations view processes from a student's perspective. Many processes found in student services cross multiple organizational boundaries. As a result, these processes are complex and cumbersome due to the number of handoffs, sign-offs, and tasks required within each process. Each handoff is an opportunity for delays, errors, and unnecessary work. It is important to get input from the customer throughout the redesign process. The case studies that are included in this book all used survey, focus group, and ongoing communication strategies as part of their planning to understand their customer needs and ensure they incorporated these elements into their redesign. You will see that common themes emerge within the case studies. Student comments consistently point to the same issues: processes that are overly controlled, complicated, and punitive or processes that are fragmented, bureaucratic, inconvenient, labor intensive, and inconsistent. These common themes point again to an inherent problem in the model rather than the way any particular institution was delivering its processes.

To be successful redesign must include three key elements: people, process, and technology. Institutions that successfully redesigned their processes recognized the need to reinvent these processes, throw out their old assumptions, and redesign around student requirements and measurable outcomes. These institutions fundamentally rethought what they do and why they do it, and identified their customer.

The scope of these projects and the changes they require can be immense, yet steps can be taken on a smaller scale. Departments that recognize the need to change but do not have campuswide initiatives in place can take incremental steps by introducing innovative improvements to discrete processes. Although these do not result in dramatic change, they are a first step toward moving the institution forward. Other areas see benefits of process improvements that they can use to create a case for change. Ultimately, the more challenging tasks of cross-functional change are taken on.

Oregon State University (see chapter 8) has taken this approach to deal with some of the recruitment and retention challenges it experienced in admissions. Through departmental redesign of the admissions processes, Oregon State was able to do the following:

- Reduce the time required to process an admissions application to one week
- Reduce response time for requested admissions information from five to two days
- Reduce recruiting costs per student by 10 percent
- Increase the number of new freshmen by 22 percent

It is now recruiting more students for less money and is looking at these positive results as a first step on a continuing journey to provide better service to students.

One-Stop Service Center and Cross-Functional Teams

When students are asked in focus groups and surveys what services they want, among the most common responses are direct access to their own information and the ability to conduct their own transactions. In addition, students want access to high-quality personal service when needed. Many schools are planning services with these goals in mind, developing one-stop service centers. One-stop service centers often go hand-in-hand with cross-functional teams. Building cross-trained, cross-functional work teams helps ensure that front-line professionals can answer learners' questions in the first contact and optimizes the one-stop service center structure and philosophy.

A one-stop service center allows students to conduct business at a single location. Generally, the core student service functions of admissions, registration, and financial services are integrated into one facility to improve service and efficiency for students. Student service staff members are organized by teams that include generalists, who are cross-trained to handle most requests at the service desk, and specialists, who answer nonroutine questions. In addition, stu-

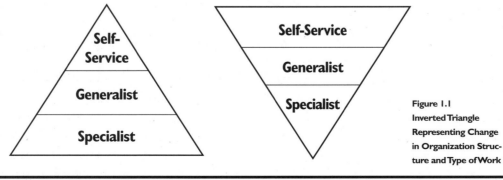

Figure 1.1
Inverted Triangle Representing Change in Organization Structure and Type of Work

Traditional Model	New Models
Functional silos	Cross-functional teams
Segregated departments and processes	Integrated systems, organization, and processes
Lack of communication across departments	Cross-trained teams
Lines and multiple offices	"One or None" philosophy
Limited access (8x5)	Anytime and anyplace (24x7)
Bureaucratic, paper-driven processes	One source of data, electronic
Sometimes-inconsistent information	Consistent information, integrated, and common interfaces

Figure 1.2
Shifting Student
Services Model

dents can take care of most business directly with self-service tools, usually voice response systems or Web-accessible services. A key element of this model is a "one or none" philosophy: Students who need or prefer personal assistance to complete a transaction require only one student service contact. Students who can complete a transaction on their own require none.

The following common themes have emerged and are being designed into new student services models:

- Routine transactions should be automated.
- Students should have the choice to initiate transactions and have direct access to their own information.
- Students should have high-quality personal assistance when needed.
- When students prefer personal assistance, it should be available at a single location.

The University of Delaware's model (see chapter 10) is based on a branch banking model, which includes student workstations and cross-trained generalists to staff the service desk, and specialists available to handle more difficult problems. The university has also made good use of Web tools, including student self-service workstations that provide access to course schedules, financial status, unofficial transcripts, and other academic information. During the planning stages, the university estimated that 20 percent of transactions would be self-service transactions, 60 percent would be handled by generalists, and 20 percent would require specialist assistance. The new model was so successful that self-service transactions account for 60 percent of the business, and the university is estimating that this will rise to 80 to 90 percent.

The University of Delaware, one of the pioneers in the design of the one-stop service center, is continually evolving its design and moving many of the services from the physical one-stop shop to its electronic equivalent on the Web.

Carnegie Mellon University (see chapter 6) created The HUB, a one-stop shop that merged several separate offices to create a single, integrated Enrollment Services organization of self-directed teams to service students and parents. Since it created the new structure, 60 percent of the staff are in different positions and 60 percent of the positions are different, requiring staff to go through an extensive cross-training and interviewing process. Each staff per-

son was guaranteed a position within the new organization and commensurate compensation to assist in adapting to the new model. Staff members have experienced dramatic growth in their skills and ability to resolve students' problems in one step.

Cross-functional teams are comprised of individuals who are cross-trained and can answer questions and provide support in more than one specialty area. Team members may be stronger in one area (such as financial aid) than another and assist other team members when necessary. These individuals become facilitators of information and focus their efforts on value-added advising rather than on performing routine transactions and tasks. In the future model, routine transactions are automated or performed directly by the customer through self-service tools. The makeup of the student service organization shifts as institutions transform from a traditional model to a new model. Self-service transactions play an increased role in how services are delivered in the 21st century model (see figures 1.1 and 1.2).

These new team-based designs for service delivery flatten the organization. Seton Hall University's new enrollment organization is comprised of three teams of cross-trained student enrollment advisors (SEAs) (see chapter 3). At Seton Hall each team consists of the following:

- One lead SEA to head the team
- One recruitment and admissions specialist
- One registration and records specialist
- One student finance specialist
- One information and technology specialist
- Four generalist SEAs

This model is based on the concept that everyone in Enrollment Services is a generalist who understands the ordinary business of each area. The specialists add depth and expertise to the teams to handle special situations and train other team members.

Self-Service Objectives and Web-Enabled Services

Self-service is at the core of the changes we are seeing in student services today. The move toward self-service transactions is not new; it has evolved as technology has progressed. Many institutions successfully introduced self-service options more than 10 years ago when they began using touch-tone technology and kiosk applications. Touch-tone technology was most commonly used to register for classes, eliminating the need to stand in long lines and go from office to office for signatures.

Brigham Young University (see chapter 11) was a pioneer in planning for self-service tools to improve service to students. It implemented its touch-tone registration system in 1984 and added kiosk applications and Web services following technology advancements. The university has more than 700 access points available to students throughout its campus and now offers many academic, financial planning, and career services online. The philosophy is that students are not only capable, but they thrive in an environment of self-directed learning and service options.

The introduction of the Web has allowed us to put information directly into students' hands, dramatically changing the nature of work in student service offices. The Web has enhanced self-service applications by providing students with the benefits of a visual display to review schedules, courses, and other student information. This has greatly increased self-service applications' ease of use and their speed and flexibility. Touch-tone applications still have benefits because some individuals prefer to use the phone or do not have access to a computer. Most institutions recognize this and implement a strategy that allows choices for students.

Many institutions have established a Web presence in response to the demand for self-service applications. Only the most innovative schools had applications such as online admissions and registration three years ago; now most schools offer some level of these options. In addition, the number and quality of Web applications continue to increase. For example, Indiana University developed a Web-based student system, *insite*, that provides a common access point and consistent user interface for student information across the traditional silos (see chapter 12). One of the services *insite* provides is the advising application, which students can use for course selection and academic planning. Students view their course history and compare it to the course requirements of their degree program or to any other degree program. The university has received more positive feedback and comments regarding *insite* than for any other information service it provides.

Institutions are also looking more closely at linking the academic and administrative aspects of a student's life. They are assisting the student with enrollment, contact with faculty, interaction with the

Table 1.1 Student Services Trends: The best practice partners listed are at various stages of implementation, as shown in this table. Tables for individual institutions appear in the case study chapters.

TRENDS	Babson	Ball State	Boston College	BYU	Carnegie Mellon	CECC	IU	JCCC	NTU	Oregon State	UDel	UMinn	SAIT	Seton Hall
Student-Centered	◐	●	●	◑	●	◐	○	◐	○	●	●	●	◐	●
Redesigned Services	◐		◐		●			◐			●	◐	◐	◐
One-Stop Service Center		●	●	◑	●			◐			●		●	●
Cross-Functional Teams	●		◑	◑	●		○	◐			●	◑	◐	◐
Self-Service Objectives	●	●	●	◑	●	○	●	◐			◐	●	●	◐
Department Process Improvements	◐		◑	◑		◐	○	◐		●	●			
Web-Enabled Services	●	●	●	●	◐		●		●	●	●	●	●	●
Admissions	●	●	●	●	◐	●	◐	●	●	●	●	●	●	◐
Registration	●	●	●	●	◐	●	○	●	●	●	●	●	◐	●
Advising	◑	●	○	●		◐	●	●	●	○	●	●	◑	
Financial Aid	●	◐	●	●	●	◐	◐	●	●	●	●	●	●	◐
Billing	●	◐	●		○	◐	●	◑	●	◐	◐	●	◑	◐
Career Services	◐	●	◑	◑		○	●	○		○	○	○	◑	○
Systemic Change	◑	◐	◐	◑		○	○	◐	●		◐	●	●	◐
Replacement of Student Information Systems	●		○	●			◑	●		●	●	◐	●	

Codes for Implementation Phase: ● Production ◑ Implementing ◐ Designed ○ Planning classroom experience, and access to library resources. Institutions will continue to enhance and offer these applications at a rapid rate.

A "Web year" is considered to be six months, reflecting the speed at which technology is being developed and introduced into our day-to-day lives. Institutions now know that more planning must occur before they introduce Web applications. This is because some of the same problems that existed with the physical design of student services are occurring now with Web applications. It is important in planning Web applications to consider the student's perspective and look at the overall processes they need to complete when using institutional services. Web applications should be presented in an integrated fashion and not re-create silos that require skilled navigating through the Web site and force students to deal with an overwhelming amount of sometimes inconsistent information. The concept of user-centered Web design is discussed in chapter 16.

Systemic Change and Replacement of Student Information Systems

The new model for the delivery of student services in the 21st century requires *dramatic* systemic change that cuts across traditional academic and administrative boundaries. As institutions construct their vision for the future, they are rethinking how they will deliver student services as well as education and other administrative services. This new model requires a new culture of collaboration and a common institutional vision. The traditional practice of focusing on one's individual department, college, or school will no longer work.

One trend we have seen evolve over the past 10 years relates directly to the move toward systemic change. During the 1980s it was quite common for institutions to have separate applications for separate areas (one package for financial aid, another for student accounts). Even more common was the distinction between student systems and other administrative systems, such as human resources and finance. These systems, which had been adapted to each department's needs, required multiple interfaces and separate databases, and were often difficult and expensive to maintain. This structure perpetuated the silo mentality and departmental data control and ownership, and it contributed to service and data access problems.

Institutions recognized the problems of maintaining all of these interfaces, the difficulty of getting institutional data, and the barriers to providing holistic services. They also saw the benefits of campuswide initiatives, integrated data, and common interfaces. They began to move toward selecting a common platform across all applications and toward enterprise resource planning (ERP) solutions that provided integrated enterprise-wide systems for human resource, finance, and student applications. These systems provided all departments and users with access to their data from one place. The move in this direction helped to eliminate many data ownership, redundancy, and integrity issues as well as reduce costs.

Additionally, advancements in software packages allowed relational databases and easy access to integrated information. Web front ends could be built to provide a common interface for applications that were already in place. Student-centered institutions began to see the benefits of planning for the goals of the institution as a whole rather than for varying needs across individual departments.

Summary Discussion of Trends

You will read in the following chapters about institutions that have a common vision for the future of student services. Table 1.1 demonstrates that this vision has become a reality and these concepts have been fully implemented at many institutions.

REFERENCES

Green, Kenneth C. 1996. The Changing Profile of Undergraduate Business Students. *Journal of Career Planning and Employment* (Spring): 21–26.

Heller, K., and L. Eng. 1996. Why College Costs So Much, Pushing Man Out of the Market. *The Philadelphia Inquirer*, 31 March.

Marks, Joseph L. 1994–1995. *SREB Fact Book on Higher Education*. Atlanta: Southern Regional Board.

2

Barbara Krauth

Trends in Support Services for Distance Learners

As most higher education administrators know very well, distance learning is exploding. A U.S. Department of Education study based on data from 1994–95 reported that three-quarters of large higher education institutions and two-thirds of medium-sized institutions were then offering courses or programs at a distance. In the few years after the study was conducted, the numbers continued to grow steadily. The reason for the rapid expansion of distance learning is that students have demanded it.

Why the Exponential Growth?

Students enroll in distance learning (sometimes known as distance education) programs for a variety of reasons, but they are principally interested in the convenience such programs offer. The greatest appeal of distance education programs is that they enable someone to go to college for the first time or pursue a technical or advanced degree without having to leave home or a job.

A variety of life circumstances can draw students to distance learning, of course. They may live in a rural area or are caring for young children. They may have a full-time job but need to get an advanced degree to develop necessary skills to advance in their career. They can pursue additional education to enter a new career field, or they want to earn a two-year degree now and transfer to a four-year

---

Barbara Krauth is project director for the Western Cooperative for Educational Telecommunications at the Western Interstate Commission for Higher Education. She directs a FIPSE-funded project titled Developing Effective Support Services for Students at a Distance and managed a previous WICHE project that developed the Principles of Good Practice for Electronically Offered Higher Education Degree and Certificate Programs. *She has a master's in English from the University of Kent, Canterbury, England.*

program later. Some have disabilities that make it hard for them to get to a campus. The point is, for whatever reasons, they are seeking an education that is free from some of the time and/or place constraints inherent in studying on campus in the traditional environment.

Student Support Services for Distance Learners

Students enrolled in distance education programs need the same kinds of student services as on-campus students, but they expect these services to meet their needs for flexibility and convenience. Some special needs also arise based on their isolation and the fact that they depend heavily on technology for learning and accessing resources.

In the past, colleges and universities have tended to handle student services for distance learners as regular on-campus processes, generally requiring distance learners to visit campus to receive services but, when necessary, making special accommodations. The mindset for serving these off-campus learners has traditionally been for local clientele, not a global market.

As long as the number of students remained small, most could be served reasonably well as exceptions to regular processes. However, colleges are now reaching larger numbers of distance learners over a wider range of academic disciplines and across state, even national, boundaries. In effect, this means that their student services must often be completely reconceived to serve these learners' needs effectively. If services are not adapted to a distance learning model, administrators and students will face many challenges in completing the most basic tasks required to get institutional business done.

Distance Learning: The Compelling Case for Change

A number of forces are pressing institutions to find new ways to provide a variety of support services to their distance learners. Among these incentives for change are both internal and external pressures:

- *It's the right thing to do.* Nearly all colleges are proclaiming themselves learner centered these days. A learner-centered mission should focus not only on instruction, of course, but also on how the institution's student services are delivered. Such a mission should also emphasize not only the on-campus community but also its students enrolled at a distance. A learner-centered mission must cut across all aspects of the way the institution serves students. It is important to design student support services for access, so as not to disenfranchise the very students intended to be served through distance education. Student services should support and promote every distance learner's successful academic progress. For example, it makes little sense to require a student to come to the institution in the middle of the day to conduct business when he or she is taking classes in a remote location and has a full-time job. Specifically conceived approaches to student services are critical to distance learners' success, their retention, and their feeling of participation in a learning community. Distance learners want to be as connected to campus as possible and to feel that their needs are being considered.

- *Competition requires it.* As distance learning opportunities continue to grow everywhere across the country, learners are discovering that they can "shop" for schools that respond to their need for convenience—for an education and services not bound by time and/or place. If your institution is disinclined to provide easily accessible and friendly services to distance learners, another one—with a vision of these students as deserving "consumers"—will be glad to do so.

- *Retention demands it.* Student retention depends on students' achieving a sense of identity as part of a learning community and on their having access to an appropriate array of support services. Studies have asked students who withdrew from distance learning programs why they did not complete their studies. The reason most commonly cited is in some way related to the pressures of their personal lives—for example, too little time, too many other obligations. The reason for withdrawing that is mentioned next is a lack of support services available to them at a distance. The institution did not adequately meet their need to feel served by and attached to the institution.

- *Technology enables it.* As institutions develop greater numbers of technology-assisted courses and programs, they are finding that, in many respects, distinctions between on-campus learners and distance learners are blurring. The technology now available makes possible better services to both groups. A technology-enabled environment is driving changes from both directions. At some institutions, on-campus students are demanding services that were originally designed specifically to provide convenience for those at a distance. A number of those interviewed through our project have pointed to this phenomenon. For example, an online registration form an institution developed initially for students enrolled in online programs at a distance is now available to those on campus—in response to demands from regular campus students for one-stop shopping. The reverse is also happening, as a growing number of institutions develop electronic student services that can serve both on- and off-campus learners—especially distance learners who are studying online.

- *Accrediting associations require it.* The higher education regional accrediting associations are currently focusing a great deal of attention on distance learning programs. Accreditors are not questioning the efficacy of learning by means of technology. Research and evaluation studies put that issue to rest long ago. Instead, the quality concern focuses on issues related to student support and to program integrity—will students in virtual learning situations be isolated, with no semblance of human contact with their instructors or other students? How can institutions make effective advising and academic support services available to distance learning students? How can students in such programs be sure that their learning experiences will equal those on campuses and that their degrees will be seen as equivalent to a traditionally delivered degree program? In trying to determine what constitutes quality in these programs, accrediting groups are closely examining the adequacy of an institution's approach to providing student services to distance learners. Within the past several years, every higher education regional accrediting group in the country has adopted a version of a document titled *Principles of Good Practice for Electronically Offered Higher Education Degree and Certificate Programs.* The Western Cooperative for Educational Telecommunications at the Western Interstate Commission on Higher Education (WICHE) developed these principles as a product of a previous project titled Balancing Quality and Access. The principles provide, for the first time, a starting point for addressing quality in distance education. The specific references to student services in the *Principles of Good Practice for Electronically Offered Higher Education Degree and Certificate Programs* are as follows:

- The program provides students with clear, complete, and timely information on the curriculum, course and degree requirements, nature of faculty/student interaction, assumptions about technological competence and skills, technical equipment requirements, availability of academic support services and financial aid resources, and costs and payment policies.
- Enrolled students have reasonable and adequate access to the range of student services appropriate to support their learning.
- Accepted students have the background, knowledge, and technical skills needed to undertake the program.
- Advertising, recruiting, and admissions materials clearly and accurately represent the program and the services available.

Although these principles do not provide concrete suggestions for how to provide high-quality services, they offer some guidance with respect to some student service categories that the regional accrediting community charged with judging quality in distance learning programs will clearly examine.

Promoting Effective Support Services for Students in Distance Education Programs: A FIPSE-Funded Project

I have directed a three-year project titled Promoting Effective Support Services for Students in Distance Education Programs. Sponsored by the U.S. Department of Education's Fund for the Improvement of Postsecondary Education (FIPSE), the project focuses specifically on improving student services for distance learners. Project activities have centered on the following:

- Discovering how colleges and universities in the West provide student services at a distance
- Identifying, through results of a written survey and extensive phone interviews, exemplary practices in providing services to distance learners
- Disseminating information on good models
- Brokering consulting services and technical assistance from those at institutions that have exemplary services—either broadly or narrowly defined—to administrators at other colleges and universities who would like assistance in improving their services to students enrolled at a distance

Survey of Student Services at a Distance: What We Have Learned

The definition of "student support services" can vary from institution to institution. The project has chosen to address all services that a dis-

tance learner might need to succeed in this different environment: preenrollment, academic advising, registration, orientation to distance learning, career counseling, library services, bookstore services, financial aid assistance, advising, personal counseling, social support, technical assistance, degree and graduation audits, and transcript evaluation.

In 1997, we surveyed more than 1,000 institutions in the West and Midwest. With 380 institutions (about 40 percent) responding, the results were quite revealing. They indicated, for example, that despite the huge growth in course offerings at a distance, only a few institutions offered full degree programs at a distance.

The surveyed schools were using a variety of technologies to deliver instruction. Live interactive video was being used by 63 percent, videotapes by 62 percent, broadcast or cable television by 54 percent, and the Internet by 59 percent. In the two years after the survey, however, the proportions changed substantially, with faster growth in the use of the Internet than of other technologies.

In terms of student services, the survey results made clear that few colleges or universities had made genuine adjustments in their services to meet distance learners' needs. There appears to be a lag between an institution's deciding to offer courses or programs at a distance and its recognizing the need to offer support services in a format convenient for their distance learners. Following are examples:

- Sixteen percent of responding institutions *required* students to visit campus to register. (They had no provisions for regular mail, online, fax, or phone registration.)
- Thirty-one percent had no special provisions for library services for distance learners (including access to online catalogs or databases, or special arrangements with community college or public libraries).
- Thirty-one percent had no intervention strategies for distance learners who were experiencing academic difficulties.
- Forty-eight percent offered no personal counseling services, either directly or through referral, to distance learners.
- Thirty-seven percent relied on *faculty* to provide technical support and answer students' questions related to technology.
- Seventy-three percent had established no social support networks (such as online coffeehouses, events at community receive sites, or exchange of student contact information).

In a less-complex world it would seem inherent in the process to offer support services that did not require distance learning students to be physically present on campus. However, many of the support services cut across various functions on campus, and arriving at an integrated solution that makes sense for these students requires collaboration, strategic planning, and, most importantly, an entirely new way of looking at things. Although there has clearly been some improvement since the 1997 study, as institutions have gained a better understanding of how important student services are to the success of their overall distance learning programs, very few institutions offer uniformly excellent services to distance learners. Thus, an institution may have developed strong core administrative services online but may have no provision for advising students at a distance or for providing them with library services. Registration and degree audits seem to be the areas with the strongest services, no doubt because a number of commercial student data packages are available to assist institutions with these services. The weakest areas are in social support, personal and career counseling, and library services.

Why Don't Institutions Provide Good Services to Distance Learners?

There are a number of reasons why institutions haven't made rapid advances in improving the broad range of services they provide to their distance learners. Among them are the following:

- *Distance learning has been seen as an add-on, rather than a central, function.* On the fringes of the institution in the past, distance education programs are now moving to the center—at least in importance and, in many cases, structurally. That is, distance learning programs may still be administratively located in a continuing education division, but they are becoming increasingly important to the institution as a whole. Despite this change in the role of distance learning programs, the excitement surrounding the use of new technologies to provide instruction to students at a distance still tends to obscure the importance of providing good services to students enrolled in these programs.

- *Entrenched practices are hard to change.* This is probably the biggest reason practices are changing so slowly. Unfortunately, those in the institution charged with helping students adapt to change—including student services personnel—are often most resistant to changing the ways they meet student needs. It is crucial for administrators interested in broadening their institution's appeal to find ways to surmount the administrative and political hurdles that can limit their adaptability.

- *Colleges and universities don't know where to begin.* They are unaware of possibilities, unsure about who needs to be involved in envisioning what services to distance learners might look like, and insecure about the time and resources that will be required.

"Good Practice" Trends

Good practice in providing services to distance learners is characterized by many of the same qualities as good practice in serving on-campus learners. That is, effective services are the following:

- Convenient—preferably accessible any time, any place
- Easy to understand and access
- Integrated into instruction, where appropriate
- Equal to—but not necessarily the same as—services provided to on-campus students
- Based on an understanding of the types of students the institution is serving at a distance and what their needs are
- Based on redesigned services, not just the introduction of technology

A Variety of Approaches

The project has identified many institutions that are doing an excellent job in supporting distance learners, although few are doing so comprehensively. Because traditional distance learning technologies are still widely in use, some institutions have found effective ways to match their instructional delivery system with the student service delivery system. That is, if your school is providing instruction via interactive television, one way to serve students at their learning sites is to offer services such as advising via desktop video. It may also be important to establish multiple approaches to meeting students' needs—for example, by backing up a Web-based service with a way for a student to access a real person quickly via phone or e-mail.

The project has made clear that a variety of approaches can be successful. These include online, Web-based services; the use of a call center; local site-based methods; and the inclusion of other technologies such as desktop video and CD-ROM. The best models, in fact, incorporate a variety of approaches, enabling students with or without access to specific technologies to receive at a distance the services they need.

Critical Success Factors in Serving Distance Learners

Reform in the area of student services for distance learners must involve major cultural shifts for most institutions in the way they conceptualize, structure, administer, and implement these services. Current staff will have to be retrained to view student support services as customer services and to make them convenient and accessible to students no matter where they are located.

Following are some specific recommendations for developing effective services for distance learners:

Convene groups representing all appropriate campus entities. Use a team approach to planning services. Bring distance learning administrators (whether they are located in continuing education, distance education, or central administration) together with representatives from the library, bookstore, registrar's office, and all traditional student affairs areas to develop a shared vision for change and a strategy for reform. Planning must begin with cross-disciplinary teams, which may, in fact, need to be more broadly representative than those assembled to reengineer on-campus services.

Match services to current instructional technologies, but with an eye on the future. If your institution is currently using interactive video to deliver most of its instruction at a distance, it makes sense to investigate how this same technology might be used to deliver some services. It is important, though, to recognize that as instruction is rapidly migrating toward the Internet, many services should also be designed to take advantage of the online environment.

Recognize the special needs of distance learners. Distance learners need the same services as on-site learners but need them delivered in a different way. Distance learners also have special needs, such as the following:

- *A sense of connection with the institution.* Retention and degree completion depend on a student's achieving a sense of identity within a learning community. Institutions have found that something as simple as issuing an identification card can be helpful in strengthening this sense of identity.

- *A sense of connection with other learners and their instructors.* Develop ways for students to interact with each other and, at times, with their instructors outside their courses. Virtual environments can make such interaction possible, as can informal meeting opportunities at a local instructional site.

- *The ability to learn via technology.* Distance students need to master the relevant technology—and they need access to help when it fails. Prospective distance students are sometimes surprisingly naïve about what technical skills they will need to succeed in a course or degree program offered via a distance learning technology. It is important to inform them of any needed technical skills. They also need to know whom to contact for assistance when something goes wrong. When no specific technology support is available, faculty become the de facto technology "help desk," an inappropriate role for them and an ineffective way to serve students' needs.

- *An understanding of the characteristics of successful distance learners.* It is important to let prospective distance learners know more about what they are going to encounter. Before a student registers, for example, he or she should understand the degree of independence required to succeed in the distance learning environment. Provide information and a self-assessment related to likely success in distance learning

to all students who are considering enrolling in a distance-delivered course or program.

Use technology to empower students. In the model that leading institutions are beginning to adopt for their on-site students, technology is used to empower students to answer the easy questions themselves. This approach also makes sense for serving distance learners, but keep in mind that you also need to provide easy at-a-distance access to a real person who can provide the "high touch" intensive advising assistance that on-campus learners have. Think carefully about where you need to keep a human in the loop.

Know your own students. Design services to meet the specific needs of your distance learners. For example, adults with bachelor's degrees and full-time jobs are likely to have different needs than 18-year-old first-time students interested in completing an associate degree in their home community and then moving to campus for the final two years of a bachelor's degree program. Determining the specific needs of your distance learners may require a careful needs analysis.

Expect rapid growth if you develop an online campus. It was not unusual for institutions interviewed in this project who had initiated a major effort at delivering instruction online to experience a 200 percent increase in full-time student enrollments over two years. Providing adequate access to services for a growth of this magnitude can clearly prove a challenge.

Learn from others. Administrators interested in developing effective services at a distance can benefit from what the institutions included in this book have learned, although it is also important to recognize the need to modify these exemplary on-campus practices based on the unique characteristics of distance learners at their own institutions. Extending the service integration and one-stop shopping model to serving students at a distance, for example, might require the use not only of Web technologies but also of phone and fax.

Assistance Available Through the Student Services Project

The full results of the 1997 study are available upon request. If you would like to receive them or want to be placed on a list to receive a forthcoming publication on exemplary practices in serving students at a distance, contact Barbara Krauth, Project Coordinator, by phone at (303) 541-0308 or by e-mail at bkrauth@wiche.edu. An executive summary of results is at wiche.edu/telecom/projects/studentservices/surveyresults.htm.

Part 2:

Redesign as the Change Agent

3

Regina Kleinman

The Reengineering of Enrollment Services: Four Departments Become One

Overview

Bishop James Roosevelt Bayley founded Seton Hall University in 1856. The first bishop of Newark, he named it after his aunt, Mother Elizabeth Ann Seton, a pioneer in Catholic education and the first American-born saint. Seton Hall is the largest and oldest diocesan university in the United States.

Seton Hall is located in the suburban village of South Orange, New Jersey, 14 miles from New York City. It has nine schools: the College of Arts and Sciences, the College of Education and Human Services, the College of Nursing, the School of Diplomacy and International Relations, the School of Graduate Medical Education, the W. Paul Stillman School of Business, the Immaculate Conception Seminary School of Theology, the School of Law, and University College. Seton Hall offers over 45 degree programs and has nearly 350 full-time faculty and many adjunct faculty. The average class size is 25 students, and the student-faculty ratio is 16-to-1. Seton Hall is fully accredited by the Middle States Association of Colleges and Schools. Of the approximately 9,000 students who attend Seton Hall, 2,000 are resident students.

The Compelling Case for Change

For much of its existence, Seton Hall was a regional school of modest aspirations. But over the last few decades, changing times and a

Regina Kleinman is project manager for reengineering at Seton Hall University. She has been a member of the Procurement Reengineering Team, has co-facilitated the Human Resources Reengineering Team, was project leader for the Enrollment Services Implementation Team, and served on the university's Core Team for Reengineering. She holds a bachelor's in English from the College of Staten Island, CUNY.

more competitive environment fueled the university to become something far greater. In 1996, a new president, preparing to meet the future, outlined a vision that aspired to excellence. Msgr. Robert Sheeran initiated a program of institution-wide transformation that touched upon all aspects of the university. Administrative and business processes offered avenues to reduce costs, operate more efficiently, and enhance the quality of services to students, faculty, and employees. Reforming these processes created the potential to redirect revenues to faculty development and technological innovations in learning. Business process redesign, or reengineering, was seen as the logical tool to use for achieving not modest improvements, but breakthrough improvements in performance. Redesigning our business processes was one aspect of reaching the president's goal of establishing Seton Hall as a premier institution of Catholic higher education.

We began by engaging in an institution-wide diagnostic review of the methods and costs of the university's business operations. The university contracted with a consulting firm that reviewed current practices and conducted interviews with the providers and recipients of services. The consultants conducted confidential questionnaires and analyzed statistical data and other quantitative and qualitative information gathered from documents, process mapping, and walk-through observations. It included a review of the state of technology. One conclusion of that study was that the enrollment stream of services offered opportunities to eliminate redundant or unnecessary work and reallocate resources to academic core activities. The study identified operating inefficiencies and lapses in service to students.

As with most institutions, the study showed that the end-to-end process of admitting, financing, enrolling, and billing students was fragmented and broken up among four different departments, and even different units within departments. No one department or administrator had ownership of the whole enrollment process. Registering for classes might cause students to wait in as many as three different lines, often more than once. Staff were overly specialized and not able to provide holistic service. Departments duplicated work by engaging in redundant data entry and did not trust each other's data. The work processes were designed for the individual departments' internal needs. The students were required to serve the processes, rather than the processes serving the student.

Project Summary

The initial study also indicated the following direction that the redesign should take:

- A consolidated enrollment service organization that would provide students with a single point of contact
- Cross-trained staff organized into student service teams for integrated delivery of services
- Technology optimized to provide self-service for students
- Streamlined processes that eliminate unnecessary or redundant work

With these recommendations in mind, the university assembled an Enrollment Services Redesign Team and engaged a consultant to lead and train the teams using a proven methodology. Starting with the previous Phase I data to get a broad understanding of the problems and a direction for redesign, the team held interviews with executives and the directors of the enrollment departments to determine their point of view on the nature of any problems and their vision for the future.

It is worth noting that the team did not include the directors or heads of the four departments. The project required intensive work over a long span of time—the team worked together three days a week for three months. It would not have been possible for a bursar or registrar to be absent from the office for that amount of time. In addition, those who created the current environment are not in the best position to participate in a process that knocks down sacred assumptions about how work gets done. Managers may not be the best candidates for the reinvention process because it may require them to flatten the organizational hierarchies by which they have advanced. That could conceivably result in the elimination of their jobs as they know them. Employees at the assistant director level, however, are in a better position to engage in out-of-the-box thinking because they are less vested in their positions. They usually have a good understanding of the work and the processes—in fact, they may have closer contact with office work flow than upper management does. They are not as apt to feel threatened by change. Quite

the contrary, they may stand to gain by a redefinition of jobs that would give them greater autonomy and decision-making responsibility. When organizational hierarchy is flattened, there can be greater ability to reward individuals without forcing them to seek a new job higher up the ladder. Also, there is excitement in being able to develop ideas for improvement that they have had for a long time but were not in a position to implement.

A critical data-gathering tool of process redesign is the focus group. The redesign team held focus groups with providers of the processes as well as with the student customers. Focus group information identified six key issues to be addressed during the subsequent reinvent phase:

- Processes were cumbersome and paper-intensive, causing student and employee dissatisfaction.
- Communications between offices were unclear and left staff and students not as well informed as they could be.
- Access to technology was not being optimized.
- Financial aid processes and funding were not satisfying students.
- The physical work environment needed improvement.
- Students desired a higher degree of customer service.

Focus groups identified opportunities for improvement and ranked them according to what was most important. Improved technology was number one, followed by one-stop service, improved academic advising, and increased financial aid funding. Strong emphasis was placed on improving customer service by providing training and offering incentives.

In addition to focus group data, the redesign team researched best practices in student services and made a site visit to one best practice school, the University of Delaware. Delaware was among the first institutions to locate the four enrollment service departments together.

Another critical tool in process redesign is the process map. Reengineering is essentially about the way work gets done and the end-to-end processes that create value for the customer. The team mapped the current processes to understand the steps needed for a student to be admitted, financed, and enrolled and for accounts to be settled. Just looking at a process map can tell you a great deal about problems in the way work gets done. If the resulting diagram looks like a bunch of spaghetti, the process is probably convoluted and inefficient. If the diagram is very tangled and lengthy, with many steps, many participants, and switchbacks, it is a virtual guarantee that the process will be difficult for students to negotiate. Process maps capture the delays that occur between steps, i.e., lag time. For instance, if a form needs several different signatures, delays will occur at each stop along the route as the form sits in various in-boxes and makes its way through campus "snail mail." It can make what should be a fast and simple matter a lengthy and difficult one.

Process mapping allows you to attach a cost to processes as well. The time an employee spends on each step will determine a cost based on their rate of pay. Add the amounts for each step and you can understand total labor costs for the end-to-end process. This is different from understanding the cost of running a department, because processes are usually not contained within a department. Costs tend to run across departmental and divisional boundaries. Until process mapping is done, you will probably not understand the true cost of a process. A process is a series of related tasks that together create something of value for a customer.

The next step was to reinvent the processes. All the research that had gone before was preparation and was incorporated into the reinvention of the enrollment processes. Reinvention is blue-sky time—time to be creative, to think out-of-the-box. It is a time to question and throw out cherished assumptions and immutable laws about the nature of the work and how it gets done, and imagine the best, smoothest, most efficient, and most satisfying processes. It is interesting, if predictable, that at the first pass most redesign teams create something that looks very much like what they already have and know. If your reinvented processes look like what you already have, you have modified, not reinvented, them. In reinvention we start from the beginning and create the world again. It is as if we had never done this before, so there are no absolutes about how things get done. The one absolute is starting from the perspective of the customer. Without the primary customer, the student, there is no business to operate. So, we start with understanding who the primary customer is, what it is that we do for them or could be doing for them, and how best to do it using technology and the organization's workforce.

When challenged to be free and creative in their thinking, members of the design team can come up with ideas that are quite elegant—on paper. Then, we do a reality check. The saying is, "First we get crazy, then we get real." In the imaginative phase of reinvention, there may have been some constricting factors that were set aside but now have to be reconciled. For instance, reinvented processes that call for a major technology installation that the university cannot afford would have to be adjusted accordingly for that constricting factor.

Following reinvention the team considered what it would take to realize the redesign. Describing those elements and drafting an implementation plan were the final tasks of the redesign team. The plan included a business case, which is an analysis of the cost of the current process versus the cost of the redesigned process. It included investments in technology or physical plant that may be required, the estimated number of employees in the new department, and total labor costs versus those in the current organization. Cost savings were balanced against investments.

At every phase of the redesign process, the stakeholders reviewed the team's work before the next step was taken. For instance, after focus group data were compiled, the data were presented to group participants to verify that we had captured their concerns and recommendations. There were interim reviews to the Core Team for Reengineering (the team that oversees the enterprise-wide reengineering initiative) to show the process maps of the current situation and the reinvented processes. This was a time when they could express any serious objections about the redesign and the direction it was taking. The validity of those objections was considered and taken into account. Eventually, when the redesign was finished there were final presentations to the concerned groups. Those groups consisted of the directors of the affected departments, the Core Team for Reengineering, and the executive cabinet. The more people who review the redesign, the better. It is a vital component of achieving buy-in and support that will be critical when going forward into implementation. Also, you never know where the good ideas will come from. During these reviews, some factor may come to light that may have been overlooked but is important to the project. Interim reviews for the provider groups—the people who do this work—will inevitably be a vital reality check.

Ultimately, the completed redesign formulated a vision of a one-stop, one-step environment to meet the enrollment service needs of the student customer. It envisioned a level of customer service that would provide students with access to information and the choice to seek personal assistance or to self-initiate transactions.

Technology plays a key role in reengineering. It allows work to be performed in ways not possible before. In our blue-sky thinking we imagined a process highly enabled by technology. It included application for admission over the Web; scanning technology to streamline the input of admission application data; student self-service for online registration, add/drop, obtaining grades, updating demographic data, and obtaining other data needed to complete routine interactions; and the use of electronic forms and routing for routine sign-offs. If routine transactions could be automated, employees would have more time to spend on more value-added activity and meeting students' needs.

The reinvented processes imagined eliminating unnecessary holds and handing responsibility for releasing holds back to the originating department. The redesign asked for clear documentation and communication of required process inputs and outputs, envisioned communicating as much information as possible (such as scholarship offers, class schedule, tuition and fee charges, residence hall assignment, and advisor) along with the acceptance to the university, and wanted to put an end to transferring students from one office (in person or on the phone) to another to get answers. In the redesigned organization, students would receive answers from one person in one visit 90 percent of the time. Mechanisms would be put in place to gather customer satisfaction data, define the gaps, and design staffing and training accordingly.

The redesigned organization, Enrollment Services, combined four separate functions into one cross-functional process. This process would require a new structure and work roles. The combined organization would be more horizontal and report to one cabinet member. An executive director would lead the organization, and three teams of cross-trained student enrollment advisors (SEAs) would comprise it. Each team would consist of the following:

- One lead SEA to head up the team
- One recruitment and admissions specialist
- One registration and records specialist
- One student finance specialist
- One information and technology specialist
- Four generalist SEAs

The concept was that everyone in Enrollment Services would be a generalist; they would be expected to know all the ordinary business of the four functional areas. However, the specialists would bring depth of subject matter expertise in their functional areas. This was envisioned as a totally professional organization, presuming that much of the clerical work would be automated.

Among the ranks of the specialists, one in each functional area would be considered the lead specialist, the person who would have the greatest degree of subject matter expertise in one of the functional areas. The lead specialist would be responsible for training other employees and coordinating the processes across the teams. Each team would be complete in itself, i.e., able to handle the full range of student enrollment needs. The student would have easy access to specialists, who would be ready to answer questions and resolve problems that an SEA could not handle.

A new physical environment would be needed for the combined organization. One-stop service would require the Offices of Admissions, the Bursar, Financial Aid, and the Registrar to be integrated and easily accessible in an open environment that would be inviting to current as well as future students. This would help eliminate student runaround to get information, approvals, and answers. The new location was to be equipped with student access stations, with computers and printers available to students to update their personal data, to query data, and to initiate transactions. Work areas would be consolidated so that those who have contact with students would be conveniently located in one facility, improving service and fostering the team-centered approach the phase I study recommended.

Redesigning processes, while requiring a lot of work, can be fun. Implementation is very, very difficult. It takes courage to reengi-

neer—it is not for the faint of heart. It is also necessary to have the requisite skills at hand and strong executive leadership and support for the changes to be successful. Institutions often engage consultants for the redesign phase but undertake implementation on their own, figuring they now know what to do. If consultants are used on the project it is critical that facilitation and transfer of skills to the internal team occurs during the redesign phase so they are prepared to move the project forward in implementation. Unless there is fairly sophisticated in-house talent for team and project management, you may want to save some of your consultant budget for the implementation phase. Even with those skills in place, there are benefits to having an outsider without a personal agenda or political allegiances. In implementation, the forces of resistance to change will come on strong and, if allowed to prevail, will sidetrack or derail the project. It is realistic to allow 18 to 24 months for implementation of the redesign.

Unlike many institutions, our implementation did not revolve around the installation of a new software application for student information. We found that most of the technology requirements for the redesigned processes could be met by adding a Web front-end interface to our current administrative software.

At Seton Hall the implementation phase is still under way but the basic idea has been achieved. We started by setting up an Implementation Team. The makeup of an implementation team is different from that of a redesign team. The redesign team included employees inside as well as outside the four enrollment areas. An implementation team needs to be composed of the people who will own the work and who are in the best position to take implementation into operation. The team should also include members of the redesign team, who have the vision in their hearts and minds in a way that cannot be easily communicated in a plan or report.

During implementation, you might need to make adjustments to the redesign. Reengineering is said to be an improvisational and iterative process; if you try something that doesn't work quite as planned, you change it. Enrollment Services was redesigned as a totally professional organization. In reality, the university's clerical workers are unionized. The organization was going to be smaller with the introduction of self-service technology and a cross-functional staff, so some union and administrative jobs would be lost. We did not choose to go to battle to eliminate all unionized clerical jobs in Enrollment Services. Ultimately, the generalist jobs were defined as the unionized clerical positions, rather than entry-level administrative jobs. It can be said that this has changed the tenor of the organization somewhat.

The Implementation Team knew that the first task was cross-training employees, because it would take time to develop cross-functional skills. The next priority was to create a prototype for testing the concept and identifying problems. Within a few months the Implementation Team had set up a prototype SEA Team and used it during preregistration. The team was comprised of representatives from all four functional areas and had full access to the student administration system. Students could choose to visit the SEA Team or go the conventional route. If a student experienced a problem, such as a hold, the SEA Team identified and resolved the problem and the student was registered—in more or less one easy step. This proof of concept and the student satisfaction that resulted convinced us that we were on the right track.

While that was going on, architects were hired, a design created, and a building renovated to house the new organization. The Web interface for student and faculty access was installed. The new jobs for Enrollment Services were developed, and current employees got first shot at applying for the positions. Many were placed in the new positions.

The difficulty and pain of eliminating all the old jobs and having the employees apply for the new jobs cannot be underestimated. Any institution considering reengineering should recognize that this could be an outcome. Indeed, some institutions are counting on it to pare away at administrative departments that have expanded over time. Envisioning ways to reduce operating costs is quite a different thing from actually eliminating jobs. In higher education we pride ourselves on being more humane than the business world and on answering to a higher calling than the profit motive and the bottom line. Any institution going into reengineering with the understanding that streamlining its operations will result in fewer jobs has to look closely at itself and be sure it has the stomach for doing so. It could mean eliminating work that has been performed by employees who have served the institution for many, many years. However, another point of view is that reengineering offers an opportunity to address performance issues that went unattended in the past. There is also a tremendous opportunity to provide new growth opportunities for staff and allow them to rise to new levels of performance. This is why change management and human resource issues are so critical in focusing on the positive aspects and opportunities of redesign.

In our case, the new organization had fewer jobs, so some people inevitably lost their jobs. The university had been planning for this since it first considered reengineering. Vacant positions were left unfilled so that anyone losing a job because of reengineering might be able to take another position in the university. The severance package was reviewed, improved, and articulated. Job outplacement services were offered. As it happened, no one ended up without a job—some stayed with the university and others located positions outside.

There is room for discussion about the virtues of letting people know well in advance that they might not have jobs in the redesigned organization. The Seton Hall redesign had originally proposed selecting the best and brightest from the university at the start and putting them in place as the members of the SEA teams. In this way, everyone would know where he or she stood, and the selected individuals would have motivation and commitment to the redesign. The remaining employees would be phased out over time as the organization's labor needs diminished. Ultimately, we chose not to follow that path. One reason was that we had to give the unionized employees time to acquire cross-functional skills before we could say who were "the best."

There is also room for discussion before making any hiring decisions about the desired characteristics of employees in a process-centered, customer-oriented organization. They may be quite different from the characteristics of employees in a traditional, hierarchical, command-and-control organization. These new characteristics include the capacity to work in teams, exercise judgment, take initiative, and function outside the narrow silos they have been used to. The new environment requires good interpersonal skills to deliver excellent service to internal as well as external customers. The employees must have the capacity to understand the complete, end-to-end enrollment process and be willing to feel responsibility for the whole, not just a part of, the process. Institutions may find conflict in trying to save as many of the current employees as possible, while addressing the critical need to staff the organization with people possessing the new skill levels and behaviors.

What Worked. The following aspects of the reengineering project worked:

- We had leadership and support from the top—the president and the executive cabinet.
- We put together a strong redesign team and excused team members from much of their regular work so they could concentrate on the work of the redesign team.
- We allowed the team to be visionary. As a result they produced a first-rate design for a student-centered, process-based organization.
- We created a redesign that referenced not only the best practices in the field, but the particular style and needs of our campus.
- We used consultants who had a proven track record in this area and a well-developed and tested methodology for reengineering.
- We communicated a lot to the university community—how the redesign was progressing and what were the intended benefits.
- We planned for ways to accommodate any employees displaced by reengineering.

- We tested a prototype to show that our idea would work and to build momentum from its success.

What Did Not Work. The following aspects of the reengineering project didn't work:

- Our information technology strategic plan was developed before reengineering and did not anticipate what would be needed for reengineered administrative processes.

- Managerial opposition is inevitable and if allowed to go unchallenged can sabotage a redesign. Even knowing that intellectually may not fully prepare one for the depth and extent of the resistance.

- This kind of upheaval can cause employees to think about finding new jobs. It will be vital for success to identify key individuals with vital skills and pay attention to them so they stay on board. It is much harder to replace those skills than to keep them.

- The redesign called for a new executive to lead the merged organization and the implementation. We started implementing the redesign before that person was in place. Implementation is difficult and changes everything about the way work gets done, upsetting old routines and habits. It requires powerful leadership by someone who believes in the vision and can inspire others to believe as well. In addition, the leader must have strong project management skills and subject matter expertise in more than one of the enrollment areas. Because we launched implementation without having that person in place, resistance was more difficult to deal with.

Student Services Trends

At Seton Hall, we have merged the Offices of Admissions, the Registrar, Financial Aid, and the Bursar into one cross-functional department. Web-based technology has been installed to allow student self-service and automation of some data entry functions. Staff have been and continue to be cross-trained. A new physical environment has been provided to house the consolidated department and to give students one place to go for their entire enrollment needs. Processes have been redesigned and their implementation is under way. The reengineering of Enrollment Services is part of a larger, enterprise-wide transformation initiative.

There are two major trends in student services, as I see it. One is one-stop, one-step service to eliminate student runaround and improve operating inefficiencies. Students and their parents are becoming increasingly savvy and educated customers. As the cost of education is at an all-time high, and as the available choices of colleges are many, they are increasingly demanding better service and maximum value for their dollars—or they will go elsewhere.

Student Services Trends

TRENDS	IMPLEMENTATION PHASE
Student-Centered	●
Redesigned Services	◑
One-Stop Service Center	●
Cross-Functional Teams	◑
Self-Service Objectives	◑
Department Process Improvements	N/A
Web-Enabled Services	●
Admissions	◑
Registration	●
Advising	N/A
Financial Aid	◑
Billing	◑
Career Services	○
Systemic Change	◑
Replacement of Student Information Systems	N/A

Codes for Implementation Phase:
- ● Production
- ◑ Implementing
- ◑ Designed
- ○ Planning

The customer-service orientation is being incorporated into the service areas of higher education in recognition of this increased power of the student-customer.

The other major trend is Web-enabled self-service technology. As the Nintendo generation comes of age, the old paper-intensive processes, requiring students to stand in line, are often not acceptable. If the student can fill out a form to turn over to an employee for data entry, why not just let the student fill out an electronic form that automatically updates the database? Students prefer to avoid standing in line and dealing with a middle person.

Perhaps the most profound change is in the way work and the people who perform it are viewed. An emphasis on process means that we have asked and answered the questions, "What is our purpose in being here?" "Who are the beneficiaries of our work?" and "How best can we do it?" A process-centered organization recognizes the potential of the employee to perform the entire process, rather than only one or two tasks repeatedly. Work is viewed holistically rather than as fragments that barely relate to each other. The employees may find more gratification and significance in their work. They are authorized to use their creativity and intelligence to perform work that is no longer confined or restricted to one area, to participate in the whole, well-designed process. As employees see how their work fits into the broader context it is easier to see the connection between what they do and the overall success of the organization. They make take more pride in themselves and more responsibility for the success of the organization as they become team players who participate in decision making, are increasingly self-managed, and are asked for their solutions to problems. To this extent, there is the possibility of restoring some of the dignity to work that is lost when employees are limited, confined to their functional silos, endlessly supervised, removed from the eventual outcome of their efforts, and not employed to their fullest ability. This does not mean that employees' work lives become easier— quite the contrary. Process-centered work is harder and more consuming than repetitive task work. Those in a consolidated Enrollment Services organization may find that they have never worked so hard before. But it can make work more rewarding intellectually, emotionally, and financially.

Critical Success Factors and Key Considerations

In my opinion, the single most important success factor in reengineering is strong leadership and support originating from the highest levels of the institution. Without support from the top, the drastic nature of the changes reengineering produces will be so strongly resisted as to make it difficult, if not impossible, to proceed.

Technology is the tool that allows work to be performed in new and innovative ways. The ideal is to redesign the processes first and then define the technology that will support them, but this is not so commonly found. Many institutions start with the implementation of a Web-enabled software package and then see the potential for streamlining processes. Either way, it is perilous to proceed into implementation on a promised delivery date rather than waiting for the supporting technology to be up and running. It is also perilous to reduce the size of the workforce before implementing technology that automates work or shifts it to the student.

The impact that change has on the people in the workplace cannot be overstated. Whatever can be done to manage change should be done. Resistance is inevitable, predictable, and very human. You will need to anticipate how it will manifest itself and plan how to deal with it. The thinking is that if resistance to change is not forcefully dealt with it can easily reach the level of sabotage and the project will be doomed. People have a lot of themselves invested in their jobs, and any attempt to redefine those jobs, especially where it reduces authority or affects prestige, will strike at their hearts and they will fight it.

In the student service area there is not as much potential for savings as there is in other processes, such as purchasing. The desire to cut the budget in itself is not enough reason to reengineer this area. If processes are streamlined and the size of the organization is reduced, there will be some initial savings. However, those savings have to be balanced against expenditures necessary for supporting the new environment, such as technology, renovations, and increased pay for more highly skilled jobs. Instead, this should be viewed as part of an overall, institution-wide effort to enhance revenues by providing better service and competing more effectively.

Training and professional development of the staff are absolute requirements for success. Cross-training is the key to a one-stop, one-step level of service and to employees understanding the processes in a holistic context, as part of a continuum that crosses over departmental boundaries. Those who are charged with managing a process-centered organization will also need training, because this approach is still relatively new. Managing processes from end to end is a new skill in our environment, as is managing the teams that perform those processes.

Putting the right people in place is critical to success, whether it is the generalist who has the most contact with students or the administrator who has become a team leader. The rule is to get the best and brightest. A reengineering project can be brought to its knees if the wrong people, meaning those with different skills than those required for the new jobs, are put in place. And it is not compassionate to set up employees for certain failure by placing them in jobs for which they do not possess the skills. This has to be balanced against considerations of who has key knowledge or vital skills that are not duplicated elsewhere and that the organization cannot afford to lose.

Interestingly, some institutions start their reengineering initiative by building or renovating a new facility for co-locating or consolidating student service departments. Generally speaking, this is ill advised. The architect will first want to know what work will be performed there, how many people will perform the work, and how the work will be organized into a work flow. These questions cannot be answered unless the processes have been well described, the jobs defined, and the work flow imagined. Start with the process—everything else comes from and supports that.

The best advice I can offer administrators considering reengineering enrollment or student services is to redesign according to the unique and particular needs and situation of your campus and its population. No two schools are exactly alike, no two have approached this in quite the same way. The trends in the field must be understood, the best practices researched, and the impact of technology analyzed. It would be a mistake to buy one school's redesign whole cloth and try to fit it onto another institution. Reengineering always starts with the customer and with the processes that are used to create something of value for them. That will not be the same in all times and places. In fact, it is quite mutable. Reengineers expect to engage in process improvement indefinitely, in response to increasing or changing demands. Know who your customers are, what you do for them, the best way to do it, and the way that will satisfy them most and be most efficient. The rest follows.

Conclusion

The higher education environment is very traditional. We enjoy and cling to our time-honored and well-worn ways of bringing students and faculty together in the pursuit of knowledge. But fast and major change is not merely in the wind—it is upon us. The widespread use of Web-based technology; the pervasiveness of the Internet; increased competition among schools for the best students and faculty; increasing costs for maintaining and building infrastructure; a consumerist approach by parents and students to college selection; and trends in the business world for performing work that influence our administrative practices—all these factors are being felt. We are being challenged to shake off dusty approaches from a time when colleges and universities were few and students were to feel fortunate they were admitted and tolerated. These times demand that processes and systems serve the student, rather than requiring the student to serve unwieldy and frustrating systems. We have had no choice but to become less rigid and punitive, and to become more service-oriented.

As it turns out, the processes that are most satisfying to the student will often be those that are also most efficient. It is satisfying to students to go to one place or person for all their enrollment requirements. It is efficient to have cross-trained, multifunctional staff working in teams to handle the whole end-to-end process. It is *not* efficient to staff independent and uncoordinated offices with employees limited to one or two functions. It is *not* efficient to require many authorization signatures that create numerous handoffs and consume time. It is *not* efficient to maintain paper-based transactions that require large amounts of data entry when students can access the system and perform the transaction themselves. It is *not* efficient for students to ask for their own data when they can look it up themselves if given access.

Undeniably, student service delivery is undergoing a transformation. Higher levels of customer expectations have been created. Colleges and universities will need to engage in creative, even original, thinking; invest in the latest technology; and reinvent the way work is performed and services are delivered if they are to meet higher expectations.

4

Madge Lewis

Reengineering Student Administrative Services

Overview

Roger W. Babson founded Babson College in Wellesley, Massachusetts in 1919. The college grants bachelor of science and master of business administration degrees in addition to programs offered through its School of Executive Education. The American Assembly of Collegiate Schools of Business and the New England Association of Schools and Colleges accredit its undergraduate and graduate programs. *U.S. News & World Report* ranked Babson's undergraduate program the best business specialty school in the country, and in its 1998 ranking of graduate programs, the publication placed Babson first in entrepreneurship and among the top 10 part-time business programs nationwide.

The college's combined student body is made up of approximately 3,300 students. The School of Executive Education has more than 8,000 alumni, drawn from 400 organizations and 23 countries. The faculty, numbering approximately 200, teaches in all three programs and is supported by an administrative staff of nearly 500 employees.

The Compelling Case for Change

When Babson began considering reengineering its student services, it faced the same obstacles as the rest of higher education, namely, a cost structure that typically ran ahead of inflation and a revenue base that was more or less static. Moreover, we had adopted a long-range strategic plan that would propel us to the forefront of business

---

Madge Lewis is business process consultant at Babson College, where she led the implementation of the college's reengineering initiative. In 1997, she stepped in as project manager to oversee the conversion of the student information system and has been serving in that capacity with other business system replacement projects ever since. She has an M.Ed. from Northeastern University and a bachelor's from the University of Hartford.

education. This approach has and will continue to require tremendous resources, both human and financial, far exceeding our means. While the capital campaign (announced in October 1994) would likely address some of these inadequacies in the long term, the college did not have the resources to accomplish its immediate goals, nor would a successful endowment campaign, in and of itself, provide all of the resources needed to meet Babson's objectives.

Cost and service issues are built into our long-term strategy for success. For example, the remaking of the two-year MBA program has positioned Babson College at the leading edge of curricular innovation. However, the delivery of this program costs considerably more than its predecessor, given the integration of the curriculum and necessity for additional faculty to spread the load of planning, classroom, and assessment time. The graduate school dean had documented nearly a doubling in faculty contact hours in the new MBA program even as we were completing the redesign of the undergraduate program and were finding a similar cost structure and need to invest in faculty there as well. Though both of these efforts are critical to the immediate and future viability of Babson as an institution, neither will, in and of itself, generate significantly increased revenues to cover the added costs of development, implementation, and ongoing support. At another level, the college requires facilities, information technologies, and library resources far beyond those that complemented past modes of program delivery. These enabling services further raise the cost of operations. This scenario cannot be offset by a growth in tuition and fees. In fact, to be competitive today, Babson is committed to annual increases in tuition pegged to the Consumer Price Index.

In quantitative terms, the college required an addition of nearly $1.4 million annually to develop and run its new educational programs. Capital requirements were underfunded by approximately $1.5 million per year, and our library and technology services were also underfunded by 50 percent. The college's strategic plan established a goal to reduce undergraduate enrollment to around 1,600 by 1997–98, in line with the capacity of our present and planned facilities. This action, along with a tuition cap, limited our options.

In summary, while essential costs were going up dramatically, we lacked the ability to generate significant added revenues. Finally, since our dependence on tuition dollars would continue, we needed to ensure that Babson could maintain its ability to attract and retain high-quality students. While the redesign of both the graduate and undergraduate programs addressed the academic requirements of our customers, we had data to indicate that the delivery of student-related business services did not meet their needs.

It was therefore clear that a dramatic step was required to reduce the structural costs of Babson College operations and to redirect those resources toward the delivery of academic programs. At the same time, and equally important, it was necessary to examine the delivery of student services and to redesign those processes beginning with a clean sheet of paper and direct input from our customers.

Project Summary

Project Goals. When the college decided to embark upon its reengineering project, it was for two significant reasons. We needed to find a way to reduce our operating costs dramatically to fund our newly designed, innovative academic programs, and based upon feedback, we knew there was room to improve our service levels to students, parents, and employers. A third, and unofficial, goal of the president at the time was the desire to be best in class in terms of customer service. I will spend the majority of this chapter discussing the design of student services since most of our effort was in this area. The reduction of operating costs was in effect a lever used to challenge the teams and hold them accountable, although the goal was indeed a real one.

In the spring of 1993, the president appointed a task force to become educated on reengineering and to determine whether there was an opportunity for the college to accomplish its goals. The task force was comprised of roughly half of the college's executive team. Along the way, it was determined that we needed a more operational-level perspective, at which time two senior managers and a faculty member were added to the group. The task force was focused solely on the administrative operations of the college; the faculty was already reengineering the academic programs, although that language was not being used. The group, after several months of reading and discussion, focused on the core administrative process that affected its primary customers—students. At the end of December 1993, the task force recommended to the president that he establish a design team to reengineer the enrollment process.

The Design Phase. As set forth in the Reengineering Task Force's Case for Action and subsequently endorsed by the college's president and cabinet, the Reengineering Design Team's assignment was to develop a detailed plan for the redesign and delivery of student administrative services. Those services were all of the services that complement classroom academic experiences, including admissions, financial aid, registration, student billing, student loans administration, academic planning, field-based learning administration, career services, and so forth. The document was to include descriptive scenarios for a desired state, a plan for their attainment, and an operating computer system prototype of some of these redesigned business processes. The detailed action plan was to include an organizational design, staffing levels, operating budgets, process policies and procedures, and information technologies.

The chief information officer, who was known for his vision and his ability to get things done, chaired the team. Other members of the team included the graduate school registrar (who was designated to lead the implementation phase of the project), the associate dean of undergraduate admission, the associate director of financial aid, the associate dean of the undergraduate program, a systems analyst, and a project manager who was working at the college on a one-year contract. Three of the seven were assigned to the project full-time; the rest of the team received a 20 percent workload reduction, but in reality it was closer to 40 percent.

The design team worked for five months conducting best practice research both within higher education and in the corporate sector. For instance, we looked at Disney for its model customer service operation and at Deloitte and Touche for its recruiting process. Focus groups were held with every constituency—parents, corporate recruiters, current and prospective undergraduate students, full-time and part-time graduate students, and the faculty. The purpose of these focus groups was to solicit input about the desired state and to learn what was not working in the current process. In the private sector, the pressure for restructuring and renewal has come from increased competitiveness and the unforgiving nature of high costs. Many argue that consumers have become more demanding as they look for better service and quality at a lower price. For those of us who work in higher education, the pressure is similarly for better service in the face of reduced (or at least stagnant) revenues. Furthermore, our customers have lost their tolerance for bureaucracies and are increasingly of a mindset that if banks, hotels, and airlines can focus on the voice of the customer and deliver quality, colleges and universities are also capable of delivering a quality product at an affordable price. Indeed, focus group–based data clearly indicated that the customer's perception of value delivered declines markedly after the first year of attendance and that this sense of poor quality and neglect continues through to graduation.

The other significant part of the team's process was to interview key stakeholders working in the departments that would be affected; we wanted to gain a general understanding of their work process but not spend too much time mapping it all out. We knew that the more time spent on the current state, the more invested we would be in it and the less able to effect real change. It was simple, ordinary brainstorming to develop the high-level customer service model that would become the framework for all future work. Finally, we hired a local software development firm to help us map out the new processes and to build our information system prototype. This was one of three instances when we utilized outside consulting services. A consulting firm that specialized in reengineering reviewed the design team's work plan at the outset to make sure we were on the right path. And once the team's work was completed, we reviewed it with this same firm and asked for its advice on how best to "sell" the plan to the president's cabinet.

After five months, in July 1994, the president's cabinet approved the Reengineering Design Team's plan to accomplish its goals. The plan called for the following:

- A redesign of administrative processes in several key areas of the college that would reduce, streamline, and simplify operations while providing improved levels of service
- Heavy investment in enabling technology
- Utilization of our human resource talents while providing for a flatter, less hierarchical structure
- An overall reduction in operating costs with a 30 to 40 percent target goal

This last point was in part a message to the team and to the community that any significant reduction of operating costs could not be achieved by tinkering around the edges; radical redesign was necessary. The following is an excerpt from the design team's executive summary, which was distributed to the community just prior to the launch of the implementation phase of the project.

An Overall Statement of Purpose:

Recognizing the many challenges that confront Babson College as we strive to achieve our educational mission, we are now committing ourselves, over the next twenty-four months, to a major reengineering project whose purpose is to reduce, streamline, and simplify the administrative operations of the institution, freeing students, parents, employers, faculty, and staff from bureaucracy and paperwork so that they may devote more of their time and resources to learning and teaching. To this end, we envision a work place which focuses upon the delivery of high quality services to our customers through the efforts of cross-functional, self-directed teams, and responsive, easy-to-use, information systems and technologies.

The Implementation Phase. This phase of the project began in August 1994 with a series of community briefings in which the director of reengineering described the work of the design team, the high-level model, the implementation strategy, and the college's decision to freeze all open positions for the duration of the project. This was an effort to create flexibility in the organization so that when it was known which positions would disappear as a result of reengineering, those employees affected would be able to move to another part of the organization if they chose. In the meantime, any position that became open, for whatever reason, was filled with temporary staff. The announcement of this policy immediately lowered the visible signs of anxiety in the staff; the first time a position opened up and was filled with temporary staff, the anxiety level lowered once more.

As Michael Hammer, an authority on reengineering, has said many times, "Reengineering is a four lane highway to hell." By definition, reengineering asks people to accept an enormous amount of change in a short period of time. It's a journey into uncertainty as we travel down a road we've never traveled before. Naturally, people are very nervous as sacred cows are attacked, rules are changed, and ambitions are threatened. Resistance to change is part of the human condition; even while you may be able to recognize the good on the horizon, you are still losing something and that makes people very uncomfortable. This change in college policy was a recognition of that discomfort and fear.

In September, the implementation team was formally launched. It was comprised of more than 75 employees and was structured in nine working groups as follows:

- Academic Records/Registration
- Admissions
- Undergraduate Advocacy
- Graduate Advocacy
- Field-Based Learning and Career Services
- Student Financial Services
- Information Technology
- Change Management
- Core Team

The first six teams on this list were called "business prototype teams" and were charged with creating detailed work flow diagrams for the respective pieces of the overall framework given to them by the design team. They received the following team charter, which detailed the scope of their assignment:

- Design business processes to take advantage of a high level of automation
- Test process designs and conceptual models with all stakeholders
- Reduce operating costs by 30 to 40 percent
- Develop a set of performance metrics to be used in assessing the success of the processes designed
- Determine staffing requirements
- Outline the training necessary to support employees in new roles

We recognized at the outset that in order for us to achieve success we needed to have adequate representation in the teams and involve as many employees as possible in the process to achieve buy-in. The director of reengineering and the cabinet recommended the team members, and the vice presidents asked them to participate. In the end, each team was made up of subject matter specialists, other administrative stakeholders, faculty, students, an IT representative, and a quality specialist. Quality specialists are staff with advanced training in quality tools and principles whose role here was to facilitate team meetings. This structure worked very well for several reasons. First, it is critical to involve as many stakeholders as possible in a change initiative of this kind in order for them to feel a sense of control and to achieve the buy-in essential to success. Second, since we were trying to improve student services, we wanted to include the voice of the customer at every stage. And third, we created a vehicle to challenge the status quo by including representatives from other departments on each team. These additions to the teams were what allowed them to think out of the box and to be creative in their work.

The IT team's job was obvious: to design and build the applications specified by each of the prototype teams, which were at the core of the overall customer service model. Concurrent with the process design work, the IT team was developing a new model for Babson's computing environment as the industry was moving toward a client server standard. Babson decided on a "best of breed" model, which meant that we would purchase the best student information system, the best admission system, and so on, and focus internal efforts in two areas. The first area was the integration of the data in a central operational data store; the second was building a common storefront of Web-enabled applications for the end user. In the end, we had a build-and-buy model; the back-end applications were purchased while the middle data layer and the front end were built in-house. This architecture afforded us the greatest amount of flexibility. At any time, we could swap out a transaction system without disrupting everything dependent on it, and we were free to engage in continuous improvement efforts on the front end.

The director, recognizing the extent to which changes would be necessary to the college's human resource policies and programs, created a change management team to determine and develop the human resource programs needed to support the reengineered environment. During the spring, this team conducted surveys to gain a better understanding of the current environment on campus and to identify the opportunities and barriers to change. A new model (competency-based) was developed that would enable us to focus on knowledge, skills, and behaviors. The model was intended to be used as the foundation for new programs in selection, training and development, compensation, and performance management. All of these changes were meant to support new team-based behaviors that were essential to the success of the new service model. In addition, this team was responsible for developing an ongoing communication strategy for the project targeted to the Babson community as a whole, another key ingredient for establishing buy-in on the campus.

The Core Team was responsible for the overall results of the reengineering project, including the approval of prototype team process designs, launch plans, staffing levels, and integration across processes. The team was made up of the prototype team leaders, the CIO, the director of human resources, the process owners (the vice president of academic affairs, the vice president of business and financial affairs, the vice president of student affairs, the graduate school dean, and the associate dean of undergraduate studies), and the director of quality. The director of reengineering chaired this group. Over time, the membership was modified somewhat based upon appropriate representation and need (for example, the budget director was added to the group several months into the process).

Figure 4.1 shows the areas of work necessary to achieve our objectives. The "prototype" teams as stated above carried out the process design work while the Information Technology, Change Management, and Core Teams did the support work.

Sensing that the Core Team would be unable, given vested interests, to come to consensus on organizational design and that the attempt would cause serious damage to the group, the director urged the president to make this set of decisions unilaterally. In June, the president held an all-day meeting with the Core Team and the cabinet with the express purpose of providing him with a variety of opinions and scenarios. It was the consensus of this group that the new organization should reflect the college's commitment to customer service, quality, community responsibility, teamwork, and team and individual empowerment. Curricular and cocurricular programs would be guided by a holistic view of students. In the past, particularly in regard to the organization of undergraduate student services, some administrators were responsible for academic counsel-

Support Structures ⟫⟫➡	Process Design ⟫⟫➡	Results

Human Resource Programs
Training and Development
Organizational Design
Information Technology
Facilities Renewal
	Admission
	Academic Records
	    and Registration
	Student Financial Services
	Field-Based Learning
	    and Career Services
	Advocacy
		Cost Reduction
		Increased Student
		    Satisfaction
		Enriched Employee Roles

Figure 4.1 Areas of Work Necessary to Achieve Objectives

ing and some for personal counseling and cocurricular programming. These two groups were separated not only geographically, but organizationally. From a student's point of view, however, he or she simply needs someone to talk to. A student chooses a college for the whole experience—academics, cocurricular programs, and other aspects of student life—not to run all over campus looking for the right person with whom to talk. The new organization was to be built around cross-functional teams and processes that relate to students and stakeholder groups. Coordinators and teams, while reporting to a single executive, would be held responsible for servicing all internal and external customers. The position of vice president of student affairs was eliminated; the new dean of student affairs now reports to the undergraduate dean as part of the Academic Affairs Division. This reorganization helps the college achieve its goal of greater integration of academic and cocurricular life and enhances our ability to use a more holistic approach in the education of students. The other major change was the formation of a student services cluster reporting to the associate vice president for academic affairs. This new cluster consists of the Admissions, Academic Records/Registration, and Student Financial Services Teams.

What Worked. Team composition turned out to be very important in two respects. First, the inclusion of faculty on the prototype teams was important from a political perspective. It gave the project some additional legitimacy in the eyes of the faculty as a whole even though we were staying away from the curriculum itself. Second, expanding the team beyond those currently working in a functional area allowed for challenges to the status quo, which would have been much more difficult otherwise.

By forcing teams to map out their new business processes fully, we standardized on a single tool. Because of that decision, we now have a full set of process maps that can be updated as processes change through continuous improvement. These maps can be used to identify and diagnose problem areas and provide very useful training for new employees. The act of writing these maps forced the teams to really think through the way they were going to do business in the future.

One of the most critical pieces of any change initiative is communication; you simply cannot communicate enough. Throughout the course of Babson's project, I produced a weekly newsletter titled *Partners In Change*, which was distributed to the entire cam-

pus. It described what work had been done during the week by the various teams. It was also a central place to make larger announcements (i.e., the reorganization), but its main purpose was to provide information. It was very important to us that employees felt we were being honest with them and not withholding anything. I also made myself available to speak to various groups, such as departmental retreats, alumni, trustees, and academic classes studying related topics, and provided a general update to the community at large twice a year at Babson Town Meetings.

In the design, we talked about advocacy as being the human version of our one-stop shopping model. The role of the advocates was to be the single point of service for all students, assisting them with general questions and providing both academic and personal counseling services; anything that could not be provided online in self-service mode. Although the words have changed, the Office of Class Deans, which provides this service to our undergraduate population, has been quite successful. Since its staffing model was built around the promise of technology that has not been fully met to date, it is at times quite overloaded and students have difficulty getting an appointment during peak cycles. The office is, however, providing a whole range of services to our undergraduate students and has become the essence of our one-stop shop for students. To some extent even faculty deal frequently with this group to discuss and resolve student issues. Students are no longer running all over campus to do business.

What Didn't Work. A different story can be told about advocacy for graduate students. Midway through process mapping, this prototype team brought its ideas to faculty and students for feedback. The result was a complete redesign that called for integrating academic and career counseling and was based totally on feedback from its constituents. The new model called for placing this role with the career service professionals who have training in this area and who could easily learn about academic advising. Although some circles enthusiastically supported the new plan, it became extremely political and never went anywhere.

Our attempt to flatten the organization seemed promising at first. We hired an outside consulting firm to assist us in building a competency model, and we designed new team member, team leader, and coordinator roles. We even went so far as to hold alignment meetings with the Core Team and the president's cabinet to make sure everyone understood and accepted the cultural changes envisioned. However, as with any major change effort, there were pockets of resistance, cultural and political issues, and turnover in several key executive positions that created barriers to change that caused us to fall short of some of our initial objectives. On a positive note, however, several of our teams that were launched in 1995–96 have indeed been functioning in a team environment and a new approach to performance management has been adopted that is partially based upon the competency model.

With regard to our target of 30 to 40 percent cost savings, we did indeed reach that goal—at least on paper. However, I had made a commitment to the prototype teams that their new staffing models would not be implemented until the technology was in place to support them. At this time I can report that the initially identified savings and staffing models have held in some areas and not in others for a variety of reasons. The college, however, was able to reinvest in the academic programs and has done so over time.

Student Services Trends

In developing a model for change, the Design Team operated under certain assumptions based upon customer feedback. First among these is that the student should have easy and timely access to all information pertaining to his or her relationships with the institution. Second, we assumed that the student would prefer to draw upon this information and more generally to transact nonacademic business with the college at times and places of greatest convenience. Third, we assumed that as long as the tools in question were relatively easy to use, students would prefer to conduct business over the college's information network and through computer-based systems and tools.

The New Service Model. The design team identified the following principles as fundamental to the redesign of the college's student-related business processes (admission, financial aid, billing, registration, advising, and career placement):

- Business processes that focus on the customer (students, parents, employers)
- A single point of service
- Easy access to administrative services
- Processes that consistently meet customer requirements
- A focus on integrated processes rather than functions
- Formal accountability for quality service delivery
- The centralization of common services
- Information technology to enhance service delivery and to eliminate duplication of effort

In the Design Team's model, the single point of service was to be provided to students and parents, when personal contact was necessary, by assigned advocates, and to employers by the Field-Based Learning and Career Services Team. However, the first line of service to students for routine business matters comes through the use of our Web-enabled student services, currently dubbed "ViDi-O" for View It and Do It Online. Use of this system enables students to get most of the information they need and do routine transactions via online, self-directed systems, freeing employees to spend time on more value-added activities.

For those who prefer human to machine interaction, the team created a so-called one-stop-shopping model whereby a knowledgeable generalist (the advocate) assists the student with any inquiry or problem. Only in a limited number of instances does the student require the face-to-face assistance of an on-campus specialist. Instead, the student obtains the necessary expertise either electronically—through the college's intranet—or through the generalist, who might in turn seek expert advice.

Another part of the design was to move toward a flatter structure. We designed a model that had basically three levels: the executive (dean or vice president), the coordinator, and the team itself. The coordinator has responsibility for providing resources, information, and coaching for two or more teams. The teams themselves have a team leader who is a member of the team that is responsible for providing value-added service to our customers. The teams are made up of cross-trained people coming together from the former functional departments that are now integrated.

Reengineering is about processes, not functions. A process is a set of activities that have inputs and that create a valued-added product or service for the customer. Like most organizations, we were built around functional units. We tried very hard to work well across departments, but it was difficult. The design team looked for overlaps or redundancy in processes, places where we could integrate our functional stovepipes. Most of what we found is very logical.

Business Process Synergies. During the design phase, we met with and listened carefully to both customers and service providers, looking for areas where the integration of functions and processes would lead to enhanced effectiveness, efficiency, and accountability. We discovered those opportunities in the following processes:

- Academic Records/Registration
- Admissions
- Advocacy
- Field-Based Learning and Career Services
- Student Financial Services

In 1994 we had two admission offices, one for the undergraduate program and another for the graduate school. While the recruiting and marketing function is unique to each program, given the different products and target customer groups, the data entry, production, telephone, and mailing activities are common—the process, not the product, was the focus of our efforts.

We also had two registrar's offices. In this case, roughly 85 percent of their work was redundant. So it was clear that combining the two made sense.

Our various internship offices and the Office of Career Services were increasingly interdependent and needed to be managed in an integrated manner. To do so gave the employer the one-stop shopping wanted for all aspects of his or her relationships with Babson College. In addition, the process of matching students to experiences, whether internships or paid employment, was nearly identical. We decided to take advantage of that by merging all these departments into a single Center for Career Development and Field-Based Programs.

The integration of student billing, loan processing, and financial aid to create Student Financial Services made a lot of sense and has become fairly common in the industry. For us, the idea came directly from the focus groups we held with parents and students who wanted a single point of service for all financial business with the college.

Finally, as stated earlier, the concept of advocacy as implemented by our Office of Class Deans is central to our new model and has been quite a success with our undergraduate students.

Critical Success Factors and Key Considerations

Babson's mission statement and culture played a critical role in laying the groundwork and allowing us to contemplate going down this road.

> Babson College is committed to being an internationally recognized leader in management education. Through its programs & practices, the College educates innovative leaders capable of anticipating, initiating, and managing change. In a climate of entrepreneurial spirit, creative & analytical thinking. . . .

Our mission dedicated to entrepreneurship, innovation, and managing change has certainly played a large role. Add to that the fact that we are a business school with faculty who understand the concepts and can support the need for change. It is important to remember also that our faculty had been engaged in completely redesigning the curriculum for a number of years leading up to this effort.

Another major factor is that in 1989 a new president came to Babson from Xerox, where he had initiated a total quality management program. When he arrived at Babson, he quietly began offering exposure to the concepts of quality to small groups of administrators

and faculty who were interested. Two years later, a full-blown Quality Office was in place, every administrative employee at the college had been trained, and some faculty members were already beginning to teach the subject in the classroom. By the time reengineering began at Babson, we were all speaking the same language and our culture had been changed dramatically. At the start of the implementation phase of the project, I created strong linkages with the Quality Office and its staff. They had the skills and tools, and it was important that the community understand that the two disciplines are both necessary and ongoing to effect lasting change; one is simply more radical than the other.

Conclusion

Let me offer some advice based upon my own experiences as director of reengineering at Babson College. First, expect and plan for resistance. Change is hard. Change is uncomfortable. It is part of the human condition to avoid it. That is why strong leadership and effective communications are central to any change effort of this magnitude. At Babson, I consider our communications effort to have been fairly successful. Employees understood after the first month or so that there were no big secrets and that, while they may not have fully believed in the direction we were clearly going, they had all the information they needed.

Change management is a leadership responsibility and must be actively sustained throughout the project. The institution's executive team must be willing to pull the heavy strings and to inter-

Student Services Trends

TRENDS	IMPLEMENTATION PHASE
Student-Centered	◑
Redesigned Services	◑
One-Stop Service Center	N/A
Cross-Functional Teams	●
Self-Service Objectives	●
Department Process Improvements	◑
Web-Enabled Services	●
Admissions	●
Registration	●
Advising	◔
Financial Aid	●
Billing	●
Career Services	◑
Systemic Change	◔
Replacement of Student Information Systems	●

Codes for Implementation Phase:

- ● Production
- ◑ Implementing
- ◕ Designed
- ○ Planning

vene when necessary, holding individuals accountable for behaviors not in line with objectives. In addition, other change agents and project leaders must target some of the communications to this group if they are to be supporters of the effort.

Redesign business processes that affect the customer first— that is where you will find the biggest payoff. Let customers help themselves. The value for students on any college campus is in the curriculum and to a lesser extent in its cocurricular programs, but certainly not in course selection. The time students spend on this and other administrative tasks should be minimal and convenient. That is why so many schools have taken up the anytime, anywhere mantra and are providing student services via Web-enabled, self-service systems, and students are responding. Finally, remember the job is never really done—you just transition into a continuous improvement mode until the need arises again for radical change— and you can be sure it will!

Frank B. Campanella
Rita R. Owens

Project Delta: Planning a New Student Services Model

Boston College seeks to be recognized as the best managed university in the nation by adopting twenty-first century network computing as the means to deliver prompt, personal services and information to all constituents in a do-it-yourself manner every day and all day and by deploying a highly productive, broadly skilled cadre of employees.

Project Delta Direction Statement
Summer 1996

Overview

One of the findings from a February 1998 cost study of higher education commissioned by Congress was the following: "Most academic institutions have been content to maintain a veil of obscurity over their financial operations and have yet to confront, seriously, basic strategies

Frank B. Campanella is executive vice president of Boston College. He is responsible for all internal management of the university as well as for long-range operational and fiscal planning, capital planning, and information technology. He holds a doctorate from the Harvard Business School, an MBA from Babson College, and a bachelor's from Rensselaer Polytechnic Institute.

Rita R. Owens is project leader, service strategies, for Project Delta at Boston College. She has developed her system and service management expertise in various registrar roles at Virginia Polytechnic Institute and State University, Babson College, and Boston College. She currently oversees two major redesign efforts for Boston College. She earned her bachelor's at Westfield State College and her master's at Virginia Polytechnic Institute and State University.

for cost reduction." At Boston College, however, we have been working vigorously on strategies for reducing costs. Our Holy Grail is simultaneously improving levels of services to students, faculty, alumni, and parents while dramatically reducing costs. We plan to transform the administration of the university through what we have named Project Delta. Delta is the mathematical symbol for change, and Project Delta is about creating change in Boston College's management culture and environment. While this project is ambitious, this type of change is not new to us. We have long been proactive in transforming ourselves. Our shift began 25 years ago as we changed from being a commuter school to the nationally top-ranked institution we are today.

The Compelling Case for Change

We undertook Project Delta in 1996 because we found ourselves in a "crisis of aspirations." We wanted to continue to increase our financial investment in our faculty, facilities, technology, and student financial assistance. To fully fund these initiatives and still maintain a low-growth tuition policy, we had to reduce our ongoing operating costs. At the same time, we wanted to improve our service to our constituents. We heard no significant complaints about our service, but we had learned from focus groups with parents that our processes were cumbersome and our service was not responsive. We were watching the proliferation of self-service options that the Internet was providing and knew that we should provide similar options to our students, faculty, staff, alumni, and parents. The combination of needing to reduce costs and the knowledge that we could improve our services through the use of Web technology resulted in the creation of Project Delta. The following are our specific goals for the project:

- To continue to improve our academic quality by recruiting and keeping the best faculty and adding 50 new faculty positions over a five-year period

- To improve all aspects of student life on campus
- To attract the best graduate students by increasing stipends in selected areas
- To provide sufficient financial aid so that students in different socioeconomic classes can afford a Boston College education
- To carry out an extensive plan to add to our physical facilities
- To make major new investments in information technology

The scope of Project Delta includes everything that the university does, but it stops at the door of the classroom or laboratory or other venue a faculty member uses to carry out his or her scholarly work. We are tackling our objectives through three concurrent strategies:

- Business process reengineering
- Organization redesign
- Dynamic self-studies using activity value analysis

These objectives are further broken down into projects to assist us in organizing the work.

The business process reengineering strategy includes the following four projects: student services, faculty/staff support, facilities management, and a new human resource information system. The focus of this chapter is the student services project, which is a redesign and consolidation of all of the processes that provide services to students.

Project Summary

Direction Statement. In the summer of 1996, a core team was formed to define what a transformed Boston College would look like. The team consisted of seven Boston College employees and was facilitated by a consultant. Since the group was charged with redesigning all services for Boston College except those inside the classroom and the laboratory, the group considered all aspects of faculty, staff, student, and parent services.

The team recommended in its direction statement the redesign and/or creation of a student services model, local service centers, management and use of physical plant, and the implementation of a PeopleSoft human resource information system. The student services model and local service centers specifically addressed the process, technology, and organizational changes that would be made to support service delivery to students and faculty/staff, respectively. A new human resource system and physical plant management system were recommended to provide a technology infrastructure. Although the major projects would not depend on these new systems for their creation, they could benefit from their implementation.

Student Life Model. After the Executive Team approved the Project Delta direction statement, several design teams were created. Outside consultants were not used extensively from this point on, although we did contract outside project management and commu-

nications consulting on a limited basis. The executives chose the design team members from areas around campus with the objective of creating cross-functional work teams that would bring varying skills and perspectives to the work at hand. Team members came from the Offices of University Housing, Enrollment Systems, the University Registrar, Management Information Systems, Student Accounts, the Vice President for Student Affairs, Financial Aid, Undergraduate Admission, the Dean of the College of Arts and Sciences, and University Counseling. A group of administrative advisors was also selected for the team, and each team had a designated leader. This group consisted of directors of all the targeted areas (if they were not already on the design team) and several campus representatives, including deans and technology leaders. The design team members were chosen not for their departmental representation, but for their ability to think creatively about services from our students' and parents' perspectives. Many of the team members were associate directors, not directors. Our assumption, which proved to be true, was that operational people—those closer to their offices' processes—would be less threatened by changes to the processes. The team worked on a high-level design for new student service processes two full days a week for six months.

We broke down our work into the following six segments:

- "As is" review and documentation of current processes
- Cost analysis of the current processes
- Evaluation of student satisfaction
- Design of new high-level processes
- Design of new organization
- Definition of new technology requirements

"As Is" Review. To understand all the services Boston College delivered to students we decided to document current processes. Team members worked in pairs to research service areas. At this point, we did not limit ourselves to the obvious service areas, like student accounts and registrar. We also looked at campus police, ID services, health services, and the dean of students.

Our goal was to educate team members about every process involved in student service areas and to uncover redundancies and inefficiencies. The executive vice president wrote to all the departments we would visit and requested their cooperation. His letter proved invaluable because many people were intimidated by our visits. It was also helpful that certain team members were able to provide most of the process for their areas. We assigned other pairs of team members to review these areas to provide some objectivity.

For each process we collected the process name, description, calendar time performed, and number of staff performing the function. We rated the processes to determine which were most important to achieving student/parent satisfaction and to supporting our academic mission. Next, we began to tackle the processes that were rated the highest in terms of customer satisfaction and academic mission to ensure we were directing our efforts toward the most significant areas in terms of impact.

Cost Analysis. We wanted to perform a cost analysis of the work we were already doing so that we could, after applying technology to a new organization, understand how much we had actually saved. A staff member from the Office of the Executive Vice President helped team members establish in dollar amounts how much each process cost the university. It was then clear which of our processes were the most costly and which of the major service areas should be targeted for change. This analysis showed that we should focus our efforts on the Offices of University Career Services, the University Registrar, Financial Aid, Student Accounts, Loans and Collections, and Undergraduate Admission. For each department, a master list of processes/activities was identified and then translated into a survey instrument designed to capture time and effort data for administrative, secretarial/clerical, and sometimes student staff (where students constituted a significant part of the workforce). We worked with a department representative who distributed and collected the surveys. Some representatives handed them out with a due date. The most efficient method for capturing the data, however, was developed by a proactive department that held a meeting to explain the process and had all staff members complete the forms in that session.

The aggregate results of the time and effort statistics for each type of staff were used to allocate salaries to processes and to determine the full-time equivalent staffing associated with each departmental activity. We continue to use these calculations as a benchmark for understanding the efficiencies we gain by automating or eliminating a process.

Student Satisfaction Survey. To assess the ultimate impact of Project Delta we needed to know the current levels of satisfaction with our services. A market research company surveyed our student population on a wide range of issues, from academic advising to the campus bus service. Respondents answered each question twice: they were first asked to identify the level of importance of the service and then to comment on their level of satisfaction with that service. Some students received paper copies with the option of completing the survey electronically, and others received the URL for the electronic survey. In addition to ease of completion, we offered them incentives. If they completed the survey they would be eligible for gifts ranging from football tickets to a dinner with our president. However, the return rate still only averaged about 20 percent.

Our findings showed us that students were satisfied with our service, but the purpose of many of our processes eluded them. For example, all groups indicated a need to improve the clarity of financial aid procedures. One of the goals of conducting the survey was to establish a benchmark that we could measure as we worked through the redesign effort to improve service to students. We plan to repeat the survey when we complete a majority of the implementation and will compare the results to the initial measurements.

High-Level Design. The team set out to define, in more tangible terms, the student service plan envisioned in the core team's direction statement. We started by identifying and redefining major processes according to the standards in the direction statement. These processes cut across current organizational boundaries. Once they were designed (i.e., flowed and documented), we reviewed the work required for the new processes, identified technology requirements, and created an organization to support the new work. The overall design takes into account all student service processes from a student's inquiry to Boston College through graduation. We designed the processes from a student's perspective, not from our organizational or operational model.

The processes include the following:

- *Personal and electronic communication services.* The process by which students and families communicate with Boston College, specifically leveraged by Web technology and a new service structure.
- *Student market analysis/development.* The undergraduate, graduate, and law marketing and enrollment planning component of the design.
- *Credential review and outcome.* The undergraduate, graduate, and law compilation and evaluation of academic and financial credentials upon admission to Boston College.
- *Establishment of personal service accounts.* The process by which Boston College sets up all service accounts for students and their families.
- *Family educational financial planning.* The service by which students and their families receive advice and direction on all financial matters concerning the students' Boston College education.
- *Student educational planning.* The service by which students receive advice and direction on all educational and career planning matters.
- *Renewal of service.* The process by which students renew or update all services.
- *Transitional services.* The management of services for students interrupting their tenure at Boston College.
- *Transitioning students out.* The services associated with students leaving Boston College.
- *Design process review.* The process ensuring continuous improvement for student service processes, organization, management, and technologies.

We needed to design an organization and operating model that supported this new direction, especially considering the service work and knowledge needed beyond that which technology can supply. The completed model organizes Boston College service employees in cross-functional teams to transition the current office-owned knowledge base into a more complete service model. We envision that units or teams will make up our future organization. Currently the units that we have designed will be organized into a Strategic Planning Unit, a Service Unit, and a Student Services Support Unit. The Strategic Planning Unit will be a team of individuals guiding student service policies, strategies, long-range plans, research, and assessment. The Service Unit will be a team of cross-functional generalists (some members with expert knowledge) who provide personalized service to students, their families, and other constituents. The Student Services Support Unit will be a group of individuals who provide specialty support to the organization (e.g., research, processing, systems management, data analysis). In addition, a Specialist Network will be created to provide service to special constituents, to address special issues (e.g., compliance, records management), and to perform specific functions (e.g., orientation, registration coordination).

Technology Requirements. We are relying on technology to change the way we work and the way we deliver service. The major technical requirements fall into two general categories, front end and back end. The front-end technologies refer to our Web-based service delivery. We know that up until now we have forced our parents and students to understand the way we are organized and to conduct their business accordingly. A good example occurs in the spring, when we expect our students to call or visit the registrar for registration, housing for room selection, financial aid for financial aid application, and campus police for parking sticker, for example. But we now are able to provide a series of self-service transactions on the Web that allow students to perform their business at their leisure, any time of day or night, with one standard interface, regardless of understanding what office is in what building performing what service. Further, this front-end technology frees up our staff to provide important personalized service rather than the data entry and filing processes that were required. We already know the power of self-service by the positive results we have experienced through voice registration and kiosk services that we have offered for many years. We plan to capitalize on this early experience and success in our new Web services.

The back-end technologies we are relying on include document management and electronic data interchange. We produce volumes of paper, such as registration forms and application forms, to support our business processing. We plan to eliminate much of that simply in the self-service scheme, where no paper is passed. However, we also send paper to support every activity we engage in with outside agencies, including lending agencies, other schools, and the federal government, to name a few. This paper keeps our staff very busy filing, retrieving, and filing again. It also keeps staff confined to physical locations close to the paper. By eliminating this paper, by transferring and storing the data, we intend to free our staff and our service from that bondage.

A Revised Charter. The detailed work began after the high-level design was made public. We spent a summer presenting the design to the Executive Team, our advisors, targeted departments, Information Technology, Human Resources, and the Council of Deans. Because we knew that extended debate about the model might drag on, we asked for written comments. The Executive Team reviewed these, met with us and several key directors, and rechartered us to continue our work and make the plan a reality.

Student Services Design Team. With the completion of the design for a student services system and organization, the Student Services Design Team is authorized to pursue the implementation of this design. The team is charged with creating a detailed design along with a migration plan for approval of the Project Delta Executive Team. While the current design is recognized as the desired outcome of this redesign project, the Executive Team requires that particular areas of concern be addressed. These issues, as well as others that may arise, must receive explicit consideration by the Executive Team before implementation. They include the following:

- *Admissions.* Given the critical importance of the recruiting and marketing effort to the enrollment objectives of the university, every precaution must be taken to ensure the continued success of the recruiting process. The design team is directed to work closely with the Admissions Office, the Dean of Enrollment Management, and the graduate admissions offices to create a recruiting process and organization that is integrated with the new model while preserving crucial external relationships and responsibilities.

- *Academic advising.* The creation of educational guides and their role in the academic advising of freshmen and sophomores is a concept that needs further development. The Executive Team supports the desire to strengthen academic advising and directs the design team to consider all alternatives, including an advising center, a larger advising role for the student service teams, and a broader advising role for faculty and other university staff as well as the educational guides model.

- *Career advising and placement.* Acknowledging the importance of career guidance and placement, both for undergraduate programs and for the graduate and professional schools, the design team is directed to work in concert with the deans and with existing university placement services in redesigning the university's career planning and placement programs.

- *Coordination with faculty/staff model.* In view of the extensive interactions between this design and the faculty/staff model, the design team and the team leader are directed to coordinate planning efforts and communication strategies with the Faculty/Staff Design Team to emphasize and clarify the interdependencies.

To Pilot or Not to Pilot. We thought for a long time, all through the high-level design, that we would pilot one or more initiatives. In fact we had discussed at least four alternatives, from creating one cross-functional team to working on the self-service Web component of each process. After much discussion and in coordination with the other projects that were taking off in Project Delta, we decided to abandon the pilot idea and actually phase in a new organization and new technologies. We knew that no pilot would really help us understand the total impact of our service changes. We expected that the work would not really change until our self-service Web transactions were in place, so the organizational pilots were unrealistic. We decided to forge ahead and begin by doing the following:

- Merge the central Offices of the University Registrar, Financial Aid, Student Accounts, Student Loans, Credit and Collections, and Enrollment Systems into a new configuration that would support subsequent phases.
- Create the redesigned processes and technologies required to support what had been described in the high-level design as the Establishment of Personal Services Account Process and Renewal of Service Process. These included all processes supporting the initiation of student accounts and services upon students' entry to Boston College and those renewals we required of students each year, including registration, application for financial aid, and room selection.

Phase One Design. In fall 1997, one year after completion of the Core Team's direction statement, the Executive Team approved our phased-in approach. Our teams now needed to be restructured, staffed by team members close to the existing work yet committed to the new vision. A core detailed design and implementation group, made up of a team leader and four members, was created. All but one of these members had been on the High-Level Design Team. This group worked on individual assignments, three days a week. Additionally, we asked a group of experts, most of them directors from the areas that would change, to join the team on a weekly basis for updates and advice. The project work had become more complex because we needed direct assistance from other areas on campus, including Information Technology and Human Resources. With their help, the Student Services Detailed Design Team was able to focus on defining processes and creating the

organization to support them. We had defined our technology requirements in the high-level design but would need to refine those for phase one.

Process Design. Three of the five designers focused on process and technology. They spent many hours identifying the 400 or so processes that would be affected by the organizational or technological change. They identified redundancies and work that would no longer need to be done. They targeted roles that would be required in the new organization. The result of this work was a scope document identifying exactly what work we would touch in phase one and how it would be redone.

Organization Design. One of the team members evaluated this process work and defined all the roles required in the new organization. We then configured the roles into a new organization structured into three major teams, each with a team leader and a smaller team. The result is a streamlined organization that combines student general services, technical integration and support, processing support, local support, system and Web development, and publications while maintaining expert roles in financial aid and loans. Specialists in student employment, classroom scheduling, classroom development, collections, research, and enrollment management are also woven into the organization. Auxiliary services including parking, meal plan options, IDs, PIN distribution, housing information, and orientation support are included.

We also spent time mapping staff members from their current into their new roles, with the understanding that roles would be changed or adapted to fit the new design. After the roles were identified, we created an organization that complemented both the realities of phase one and the goals of phase two. At this point, three of the executives worked with the team leader to refine the organization, especially its leadership structure.

The new functional areas of the phase one organization are shown in figure 5.1.

Technology Design. From the outset, Project Delta has relied heavily on technology to effect change. It was no surprise, then, that two Information Technology managers were brought in to review the design and to document the scope of the work required to support phase one. Our requests included the following:

- Web navigation/Web access to all services
- Student personal scheduler/university calendar
- Course waiting lists
- Automated transcript and certification
- Web room selection/off-campus housing renewals
- Enhanced degree audit
- Financial aid enhancements
- Automated account setup/creation

Student Services and Student Financial Strategies		
Technical Integration and Student Services Support • Project Management • Communications and Learning & Development • Processing • Room Scheduling • Data Analysis • Computer Production	**Student General Services** • Academic • Financial • Auxiliary Services • General Services • Records • Transcripts	**Financial Services** • Financial Aid • Student Loans • Collection • Student Employment

Figure 5.1
New Functional Areas of the Phase One Organization

- Cashier services enhancements
- Online shopping capability

Supporting University Projects. Before moving to the implementation stage of phase one, we should set the context for the changes in student services by describing what was happening across campus. Clearly, Project Delta is not just about student services. During the Core Team's work in 1996, several other projects were defined that would support both the student life model and the faculty/staff support model, the project's two major initiatives. Those that directly supported phase one of the student life model included a vacated slot management process; a new human resource classification and compensation system; the formation of a learning and development organization; and the initiation of AGORA, our name for a system of Web-based services.

- *Slot management.* When Project Delta began, we promised the Boston College community that, while we were committed to changing work and shifting roles, there would be no resulting involuntary layoffs. Because of this commitment, the vice president for human resources initiated a policy whereby every vacated position would undergo a review. When staff left they would be replaced with a temporary employee whenever possible. Permanent employees whose work or roles were eliminated would be moved into those positions held by temporary staff. For student services this strategy proved successful. In our phase one move we reduced our staff by approximately 8 to 10 percent. In most cases, we simply did not renew a temporary employee's position when it expired. In one case, we were able to move an employee to another division. In other cases, employees who were given temporary assignments will be redeployed elsewhere on campus.

- *Human resource classification and compensation system.* In response to Project Delta's organizational goals, Human Resources is implementing a new classification system. We are moving from 30 classes to five broad bands. We expect this banding will be effective for the new team structures in

phase two of student services. And an employee's performance will now be measured against university competencies, especially customer service and teamwork. The plan also calls for a variable pay component by which a manager will be able to give spot bonuses to staff for achievement.

- *Human resource learning and development.* From the earliest stages of Project Delta, we understood the magnitude of the change we were about to bring on the university. We wanted to be able to support our employees during this difficult transition as well as give them the skills necessary to support the service models. Learning and Development, the new arm of Human Resources, has been charged with providing training and organizational support. The student service organization, however, provides its own functional training.

- *Project AGORA.* For many years, Boston College has benefited from the expertise of our Information Technology Department and its innovative self-service projects. Project AGORA is Boston College's recent initiative for Web-based service. Delivery was built based on the following concept, which appears on the AGORA home page at agora.bc.edu/start:

  > In Ancient Greece, the agora was where the community gathered for discourse and trade. At Boston College, AGORA is where the University gathers to communicate electronically, conduct business, and retrieve personalized information at any time, from anywhere.

  For the past 10 years, we have offered our students services such as ATM and telephone student information access to voice response registration and telephone credit card payments. The self-service goals of Project Delta were a natural step for Information Technology staff, and AGORA is the direct result of their commitment and expertise. AGORA is a secure intranet site that provides members of our community with a personalized set of Web-based services. AGORA dramatically shifts the way work is done by providing self-service capabilities to all students, staff, and faculty. It gives them the opportunity to view and update their information and to conduct business as they like.

Phase One Implementation. From April until October 1998 we put all our efforts into shaping the organization and starting our technology rollout.

Our Job Hiring and Appointments. Working closely with the vice president for human resources, we decided that all the new roles that needed market reference points would be posted. However, staff members would only have to apply for jobs if they wanted one of the new positions or if their current position had been eliminated and they needed to find something else. By the end of the organizational shift, approximately 10 percent of the staff did not have work or roles in the new organization. Several of the positions were captured as staff left the university; others were given a transitional assignment until another job on campus could be found. While most staff members' job content did change, their actual roles did not. For example, the financial aid counselors continued in that role but took on new responsibilities in Student Loan Services.

Learning and Development. Over the summer, Human Resources helped develop and execute a session titled "Working in a Rapid Response Environment" for all staff members who would be affected by phase one. The purpose of the session was to explain why we were making changes and to give the staff some skills for coping with change. Because hiring was not complete, we could not do much functional training over the summer, but we did ask several service staff members if they would be willing to cross-train with financial aid and student account personnel. Those who agreed to do so felt that the training was valuable.

Technology Rollout. Our technology requirements for phase one are extensive. We began to work on deploying Web services first, and that remains our current focus. Over the summer Information Technology began to roll out AGORA services and especially those that would positively affect the phase one organization. By the time we sent out our fall bills in late July 1998, we were able to promote AGORA services. By October students were able to serve themselves on the Web in the following ways:

- View course history, current schedule, and grades
- View exam schedule
- View financial aid application and awards
- View status of Stafford Loans
- Complete medical insurance waivers
- View/change addresses and directory publishing preferences
- View library withholdings
- View undergraduate degree audit
- View student account
- View advisor information
- Create/add to Convenience Bucks Dining Account (charged to the student's account)

- Complete Stafford Loan entrance counseling requirement
- Complete Stafford borrower authorization statement
- Request a reprint of a student account bill
- Request student enrollment certification
- Order a replacement ID and deactivate a lost/stolen ID
- Change Eagle-One bill address preference

Space Reconfiguration. Boston College has a suburban campus with extremely limited growth potential. We knew we would not have the luxury of dedicating a full building for student services. In fact, we didn't know if we could even fit the new organization in one building. While it is our hope that the fully developed student service organization will not require all service teams in one location, we also know that our shared paper files forced the phase one organization to be in one place. With our limited options, we chose to do a temporary rehab of the floor shared by the Offices of the Registrar and Financial Aid. We gained a small space on the fourth floor for the systems support group, created a service area in the front of the building, and gained a workroom in the basement. For students it has created one central place to visit, or at least start from, for most business. In summer 1999, we move the staff out of the building and completely renovate it. We are working with an architect not only to properly configure and appoint the space for student services, but also to create a more workable staff space. We expect this organization to change again in the following 24 months, so we are using movable wall units to provide both the private office space we need for many employees and the flexibility we need in this ever changing organization. The plans also call for a face-lift to the outside of the building as well as a self-service area furnished with network computers and ATMs.

Work in Progress. There are many unattended details that have fallen out of the phase one implementation, and so much more is needed to support our students and staff. We are, then, continuing our efforts to support phase one, and some of the projects we are working on include the following:

- *Functional training:* Because of the tight time line for moving the organization, there was little time to prepare staff for their new roles. The team leaders are now working together to prepare a series of modules that will teach all staff what a student encounters, from admission through graduation.
- *Learning and development:* Human Resources' learning specialists have designed a curriculum for all staff, ranging from leadership sessions to leading and living with change. We expect to send several of our service providers to such nationally acclaimed service institutes as Disney's. Also, several members of Human Resources recently completed interviews and/or focus groups with all student service staff and reported on their findings. We were able to learn how the staff felt about various

elements of the change, including the actual hiring process, functional training, and communication. We are now working on an action plan to address many of these concerns.

- *Space:* Our Planning and Construction and Space Planning groups are supporting our design for renovating our space.
- *Classification and compensation:* Student services is a pilot for the new Boston College Classification and Compensation System. The new roles created have, in fact, not been classified under the old system and will be some of the first positions under the new broadband scheme. As part of the pilot, the director of student services is helping design a new performance management system that will focus performance improvements around the new competencies we want to stress as part of our service organization.
- *Technology deployment:* We continue to deploy AGORA services, especially those that support the renewal of services process. We are planning to study and execute document management support for our student financial processing. Also, our director of financial strategies is pursuing several technology-based services that will assist us in student loan processing, further dramatically changing our work.

Student Services Trends

Throughout this work we have been very aware of our colleagues' student service work. We have tried to take the best of what Boston College can offer, for example, good self-service and innovative technology deployment, and couple that with space and organizational changes we had not emphasized in the past but felt were necessary as part of our overall vision. The student services trends chart demonstrates where we are in relation to the broader trend we are seeing in student services today.

Critical Success Factors and Key Considerations

Projects of this magnitude and complexity require much attention and commitment from everyone involved. And while it is impossible to predict what will work in every situation, we are convinced from our experiences that these basic elements are required for success:

- *Align leadership.* It is important that a senior officer of the college, the executive vice president, or the provost lead the change project. It is equally important that the CFO, the CIO, and the chief human resource officer be a part of the Executive Team and buy into the project. The president must stand fully behind the project, as must the Finance Committee of the Board of Trustees and the trustee leadership.
- *Will to change.* It is important at the outset that the Executive Team members understand that to accomplish the change

Student Services Trends

TRENDS	IMPLEMENTATION PHASE
Student-Centered	●
Redesigned Services	◐
One-Stop Service Center	●
Cross-Functional Teams	◑
Self-Service Objectives	●
Department Process Improvements	◑
Web-Enabled Services	●
Admissions	●
Registration	●
Advising	○
Financial Aid	●
Billing	●
Career Services	◑
Systemic Change	◐
Replacement of Student Information Systems	○

Codes for Implementation Phase:
- ● Production
- ◐ Implementing
- ◑ Designed
- ○ Planning

process it will be necessary to make a number of difficult decisions. From the beginning, therefore, they must determine and agree that they have the will to make the required changes.

- *Respect for culture.* In carrying out a major change effort it is important to preserve those aspects of the culture that are part of the college's tradition and that have been instrumental in its success to date. Great care must be taken to do this and to communicate to all constituencies the concern of the Executive Team about this issue.
- *Involve employees.* Many change efforts are characterized by large numbers of outside consultants actually leading or carrying out the work of the change effort. With confidence in the employees of the college, in their experience, in their expertise, and in their sense of responsibility to the institution, it is essential that they, rather than consultants, carry out the work. This is not merely to accomplish buy-in, but also to put the work in the hands of inside experts. It also demonstrates executive confidence in the competence and loyalty of the employees. Consultants should be used when there is no on-campus expertise. In our case, at the beginning we had no experience in launching a business redesign project, so we hired a consultant to work with us for three months to develop a plan. We have no on-campus project management expertise, so we have employed consultants for that purpose. And finally we have employed consultants to develop a communication strategy and to actually perform the work to implement that strategy.

- *Empower teams.* It is important that the team leaders be empowered to accomplish their objectives. In our case, we suspended the normal hierarchical structure to allow the team leaders to blast through resistance to change, political battles, and hierarchical disagreements.

- *Understand costs.* The Boston College objective is not to downsize, but to eliminate work and thereby pull costs out of the system. To accomplish this, we had to determine up front the then-current cost of major processes and sub-processes and the other activities and end products that were required to accomplish departmental objectives.

- *Communicate.* Major change efforts create uncertainty. Uncertainty, in turn, creates anxiety. While it is never possible to relieve all such anxiety, an effective antidote is frequent and effective communication. Newsletters and Web pages can be helpful, but clearly the best way to communicate is by having members of the Executive Team meet on a regular basis with various groups of employees to update them, respond to questions, and squash the latest rumors. In our effort, I had serious concerns about our effectiveness in communicating and brought in two people on a part-time consultant basis to assist us in developing and delivering timely messages.

- *Plans for implementation.* Once a decision is made to change a process, to eliminate work, or to reorganize, the job is still not done. A detailed implementation plan must be developed and built into the traditional managerial and budget processes of the college. In no other way will costs and budgets actually be reduced.

- *Build an environment for sustaining change.* Recreating these sorts of major change efforts is definitely not something you want to keep on the management agenda. It is, therefore, important that the major change effort itself plant the seeds for its continuation. Departments, for example, could be placed on a five-year cycle for an activity value analysis review, much like a reaccreditation visit. Teams can be established with the responsibility, for example, of consistently reviewing business process design.

- *Acknowledge the difficulty.* This is really hard work! It is especially hard when you are in the middle of it. It is impossible to anticipate every problem. Even if you do anticipate most problems and develop plans for them, ultimately it is necessary to deal with people who are experiencing changes to their work life and to understand and work with their feelings and insecurities. You also have to deal with the naysayers, the articulate, politically adept critics who most often are not themselves contributors. Expect some down days. Rely on your teams. And persist!

- *Set an end date.* Finally, it is important for everyone—from the Executive Team to the dining service employee to the faculty member to the secretary—to know that the major change effort will some day end.

- *Say thank you.* There are many big ways and little ways, financial ways, and other ways that the Executive Team can thank all of the people who have made material contributions to the change process.

Conclusion

Since the beginning of Project Delta all of us involved have felt we are crossing uncharted territory every day. No matter how much we tell you here of our approach, your own attempts at such change undoubtedly will be different. Every employee you involve in your initiative will bring his or her own unique perspective, a true benefit of this work. We can all learn from one another about the best way to service students, but we can also bring to it our institution's individuality.

6

Linda M. Anderson
William F. Elliott

The Evolution of Enrollment Services

Overview

Carnegie Mellon University is a national research university of about 7,500 students and 3,000 faculty, research, and administrative staff. Industrialist and philanthropist Andrew Carnegie, who founded the institution in 1900 in Pittsburgh, wrote "My heart is in the work" when he donated funds to create Carnegie Technical Schools. His vision was to open a vocational training school for the sons and daughters of working class Pittsburghers. When the school was renamed Carnegie Institute of Technology in 1912, it took another important step in its transition into one of the nation's leading private research universities. In 1967, Carnegie Tech merged with the Mellon Institute to form Carnegie Mellon University.

The university consists of seven colleges and schools, the Carnegie Institute of Technology (engineering), the College of Fine Arts, the College of Humanities and Social Sciences, the Mellon College of Science, the Graduate School of Industrial Administration, the School of

Computer Science, and the H. John Heinz III School of Public Policy and Management. Carnegie Mellon's position of leadership in the arts and in technology is unusual in higher education today. The institution's prominence in the arts dates back to 1917, when it awarded the first undergraduate degree in drama. And it has become a national leader in technological fields such as computer science, robotics, and engineering. The university is a diverse blend of academic disciplines, including nationally recognized programs in cognitive psychology, management and public policy, writing and rhetoric, applied history, philosophy, and biological sciences. Carnegie Mellon is recognized as a pioneer in the uses of computing in education. Its Andrew computing network, named for benefactors Andrew Carnegie and Andrew Mellon, is among the most advanced on any campus today.

The Compelling Case for Change

In the early 1990s Carnegie Mellon, like most other colleges and universities, was challenged by trustees and the general public to adopt business practices to improve the management and delivery of services. One of the several ways to achieve such improvements was to adopt quality management techniques. The Quality Round Table, a membership organization of corporations, initiated the University Challenge by inviting colleges and universities interested in adopting total quality management techniques to submit a proposal. We submitted a proposal, were selected, and were paired with Xerox to undertake the implementation of quality management at Carnegie Mellon. After extensive planning and preparation a large number of faculty and staff spent five days in Rochester, New York, the home of Xerox, to attend presentations and participate in workshops to educate and train members of the Carnegie Mellon community in the tools of quality. At that time, the ideas of process improvements, problem solving, and reengineering became part

Linda M. Anderson is leader/partner of enrollment services at Carnegie Mellon University. She is a past president of the Northeast Association of Student Employment Administrators and has served on the executive board of the National Student Employment Administrators. She holds a bachelor's and a master's from Indiana University of Pennsylvania.

William F. Elliott is the vice president for enrollment at Carnegie Mellon University. He has served as president of the Pennsylvania Association of College Admission Counselors, as trustee of the College Entrance Examination Board, and as a member of several Middle States Association accreditation teams. He holds a bachelor's from Worcester Polytechnic Institute, a master's from Clark University, and a Ph.D. in higher education from the University of Pittsburgh.

of our vocabulary and part of the way of thinking at the university. While process improvement, problem solving, and reengineering may have been new terms for the Rochester experience, these terms were not new to the university. In the mid-1940s the original Carnegie Plan for Education conceived of problem solving in a formal manner and generated a curriculum based on this concept. Much of this early thinking is incorporated into what we know as "quality" today.

About the same time that we began to adopt quality management, and for entirely different reasons, a group named the Enrollment Group was created. The goal of the Enrollment Group was to "Make operational the vision, mission and core values of Carnegie Mellon as they pertained to the distribution of financial aid to prospective students and currently enrolled students." To achieve that goal, the immediate objective of the Enrollment Group was to "Create a climate and culture of change by recommending process changes with technology as an enabler and to articulate in relevant and persuasive terms the case for change."

With the Rochester experience as background, the Total Quality Steering Committee (TQCommittee) was established. The TQCommittee membership included the president; the provost; the vice presidents of business, development, university relations, and enrollment; the dean of the business school; the heads of the English and Electrical Engineering Departments; and the director of the president's office. The objective of the TQCommittee was to monitor and assist with the implementation of total quality techniques in the management of the university. Business affairs and student services were two areas quickly identified for the application of this new knowledge. In business affairs the purchasing practices of the university were selected and in student services the processes of registration, financial aid, and cashier operations were selected. The student services project was known as Enrollment Process Reengineering (EPR).

Project Summary

By means of reorganization the cashier and all of its responsibilities were transferred from business affairs to the Enrollment Group. As a result, the group became the process owner of registration, financial aid, and cashier operations. To initiate the reengineering process, the associate vice president for planning and budget was appointed the leader of the reengineering team. This team was charged with setting the objectives of the new organization and developing the organizational design to achieve the stated objectives. With the leader being outside the Enrollment Group, the key people from the Offices of the Registrar, Financial Aid, the Cashier, and the Vice President for Enrollment, were able to be members of the reengineering team.

The associate vice president for planning and budget, director of planning, registrar, director of financial aid, and cashier spent the

summer and fall of 1994 collecting operational data concerning financial aid awarding, course registration transactions, and billing and payment cycles. Data had never been collected and displayed in such a manner to measure the end-to-end process of enrollment. Time measurements of the process life cycle, the number of steps needed to complete a process, and the number of times a person in each of the three offices touched the data to complete a process were compiled. In addition to the collection of the operational data, focus groups were held with students, faculty, and staff to obtain an accurate description of the current state of the registrar, financial aid, and cashier operations. Benchmark visits were made to the Massachusetts Institute of Technology, Boston College, the University of Delaware, and the University of Pennsylvania in December 1994. Fully understanding the organization, processes, and best practice examples was critical to the success of the reengineering effort.

Enrollment Process Reengineering Team

The Enrollment Process Reengineering Team (EPRT) formed in January 1995 and brought people together from across the university. It consisted of the following:

- Associate vice president for planning and budget (chair)
- Professor of electrical and computer engineering
- Associate vice president for computing and information systems
- Vice president for enrollment
- Associate dean for undergraduate affairs, Mellon College of Science
- Director of enrollment systems
- Student in the College of Humanities & Social Sciences
- Cashier
- Senior research scientist in statistics
- Registrar
- Director of housing
- Assistant dean for undergraduate education, School of Computer Science
- Members of the preplanning team

Based on the following vision statements of Carnegie Mellon and the Enrollment Group, the EPRT went about its work.

Carnegie Mellon University Vision Statement
Carnegie Mellon University will lead educational institutions by building on its traditions of innovation and transcending disciplinary boundaries to meet the changing needs of society.

Enrollment Group Vision Statement
The Enrollment Group is to be a recognized leader in providing student services and programs that will

complement the University's goal of meeting the changing needs of society.

The EPRT defined the enrollment process as the end-to-end process of a student wanting to enroll in a course to a student becoming enrolled at Carnegie Mellon. This was very easy to say but very difficult to define when accounting for the steps of the registrar, financial aid (when applicable), and cashier that must be completed. The EPRT defined the current state of the enrollment process as "Three interdependent processes (registration, financial aid & billing/collections) currently separate and fragmented which were . . . Inconvenient and time consuming . . . Bureaucratic, labor intensive and prone to error . . . Unstructured and inconsistent across colleges."

To satisfy student requirements, the EPRT established the objectives of the redesign process as follows:

- Process output directly accessible by students
- Process input decentralized to students
- Process convenient and coinciding with scheduling constraints, e.g., should not conflict with classes
- Process consistent across the university
- Accessible and meaningful advising
- Process recognizing the student as the responsible participant
- Clear and consistent decision rules relating to prioritizing and exception management, access to courses needed
- Financial counseling
- Decision support tools
- Reduction of the number of administrative and departmental steps and points of contact required to complete the process
- Elimination of non-value-added activities
- Reduction of process costs for both central and academic units
- Reduction of the time to complete process steps
- Elimination of redundant effort and unnecessary inspection
- Maximization of cash flows to the university

The opportunities the EPRT identified to improve the enrollment process were as follows:

- Replace authorizing signatures by
  - replacement of registration authorization with academic audit support and
  - replacement of departmental course signatures with uniform registration rules.
- Optimize scheduling.
- Eliminate separate departmentally based processes.
- Coordinate administrative functions.
- Emphasize financial planning and proactive problem resolution.

- Use technology as a critical enabler by
  - distributed access to and input of information,
  - academic audit functionality,
  - coordinated information across administrative and academic departments, and
  - communication of electronic funds transfers.

The completed Enrollment Process Reengineering report was submitted in June 1995. Immediately following the presentation, the Enrollment Services Process Implementation Team (ESPRIT) initiated activities to implement the recommendations of the EPRT. It was composed of the following:

- Vice president for enrollment (leader)
- Director of financial aid
- Director of public relations
- Employment specialist from Human Resources
- Director of enrollment systems
- Cashier
- Registrar
- Director of special projects, Enrollment Group
  - Members of the EPRT

Planning the Design of Enrollment Services

Before the reengineering effort, the admission, registrar, financial aid, and cashier operations at Carnegie Mellon looked like those at most other institutions. Each office was separate while cooperating with each other at the boundaries (see figure 6.1).

One of the objectives of the reengineering efforts was to open a student service center, The HUB, as the one-stop shop for enrollment

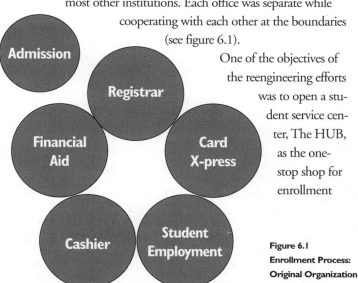

Figure 6.1
Enrollment Process:
Original Organization

transactions. The creation of The HUB eliminated the fragmented administrative processes and made the enrollment process more convenient for students to resolve their enrollment concerns in a single location and obtain direct financial counseling when required or recommended.

In a short time it was obvious that if a one-stop process was desirable for currently enrolled students, the processes of admission and financial aid for new students should also be combined into a single operation. Upon investigation, the admission and financial aid processes for new students were judged to be interdependent, separate, and fragmented. The processes were inconvenient and time consuming, bureaucratic, labor intensive, and prone to error.

To get The HUB started, staff from the affected offices (registrar, financial aid, and cashier and card express) had the opportunity to interview for the seven positions in The HUB. Seven Enrollment Services counselors were selected and provided with a week of cross-functional training prior to the opening of The HUB in August 1995. While this interviewing process took place, three program administrators for financial aid were selected. These employees remained in the Financial Aid Office.

During the 1995–96 academic year the Offices of the Registrar, Financial Aid, and the Cashier and Card Express continued their historical operational modes, while The HUB served as the student enrollment resolution center. Simultaneously, the ESPRIT continued to work on the action plans to complete the creation and installation of the remainder of the Enrollment Services Division. Those were the only personnel changes made at that time.

The design and subsequent successful implementation of the Enrollment Services model were based upon the integration of the freshman financial aid process into the Office of Admission, along with the simultaneous automation of financial aid packaging and the outsourcing of financial payment counseling. The director of financial aid designed and provided training modules for the staff of the Office of Admission. Several members of the financial aid staff and the director and staff of enrollment systems completed the system analysis, design, and testing necessary to install the internally written automated packaging process. The time line for release was March 1996 to meet the delivery requirements of the 1996–97 freshmen awarding process.

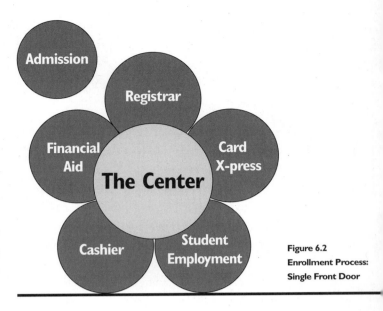

Figure 6.2
Enrollment Process:
Single Front Door

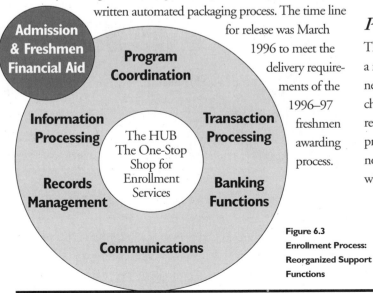

Figure 6.3
Enrollment Process:
Reorganized Support
Functions

Effective communication with students, associate deans, and heads of the academic departments was very important. Individual conversations with people from these groups and focus groups were necessary to gather feedback. Key technology initiatives and the design, testing, and implementation plans were addressed in significant detail. Tasks, responsibilities, and accountabilities of each of the functional groups within Enrollment Services were identified, and the ESPRIT human resource specialist assisted in the development of 42 position descriptions. All of the staff, including The HUB associates and the program administrators for financial aid, the registrar, the director of financial aid, and the cashier had the opportunity to interview for any of the 42 positions within Enrollment Services. The vice president for enrollment and the ESPRIT human resource specialist interviewed and appointed staff to the 42 new positions. Each staff member was guaranteed a position within the new organization, and no one experienced a loss of compensation. The selections were made in April 1996, and ESPRIT's proposals were implemented in July 1996.

Planning the Implementation

The reengineering of Enrollment Services created a new culture and a new way of thinking about the enrollment process. Design of the new process was extremely important, as was the implementation; change management is always a difficult issue. The EPR effort required change, which affected staff who operate the enrollment process itself. The change was incremental and iterative as new technology was introduced. It improved the service provided to students while requiring staff to adjust to new ways of doing business.

Figures 6.1, 6.2, and 6.3 show the development of our organization from several separate offices to a single integrated organization. The new organization is a flattened structure, which emphasizes creative and collaborative approaches to learning, problem identification, problem solving, and leader-

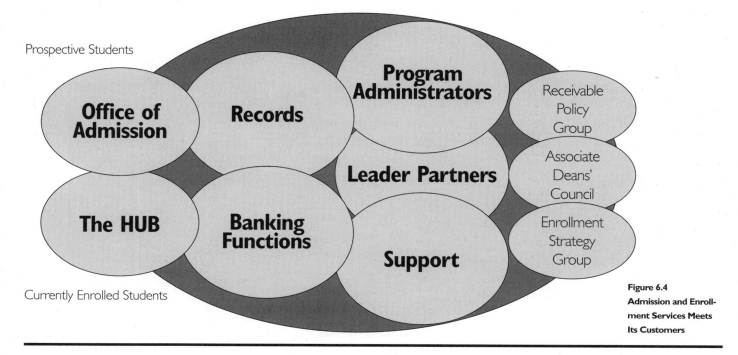

Prospective Students

Office of Admission

Records

Program Administrators

Receivable Policy Group

Leader Partners

Associate Deans' Council

The HUB

Banking Functions

Enrollment Strategy Group

Support

Currently Enrolled Students

Figure 6.4 Admission and Enrollment Services Meets Its Customers

ship development. We are organized by enrollment functions, which transcend the traditional organizational boundary lines of the Offices of the Registrar, Financial Aid, and the Cashier and Card Express. Our six main groups/teams within Enrollment Services are The HUB, records, banking functions, program administration, support, and the leaders/partners (see figure 6.4).

We are organized with an outward focus to deliver services to students and an internal focus to continuously improve the enrollment process. This focus requires both the horizontal and vertical growth of our organization, while linking policies and practices to three policy groups—the Receivables Policy Group, the Associate Deans' Council, and the Enrollment Group. Our goal is to manage processes, not people, and thus we manage without supervisors within our flattened organization.

The staff of the Office of Admission interacts with prospective students as freshmen or transfers concerning both admission and financial aid issues. The admissions staff is trained in financial aid needs analysis and packaging and is able to carry out the same conversations as financial aid counselors in other institutions.

The HUB is the front door to Enrollment Services for currently enrolled students and their parents. The HUB staff is comprised of nine Enrollment Services counselors, who address student enrollment issues. They also do the following: initiate and adjust financial aid eligibility; counsel families about loans and financing options; take payments; process identification cards; adjust tuition charges; respond to questions regarding dining plans, enrollment verifications, and transcript requests; and resolve undergraduate and graduate student enrollment concerns.

We are evolving from groups to self-directed teams, which challenges us to enhance our facilitation and communication skills and to

focus actively on process perspectives, work, and how our work gets done, rather than on the structure and who manages the structure. We have eliminated the boundary lines between the previous historical enrollment functions. Equally important for us is to eliminate the mental boundary lines, which is part of any transformational process.

One of the first objectives of Enrollment Services staff development was to define our vision, mission, and values statements. This was accomplished over a period of several months. Our next and continuous goal was and is to operationalize our vision, mission, and values through our daily operations and interactions with each other, with students and parents, and with our stakeholders. We are creating a culture of change. Our ongoing challenge is to link our vision, mission, and values to our operations, to performance evaluations, and in time to compensation.

Our Vision

To be a unified service organization that continues to pioneer and deliver innovative enrollment services through empowered staff.

Our Mission

To provide services that

- facilitate student enrollment,
- guide students and families as administrative and financial partners,
- support university academic and administrative activities,
- fulfill the requirements of our external customers, and
- emphasize commitment and professional development among our staff.

Our Values

- Accountability
- Approachability
- Dedication

- Integrity
- Outreach
- Reliability
- Teamwork
- Tenacity

Systemic Change

The financial aid, registrar, and cashier staff moved from a hierarchical office structure to an organization of groups and teams. Sixty percent of the staff is in different positions, with 60 percent of the positions being different. The staff faced tremendous learning curves, changing processes, and changing relationships within Enrollment Services and between Enrollment Services and other offices on campus.

Our focus is to continue developing the attributes of a learning organization. In our work environment we give each other opportunities to learn, exchange ideas, change, and thrive. We are experiencing an increased interdependency among groups/teams within Enrollment Services and between ourselves and other groups with which we interact to deliver better services to students. Our capacity to learn and the ways we integrate learning are important. We are changing from specialists to generalists with increasing reserves of specialized information. We continue to learn new ways of understanding student requirements and delivering enrollment services.

In our daily operations, as we address process developments and improvements, we balance competition, cooperation, and collaboration, and share knowledge and perspective freely. We identify what we do not know and how we can learn it. In this process we have to educate ourselves on how to learn, how to teach, how to share, and how to evaluate growth. Growth of expertise and perspective is both horizontal and vertical in our new organization. The leaders are responsible for this learning and this new culture.

What Worked and What Didn't

Successes. Each technology enhancement has helped reduce or eliminate routine transactional processing and standardize, simplify, and eliminate redundancies. As a result the number of administrative steps and student contacts needed to complete the enrollment process have been reduced. These technology developments include the following:

- Automated needs analysis and financial aid packaging
- Automated certification of loans
- Automated disbursement of loan funds to students' accounts
- Online registration
- Electronic grades
- Web-enabled services

- Biographical data
- Grades and schedules
- Student account information
- Ability to change address, request an enrollment verification, request official transcripts

Each year cross-functional training initiatives are more successful. The staff has experienced dramatic growth, in fundamental skill levels, knowledge base, and behaviors and perspectives necessary for understanding and resolving student enrollment process failures. Rather than refer a student from office to office in search of a solution to a problem, Enrollment Services counselors take responsibility and ownership of problems and work with students until the problems are resolved. They are also the pulse of our organization and often the first to identify enrollment process failures from a student perspective.

The analysis of student, parent, and employee satisfaction surveys has helped us to understand weaknesses and strengths of the new organization. The surveys demonstrated our growth and development over the past three years.

Groups are evolving into teams. The staff has grown to realize the interdependent relationship of processes and administrative functions. The approaches to problem identification and problem solving have changed from singular in nature to a macroenrollment process perspective.

Lessons Learned. Resistance to and fear of change is greater than you will ever expect. This resistance is independent of title, administrative level, age, race, or gender. The fear of change can be contagious and create an unexpected level of anxiety that can interfere with and delay improvements in productivity. It is necessary to articulate the case for change to the institutional community and all constituencies in relevant and persuasive terms. To overcome the resistance to change, listen and involve as many people as possible in the change process and allow time for everyone to process the information. However, there will never be enough time to alleviate all fears.

One of our greatest challenges was managing the staff's perceived loss of power, control, and competence. Communicating what the new work environment would be during the transition period and after the change was difficult, especially when the results were uncertain. Unfortunately there will never be enough communication in any change process to meet everyone's expectations.

Plan an aggressive communication strategy, including a detailed schedule of milestones. Stay on schedule, but know when to let the schedule slip when the objectives prove to be unrealistic. Discussion of a schedule brings up issues of implementation strategy. Several statements from the quality literature put the issues into perspective. "No time is a good time to implement change, so any time is a good time." Given that change is painful, ask, "Is it better to suffer a swift pain or be plagued with a constant and nagging ache?"

The Carnegie Mellon reengineering effort was undertaken with a very aggressive schedule that inflicted a swift pain on many people. There are many who say the schedule was too aggressive, but we all wear the badge of success with great pride.

Even after the change process is complete, it is important to stress a new way of thinking that constantly reminds everyone that change will continue as new ways to do old jobs are created. Constantly questioning what we do, and why we do it, is an accepted way of thinking. Answers to the question, "What do we do?" should remind the staff that the enrollment process must seek new ways to function seamlessly while providing academic, administrative, and financial services that help students. Why we do what we do must produce the reply, "to serve the customers of Enrollment Services who are students, parents, agencies, and alumni." In serving our customers we are helping students focus on their educational requirements by minimizing the time spent on administrative tasks through the coordination of academic and administrative services.

Leadership is critical and comes in many forms. The upper-level management requires periodic formal reviews of the process, forces progress, and keeps the implementation team on schedule. The implementation team sets the example for all others to follow. The individual leaders, whether they're the process owners, members of the implementation team, or team leaders, must be visionaries, storytellers, and change agents.

The leadership needs to address three tasks to be successful. These are helping each employee find meaningful purpose in the work of the organization, ensuring that each employee is constantly learning and questioning the activities of the organization, and making each employee feel part of his or her small operating unit while understanding how small operating units working together can achieve the vision and mission of the organization while adhering to the agreed-upon values.

Student Services Trends

TRENDS	IMPLEMENTATION PHASE
Student-Centered	●
Redesigned Services	●
One-Stop Service Center	●
Cross-Functional Teams	●
Self-Service Objectives	●
Department Process Improvements	●
Web-Enabled Services	●
Admissions	●
Registration	●
Advising	N/A
Financial Aid	◐
Billing	○
Career Services	N/A
Systemic Change	N/A
Replacement of Student Information Systems	N/A

Codes for Implementation Phase:

● Production
◐ Implementing
◑ Designed
○ Planning

Conclusion

When the EPR effort was initiated the objective was to improve service to students, parents, faculty, and staff. There have been many achievements to date, and many more opportunities have been identified to further achieve this objective. One of the ways to improve service is to be more efficient with the use of resources. To date we have been able to improve services without an increase in resources that were originally allocated to these areas. In the long term there is every reason to believe that services can continue to improve while reducing the expenditure of resources. This reengineering effort has produced many rewards that were never anticipated when the project was initiated. The work is demanding and at times overwhelming, but the successes have been wonderful.

7

Southern Alberta
Institute of Technology

Karen Hayward
Keith A. Pedersen
Floyd Visser

Transforming With a Learner-Based Redesign

Overview

The Southern Alberta Institute of Technology (SAIT) is a premier polytechnical institute offering training in more than 85 trade and technology programs. Founded in 1916, SAIT is the oldest polytechnic in Canada. Since its inception, SAIT has grown and expanded to meet the changing needs of employers and learners in Alberta, Canada, and around the world. Today it offers grant-funded programs as well as customized programs and courses for domestic and international markets.

The Compelling Case for Change

An important part of SAIT's vision is to continue to be a premier polytechnical institute recognized worldwide for its quality training and services. Another aspect of SAIT's vision is future growth.

Karen Hayward is project facilitator with the Customer Service Process Development Project Team at the Southern Alberta Institute of Technology. She has a bachelor's from the University of Winnipeg and a master's from York University.

Keith A. Pedersen is vice president for administration at the Southern Alberta Institute of Technology and the project sponsor for SAIT's customer interface project. He is a chartered accountant and holds a B.Sc. from Bishop's University and an MBA from the University of Western Ontario.

Floyd Visser is project manager with the Customer Service Process Development Project Team at the Southern Alberta Institute of Technology, where he has been overseeing the redesign and implementation of admissions, registration, and student aid processes. He has a background in career development and architecture.

Maintaining status quo is not an option if SAIT is to achieve its vision for quality and growth. The challenge for the organization is how to double SAIT's enrollment and earned revenues by 2005.

Increasingly, SAIT's learners are demanding choice—in programs, services, and methods of learning. The ultimate goal of SAIT's learners is to be able to develop and build careers of their choice. Choice therefore is critical when learners decide where they want to pursue educational excellence. We want SAIT to be their first choice.

We are building our global reputation as a recognized center of applied learning. Attracting and retaining learners of excellence over a lifetime of continuous learning is both a challenge and a goal at SAIT. We have projected a learner population growth to 100,000 learners per year within five years. By 2002 we anticipate that 90 percent of our programs and courses will be available using alternative forms of delivery, with 40 percent of learners choosing the Web as their delivery vehicle of choice. To position ourselves for these changes we recognize the need to rethink how we are delivering our services. Our goals are to ensure the following:

- We have the facility and technology infrastructure in place to support this growth.
- Staff members are empowered to make decisions and find solutions with learners.
- Our curriculum is the best in the world.
- We offer a variety of delivery methods to meet individual learner needs.

Project Summary

SAIT's method to achieve these goals is to transform itself into a learner-based technical institution of choice. Part of this objective includes redesigning the customer service interface with our learners, focusing on what the learner wants and expects from SAIT. What we hope to achieve by rethinking our services is increased learner access, success, and satisfaction as well as increased staff performance levels. One of the outcomes that we hope to achieve as part of the overall effort is increased revenue.

SAIT's journey toward this transformation has been full of challenges—both anticipated and unexpected. Best of all, we have grown as an institute from the wisdom of our learners and our corporate customers, and the experience and knowledge of our employees. The following is a brief look at the highlights of that journey, our milestones, our successes, and our learning.

Getting Started. Our goal to increase our learner population and to provide choice in delivery methods for curriculum demanded that we review how learners accessed SAIT. The explosion of Web interfaces for our learners introduced another exciting element: the use of technology to enable learners and staff to access information and to provide interactive capabilities for learners to take more responsibility in the management of their academic careers.

SAIT's strategic plan and corporate culture encourage innovation and entrepreneurial behavior among all employees. In 1997 the Student Career & Development Services (SCADS) management team, the frontline access point for our learners and customers, began discussing ways to improve learner services. Two solutions to improve learner access to SAIT were to bring in transcript electronic data interface (TEDI) and scanning to convert paper information into electronic data files.

In the fall of 1997, SAIT representatives attended the IBM Innovation in Student Services Forum and learned how a number of institutions were transforming their student service operations to be more learner-centered. SAIT met with IBM after this session to discuss how to transform our current services into a more learner-focused model. Through these discussions, we derived the following three objectives:

- To develop a collaborative process to create a learner-centered environment
- To improve customer service continuously by integrating people, process, and technology elements in the best interest of our learners while providing ongoing evaluation and input from our learners/customers
- To identify and implement technology as an enabler for improved learner service and process

In simple terms, we decided to merge three learner service silos (admissions, registration/learner records, and financial assistance)[1] into one customer service area. This was the scope of the first phase of our redesign effort. We labeled it "phase I redesign" to provide clear communication to the campus that this was the beginning of

a new culture at SAIT. In the future all of our services would be designed to meet learner and customer needs and expectations.

During the redesign process and into the implementation of the phase I redesign in 1998–99 other learner service areas were brought into scope. Processes that were added to the redesign effort included learner recruitment and employment, career and program advising, bidding for new business, and scholarship development and management.

Steps for Redesign. With goals and scope determined, the next step was beginning the redesign. The approach taken included the following:

- Documenting SAIT current processes at a high level for historical reference and benchmarking
- Identifying outputs desired by learners
- Creating a customer service vision and goals
- Gathering learner needs, wants, and perceptions of performance
- Reinventing the processes, organization, facilities, and use of technology with the help of content experts
- Recording related out-of-scope issues and recommended solutions
- Building a high-level plan for implementation

The following six steps outline the methodology we used throughout the phase I redesign, including findings and learning from each step and milestones achieved. The resulting best practices and critical success factors will be summarized at the end of the six steps.

Step 1: Assign a Project Manager and Redesign Team to Work With Consultants

Methodology. For the redesign to be accepted and implemented across SAIT, a 60 percent dedicated redesign team was assembled. The team was cross-institutional and cross-functional in nature to ensure the widest representation from within the SAIT community. Areas represented included learners, admissions/registration, records (academic tracking, scheduling, and graduation), student financial aid, employment and counseling, academic departments (two faculty members), educational resources (Web master), information systems (banner expertise), and business development and international training (earned revenue expertise).

Findings/Learning. This 12-member team from SAIT together with a five-member consultant team and 17 subject matter experts from the SAIT community identified the critical success factors for the customer service redesign. These were the following:

- Ongoing executive support and leadership
- Systemic commitment to learner customer service
- Campuswide vision for learner services
- Ongoing customer input throughout the design and implementation of customer services

- Ability for all learners to access high-quality support services directly
- Extensive staff training
- Adequate funding and resource commitment to support implementation
- Building a collaborative campus culture
- Viewing technology as an enabler, not the solution

Milestone. Creation of the critical factors that served as a guide for the redesign

Step 2: Document Current SAIT Learner Services Processes

Methodology. Documentation of the current learner service processes was an important next step in the redesign. We needed to have a clear, high-level understanding of what current SAIT practices were and use these practices as a baseline of SAIT's current key services, processes, measurable attributes, and customers. This baseline would later be compared with the redesigned processes to identify potential gaps or areas requiring development.

Findings/Learning. Admissions, registration, records/learning tracking, and financial aid processes were built to a high-level detail. What became evident during this step was the following:

- The high degree of duplication existing among the services provided by each process
- The excess number of steps to communicate data from point A to point B
- The lack of access to required data by users of individual processes
- The focus on internal SAIT technical requirements and not on learner needs and expectations

Milestones

- Creation of high-level current process flows for admission, registration, records/learning tracking, and financial aid
- Identification of high-level gaps, including process duplication, inefficient communication flow, lack of access to systems, and the use of technology as a solution, not as an enabler

Step 3: Create a Learner Services Vision and Desired Attributes

Methodology. To move forward SAIT required a learner services vision and related attributes. A Customer Service Visioning Workshop was held in March 1998. At the workshop, cross-institutional representatives, including senior executive officers, the Project Sponsor Team, the Customer Service Redesign Team, and student service managers collectively defined SAIT's vision for customer service.

Findings/Learning. The vision statement resulting from the workshop states, "We take pride in being leaders in providing customer-valued products and services." The following are attributes of this service:

- Programs and support services are offered at times, in places, and in formats convenient to learners and to industry (accommodation of learner personal lifestyles).
- Standards for customer service operate in a work environment that promotes employee morale.
- Support services are learner-empowered and focus on learner needs and expectations using performance measures to evaluate success.
- Customer service is the critical link between learners, industry, and SAIT curriculum. This is made possible through the fostering of collaborative, cross-trained, and empowered employees.
- Technology enables learners and employees to access information about SAIT's programs and services, and offers interactive capabilities that allow learners to take more responsibility in the management of their academic careers.
- Ongoing executive support was demonstrated through commitment of resources to customer service at SAIT.

Milestone. Creation of the customer service vision statement

Step 4: Assess Learner and Provider Views of Current Customer Service

Methodology. The entire institution had a responsibility for the successful redesign and delivery of SAIT's customer service processes. We needed to learn and understand the needs and expectations of our learners, customers, partners, and employees and communicate our findings to the entire community. We did this through interviews, a visioning workshop, focus groups, surveys, presentations throughout SAIT, town hall meetings with SCADS staff, redesign workshops, and a newsletter produced every four weeks and circulated to the SAIT community. The following discussion identifies the primary communication tactics used, including implementation method and findings/learnings from each tactic.

Twelve focus group sessions with learner groups and service provider groups were conducted. Each focus group had from seven to 12 participants. The learner groups included two grant-funded (age 18 to 22 and 22+), continuing education, international, government-sponsored, business and industry, distance/remote delivery, and apprenticeship learners. The service provider groups included academic deans, directors, student service personnel, instructors, academic coordinators, and industry representatives.

Findings/learning. Through the focus groups we learned that it was important to separate industry customers and earned revenue sales representatives. These groups were combined in this step due to time factors and availability. As SAIT has increases in earned revenue activities as a key goal, the learning from these two groups was important. Combining the groups resulted in mixed learning as each group had a different set of needs and expectations. Another group to be targeted is prospective learners, whose needs and expectations need to be considered in all of our recruitment activities. Continuous communication with all learner groups is also critical to ensure that the design does in fact meet the ongoing needs of the learners. A balance of the various stakeholder needs is, of course, necessary. However, it is unrealistic to believe that every learner demand can be met in phase I redesign. The solutions we created were designed to generate a win-win situation for both the learner and the institute with regard to economic and other priorities, and the overall scope and objectives of the phase I redesign.

A major survey was distributed to learners and SAIT employees. The survey was announced and produced in the Emery Weal student newspaper, was made available on SAIT's intranet Web site, and distributed through SAIT's internal mail. This effort resulted in 410 responses.

Findings/learning. Multiple points of contact were critical in surveying our community. We conducted this survey within a two-week time period. Based on the results from this survey, in the future we will use a one-month time frame for target groups to respond to a survey. We will also increase the number of times the target groups are provided with access to surveys. For example, we will run a survey in the student newspaper three times, once per week for three weeks, rather than once. The survey introduction will also be changed to reflect the purpose and use of the results more clearly and to identify the benefits to the learner and to SAIT for individuals to complete and return the survey. One last point with regard to the learner groups targeted: in the next round we will also target prospective learners to identify their wants and expectations.

Overall, the results of the focus groups and survey resulted in SAIT learners indicating that SAIT's key strengths include the ability to provide an affordable, relevant, career-focused education as well as a positive campus experience. (SAIT currently holds a 98 percent learner-employment ratio for graduates.) However, we also learned that the following SAIT services needed improving:

- Handling of services remotely (Web access)
- Providing choices for self-help and personal assistance
- Providing easy access to SAIT program and service information for empowered employees (improve problem solving for learners)
- Using formal customer feedback channels
- Creating a single location for all interactions with SAIT, in person, over the telephone, via paper calendars, or using the Web (eliminate multiple referrals)
- Having access to employees who care about learners

- Providing well-communicated rules and regulations for learners and staff
- Providing high value for the investment of taking training at SAIT

In most cases, the service providers were harder on themselves than the learner was. The learners felt that the staff performance was commendable despite the poor processes in place. In fact, in many cases the staff was credited with covering up the poor processes.

Three presentations to the SAIT community were made during the February–May 1998 redesign time frame. All presentations were advertised to the community using posters, e-mail notices, and letters signed by the president of SAIT and sent to staff in the SCADS area. (The SCADS area staff had great sensitivity because the redesign had a major impact on their area. SCADS area staff members are the front line to the learner. During the course of the redesign this group's name changed to Customer Services.) The notices invited individuals to the launch and interim presentations. The *CS Update* newsletter was also used to promote the interim and final SAIT-wide town halls.

The launch presentation (February 1998) introduced the redesign to the SAIT community, explaining why we were doing the redesign, what was happening, and the future impact on SAIT. The event included presentations from the president and registrar as well as the academic coordinator, project manager, project sponsor, and the learner representative from the Redesign Team. A total of 170 staff from across SAIT came to hear and to learn more about the redesign process.

The interim presentation (March 1998) had as its focus providing time to review what had been happening with the phase I redesign and an opportunity for the community to give input and engage in discussion. The tone of the town hall was informative and fun. The first draft of the redesign was presented to the community, including a draft organizational structure that demonstrated a move from silos to a one-stop welcome center. The event included presentations from the registrar, the redesign project manager, the learner representative, and team members. More than 200 people were present and participated in 10 roundtable discussion groups. A Redesign Team member facilitated each roundtable discussion group. In addition, a scribe from the Project Sponsor Team documented questions, concerns, ideas, and suggestions.

Findings/learning. Overall the response from participants regarding the redesign was positive. Most of the attendees accepted the model presented and the overall concept. It was felt that the new model would improve learner services. Academic deans, coordinators, and instructors did, however, raise issues regarding self-directed placement testing, an innovation under review by the

Redesign Team. The issue arose from the diversity of programming at SAIT that presents a challenge to providing this service. In addition, many in the audience felt that the presentation of the move from silos to a customer service or welcome center was too cavalier and presented a pejorative view of the current service provision that reflected poorly on SCADS and SAIT as a whole.[2]

The final presentation (May 1998) provided the SAIT community with details of the redesign concept and phases, the team-based organizational structure, and the final recommendations for implementation. It was also announced that the SAIT executive officers had decided to implement the redesign and would recruit a full-time Implementation Team to begin work on the implementation by July 1998. Team members would receive a one-year "secondment"[3] to the project, to end when implementation was complete. The redesign project manager made the final presentation, with a representative from Human Resources providing input regarding the team-based organizational structure. Copies of the *Final Report Executive Summary* were provided to all attendees, with full documentation provided to each dean and director at SAIT, executive officers, members of the Redesign Team, and SAIT's Board of Governors.

Findings/learning. The major finding or learning from the use of town halls is that this type of forum was an important factor to maintain in the implementation of the redesign.

The Redesign Team also produced a newsletter, *CS Update*, at every major milestone and event. Four *CS Updates* were produced during the redesign, providing another source of information for the SAIT community.

Findings/learning. Production of *CS Update* has been carried forward into implementation as a primary vehicle to communicate with the SAIT community. It is currently produced every six to eight weeks and provides information regarding the current status of tasks, announcements, feedback forms, and answers to frequently asked questions. The newsletter is available both in paper format distributed to all SAIT employees and on a Web site.

Two town halls with SCADS staff, without supervisors present, were also held to provide an opportunity for the individuals most closely affected by the redesign to present fears, concerns, and questions as well as ideas and suggestions in a neutral environment. Fear of change and loss of jobs were the greatest concerns. The information was gathered by asking participants to write their number-one fear, number-one concern, and number-one idea on 3-by-5-inch index cards. The information provided on the cards was used to generate discussion with the participants as a whole. In addition, this format provided an opportunity to build consensus and agreement among participants regarding the content of the redesign and the recommendations for implementation.

Evaluation feedback forms were also solicited from participants at the two SCADS town halls.[4] The results indicate staff members were very supportive of the redesign concept, the vision of a learner-driven organizational structure, and the overall recommendations from the redesign. The staff also indicated that they better understood the model and felt that it would be successful if implemented (80 percent support by the SCADS staff.). This information was documented and provided to the SCADS staff within 24 hours. Timeliness of response and feedback was critical to the success of the redesign.

Findings/learning. The use of town halls with staff has been carried forward into implementation. They are now called "Talk Time" and take place twice a month or as requested by newly named Customer Services staff. The continuation of the town hall format was at the request of staff. Learning what was happening with the implementation of the redesign, the impact on staff, and next steps before the rest of SAIT was very important to the staff. In the past, they were often the last to learn of changes (programs, staffing, facility renovations, for example) at SAIT. By providing the staff with an opportunity to hear about the changes, to learn about the progress of implementation tasks, and to be able to ask questions or provide input before the changes were finalized was a significant win for the implementation. Communication throughout the redesign was a critical success factor and continues to be a critical factor in implementation.

Information gathered through all of these sources provided the foundation for the redesign recommendations. Common themes emerging from the data include the following:

- Focus on customer needs and customer service, employees, and processes evaluated by customer satisfaction and other performance measures.
- Provide technology that supports customers' desired processes.
- Create one-stop shopping/solutions on the first attempt.
- Develop a widespread communication plan.
- Foster collaborative, cross-trained, and empowered employees.
- Shift from reactive response to proactive planning.
- Hire/develop responsible and accountable process participants.
- Create a work environment that promotes employees' morale.
- Provide easy access to needed information (distributed information processing/sharing).
- Promote a single, integrated, user-friendly system.
- Provide choice for self-help and/or personal assistance.
- Create SAIT standards for effective customer service.
- Ensure ongoing executive support and commitment of resources.

The result was the creation of recommendation statements, graphic views of learner needs and expectations, and direction for the redesign workshops.

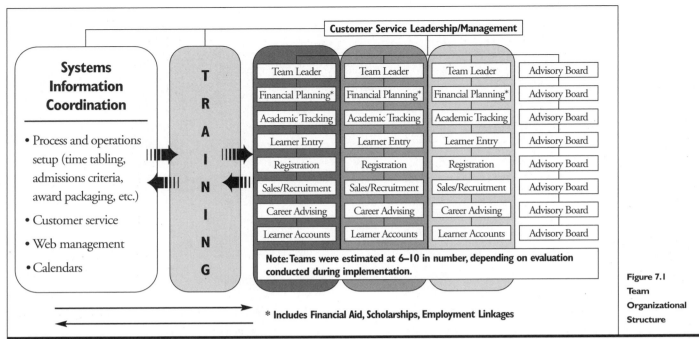

Figure 7.1
Team
Organizational
Structure

Step 5: Reinvent SAIT's Service Delivery Based on Learner Needs and Expectations

Methodology. Using the reinvent framework, SAIT underwent a series of redesign workshops in the admission, registration, record/learner tracking, and financial assistance areas. SAIT used these workshops to reinvent interaction with our learners from their initial point of contact with SAIT through admissions, classes, graduation, and future options presented by the ideal of lifelong learning. Each reinvent was handled by groups of 15 to 18 individuals, including Redesign Team members and subject matter experts from specific process areas. These groups were split into smaller work teams of three individuals, including two subject matter experts and one nonexpert. This format provided for the greatest exchange of information and out-of-the-box thinking. Members of the consulting team rotated through each group to guide participants through the process. By day three, a composite of each group's unique reinvent process designs emerged as *one* high-level redesign process flow agreed upon by all members of the reinvent team.

Findings/Learning. The reinvent workshops resulted in the creation of learner-focused processes that used technology as an enabler for choice and access to information about SAIT, our programs, and our services and provided an interactive vehicle for learners to be more responsible for the management of their academic careers. The themes discerned from the redesign efforts made it clear that SAIT needs to provide seamless, one-stop, customer-focused services through a variety of service options, including accessing information in person, by telephone, by reviewing documents, or using the Web.

As part of the reinvention, a view of how to collapse the silos of service currently in place at SAIT and move toward a welcome center of customer services at SAIT also emerged. A customer service man-

ager/registrar would manage the center. A team-based service delivery structure was created that was cross-functional in nature and provided room for external customer input. Advisory boards for specific process requirements (such as financial aid and the student finance board, program and career advising, calendars and publications, and scheduling of programs and program setup requirements) were recommended to allow for external input (see figure 7.1). Finally, the foundation for all service delivery at SAIT was the enforcement and provision of continual training for all staff on new programs; systems; and communication, empowerment, and change management skills.

A phased implementation approach was also designed to move from silos to a one-stop shop (see figure 7.2). A phased approach was recommended initially to help reduce the fear across campus regarding radical change. The idea of phases implied a longer time frame to move toward a one-stop shop. This included time to accommodate the adjustment of staff to the changes and to shift the mindset of SAIT from the current processes into the redesigned, streamlined processes.

One of the fundamental issues of change management is getting buy-in to change. Throughout the redesign we found that time was the key to the following:

- Help gain the understanding and acceptance of SAIT employees that the processes were derived systemically
- Help technology catch up to the redesign requirements
- Create a prototype for further redesign of areas on campus
- Phase in customer services across campus
- Phase in process flows to the campus and all affected user groups

During implementation this phased approach proved to be impractical for a number of reasons. First, prolonging the collapse of the silos increased staff fears regarding job loss and change in general. Second, building teams necessitated moving to phase V, the one-stop center approach. Teams could not function in the existing silo physi-

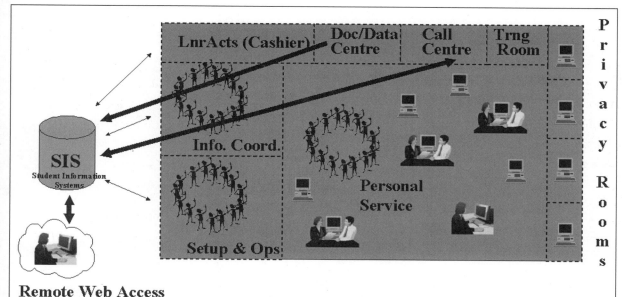

Remote Web Access

Figure 7.2
Phase V of Redesign
Central Customer
Services Area

cal environment. Third, the new processes could not be implemented without a fully implemented team organizational structure to support them with other stakeholder groups across campus. Fourth, technology caught up with the redesign requirements, eliminating the need for further delay. Based on these realities, we determined to move immediately to phase V of implementation—the team-oriented Customer Service Welcome Centre.

Milestones

■ Creation of a phased approach to implement a customer service center

■ Creation of a cross-functional team organizational structure

■ Creation of top-level, learner-focused, and learner-empowered redesign process flows for admissions, registration, records/learning tracking, and financial aid

Step 6: Develop a Customer Service Implementation Plan

Methodology. Gathering all of the learning from interviews, surveys, focus groups, vision workshops, SAIT presentations, and the reinvent workshops, the Redesign Team summarized the findings and developed recommendations for implementation of the redesign. These recommendations included identifying major goals/tasks, developing clear definitions for each goal/task, and detailing outcomes for each goal/task. These goals/tasks formed the basis for the implementation of the new learner-focused and learner-driven customer service processes at SAIT.

Findings/Learning. The welcome center concept that the Customer Service Redesign Team recommended enabled customers to define their own learning plans and provided the tools, techniques, and information needed to support and enable them to achieve their career goals. The Redesign Team determined that successful implementation demanded that the following goals/tasks be addressed and instituted:

■ Senior executive officers approve and mandate the redesign recommendations.

■ The executive sponsor assigns a full-time implementation team to address and institute the redesign recommendations.

■ The full-time team be trained and oriented to the redesign concept, goals, and tasks.

■ Assign team members to specific tasks, including

• detailing process flows and building a framework for continuous process improvement,

• defining and assessing system requirements,

• implementing TEDI and scanning systems,

• assessing skills required for new customer service positions and building position descriptions,

• recruiting for new positions,

• building and conducting ongoing training programs for customer service staff,

• designing and building a Web infrastructure for customer service processes, and

• building and implementing a communication plan for customer services staff and the SAIT community.

Following through on these recommendations will provide a strong foundation for a successful implementation. The executive mandate formalizes the approval of the redesign and provides credibility and responsibility for the Implementation Team to implement a redesign successfully. Assigning a full-time team provides the support and resources necessary to complete established tasks and next steps. Training the team to understand and live the redesign concept is critical to ensure that the spirit of the redesign is maintained throughout implementation. Finally, assigning team members to specific tasks provides a level of accountability and responsibility necessary to ensure each task is completed.

The ultimate result of successfully implementing the customer service concept and process redesign is the realization of choice for learners. Choice is made possible through the following:

- A user-friendly, front-end Web support system
- Options for subject-based registration
- Staff trained on SAIT's standard for customer service
- Cross-trained staff, empowered to make decisions
- Easy application, registration, financial aid, and academic tracking processes
- An infrastructure that supports easy access to technology
- A friendly, comprehensive on-campus facility for customers seeking personal contact
- Effective communication of the redesign process to the entire SAIT community

Milestones

- Creation of the redesign implementation recommendations
- Recommendation to move SAIT toward a holistic solution to improve customer services

Critical Success Factors and Key Considerations

To achieve the vision of holistic customer-focused services for learners, the Customer Service Redesign Team identified the following critical success factors:

- Ongoing executive support and leadership through the transformation process to address support, resource commitment, and policy issues, and a systemic view of customer services
- Campuswide view of customer services, keeping everyone in the loop during implementation
- SAIT-wide buy-in to the vision for customer services
- Ongoing provider/learner input throughout the implementation process
- Ability for a diverse set of learners to access support services directly
- Extensive and ongoing staff training to ensure their success in the new model
- Adequate funding and specifically allocated staff resource commitments for all facets of implementation of the new model
- A collaborative SAIT-wide culture as part of the process
- Viewing technology as an enabler, not the solution

Undergoing the reinvention of our front-line customer service processes demanded that we put our ingenuity and entrepreneurial spirit to work. SAIT's culture encourages innovative thinking, and the Redesign Team took the term "innovation" to its extreme throughout the four-month redesign period. The following highlights some of our greatest successes. They are founded on the critical success factors determined by the Redesign Team and are now considered to be SAIT's new best practices.

Communication. Building a SAIT-wide presentation town hall forum for interaction with all of the community, both staff and learner, ensured that everyone was kept in the know, from the launch of the project, through an interim discussion, to the final presentation of the redesign recommendations. Even more innovative was the creation of SCADS-area town hall meetings, where staff members were free to express their concerns, fears, ideas, or level of agreement with the redesign without fear of reprisal from a supervisor. Finally, the creation of the *CS Update* newsletter, produced regularly and distributed in paper and electronic formats, ensured that all SAIT was kept up-to-date on the redesign and what it meant to them as SAIT employees.

Cross-Institutional and Cross-Functional Redesign Team. The Redesign Team consisted of 12 representatives from SAIT (two faculty at the academic coordinator level, an admissions clerk, a records clerk, a financial aid clerk, a systems programmer, a Web master, an earned revenue representative/government liaison, an Employment & Counseling Services manager, a budget and finance representative, an administrative support representative, and a learner representative) plus five consultants. SAIT representatives were given a 60 percent release from current activities to provide support to the redesign. This demonstrated strong commitment to change from the executive level at SAIT and provided the team with the time to work through the redesign as an integrated team and gain a broader perspective of requirements and issues that would affect the redesign.

Executive Support Demonstrated by the Vice President, Administration. The vice president, administration, who was also the redesign project sponsor, permitted the secondment (release from duties for a specified period of time at full pay) of his executive administrative assistant to the Redesign Team for four months. This provided the Redesign Team with the level of support and knowledge of the SAIT campus and SAIT initiatives needed to ensure the success of the redesign project.

Skill Development of the Redesign Team. Team members actively participated in all aspects of redesign, including facilitating workshops, focus groups, and town halls; writing the *CS Update*; planning the reorganization of the Customer Services Center and building the team organizational structure; writing the final report recommendations and the executive summary; and presenting at all SAIT-wide presentations. The continued growth and active participation of all the Redesign Team members helped to promote the fact that the redesign was a SAIT product, not simply a new packaging of a consultant's product.

Recruiting the Implementation Team. The Redesign Team was formed based on recommendations from directors and deans who participated on the Project Sponsor Team and from supervisors from the SCADS area. Based on our experience during redesign, we recommend that redesign teams be created using an open recruitment process. This encourages buy-in from community at the start of the process and represents fair, equitable selection that is systemically based without favoritism. The Implementation Team was created using this open recruitment process.[5] And full-time secondment, rather than a 60 percent offload from current working positions, was incorporated to ensure dedication and focus on one job throughout implementation.

Conclusion

These are the principles, goals, and critical success factors that form the foundation for SAIT's implementation of our customer service process redesign. The journey was challenging, and many sets of running shoes wore out in the short four months of the redesign. We learned a great deal about what makes SAIT a strong, polytechnical institute that provides relevant, quality-based training to a global community. We discovered what we need to improve as an institute and how to offer the choice our learners are demanding. We learned how to listen and communicate more effectively with our learners, our customers, and all SAIT employees. The value of cross-institutional collaboration; the brilliance of our participants' entrepreneurial, out-of-the-box thinking; and the innovation and knowledge of our staff and learners to find solutions rather than quick fixes were little less than amazing. It was truly an experience where hard work paid off in dividends.

SAIT is currently midway through its implementation of the redesign recommendations and has found that speed is critical to success. We anticipate that the Redesign Team's structured, one-stop welcome center concept and model will be operational by the fall of 1999. Eighteen months after the transformation of customer services at SAIT began, we will offer learners a larger degree of choice in how they access SAIT; manage their academic careers; and meet their ultimate goal of successfully entering, developing, and building careers of their choice in our changing world of work.

NOTES

1 Admissions included the application process; Registration and Records included class registration, class scheduling, and academic tracking processes; and Financial Assistance included student financial planning and management processes from student application through disbursement and billing, not including compliance monitoring, accounting, and government reporting.

2 This is one of many examples of the political face of the redesign and the challenge of change management at SAIT.

Student Services Trends	
TRENDS	**IMPLEMENTATION PHASE**
Student-Centered	◐
Redesigned Services	◐
One-Stop Service Center	●
Cross-Functional Teams	◐
Self-Service Objectives	●
Department Process Improvements	N/A
Web-Enabled Services	●
Admissions	●
Registration	◐
Advising	◑
Financial Aid	●
Billing	◑
Career Services	◑
Systemic Change	●
Replacement of Student Information Systems	●

Codes for Implementation Phase:
- ● Production
- ◐ Implementing
- ◑ Designed
- ○ Planning

This political challenge was a constant factor throughout the redesign and followed us into implementation.

3 Secondment refers to the temporary removal of a staff member from one position into another position at the same rate of pay for a specified time period. Once the need for the temporary position is finished, the individual returns to his or her original position or a comparable one in his or her former department or area.

4 Thirty-five representatives from SCADS were at each town hall. Total SCADS staffing was 80. It should be noted that these meetings with Customer Services staff have been incorporated into the redesign implementation.

5 The full-time Implementation Team included eight team members. Four were from the Redesign Team (a faculty member, an earned revenue representative, a Web master, and a Student Career & Development Services/Employment & Counseling Services member). And four were new members from across campus (a faculty member, a Student Career & Development Services/Timetabling member, an International Students Admissions/Services member, and a Human Resources representative). Administrative support was provided by a SAIT graduate from the Office Administration Program, which provided a learner perspective.

8

Oregon State University

Robert Bontrager

Reengineering Admission Services

Overview

Few issues are as compelling in the day-to-day life of a college or university as its enrollment. Attracting and retaining an adequate number of students drives everything from an institution's budget to its self-image. Indeed, for the majority of schools, enrollment concerns have been at or near the top of their priority list for most of the last 20 years.

The reasons for this are fairly straightforward. Higher education expanded nearly unchecked from the late 1940s through the 1970s. Fueled initially by World War II veterans enrolling under the GI Bill, the expansion of access resulting from the Civil Rights movement, and finally the sheer numbers of the baby boom generation, the number of students participating in higher education exploded. The number and size of institutions grew dramatically to keep pace. Faculty members were hired, programs were established, and physical plants were expanded to meet the needs of the growing student bodies on virtually every campus. All of this came to an abrupt halt in 1980 when the baby boom generation finished college. This single event precipitated a free fall in the pool of high school graduates and over the ensuing years shifted higher education from a seller's to a buyer's market (see figure 8.1). The

Robert Bontrager is director of admission & orientation at Oregon State University. Before joining Oregon State in 1994, he was vice president for enrollment management at Eastern Mennonite University and assistant registrar at Arizona State University. He completed his bachelor's at Goshen College and earned his master of counseling and Ed.D. degrees from Arizona State University.

downward trend continued nearly unabated through 1992. While the number of high school graduates is now on a long-term upward trend, it will not approach 1980 levels until 2005.

Colleges and universities have compensated for these circumstances somewhat by attempting to increase their enrollment of nontraditional students. While this has proven to be a successful

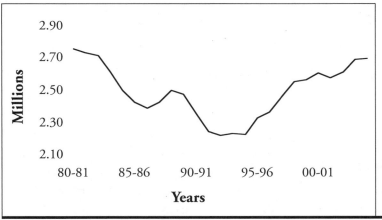

Figure 8.1 National High School Graduates 1980–2004

strategy for some institutions, few four-year schools have been able to fill their rolls adequately with nontraditional students. Instead, a large majority of four-year institutions have worked to revise their recruitment and retention practices in order to respond better to student needs and maximize their enrollment. While the nature of those efforts has varied among institutions, many schools have needed to rethink, revamp, and reengineer their business processes in very fundamental ways.

The Compelling Case for Change

The enrollment picture at Oregon State University has closely paralleled the national trend. Oregon State grew from 6,160 students in 1955 to 17,689 students in 1980. During that period, Oregon State was virtually unchallenged as the leading university in Oregon, with the highest enrollment of any college or university in the state. It attracted by far the largest number of Oregon students and enjoyed a strong international reputation based on the quality of its academic programs and research. While the reputation remains intact, enrollment has dropped significantly. As the competitive environment in higher education intensified in the 1980s, Oregon State fell into a pitfall that caught many prominent state universities. This pitfall consisted of a series of related, false assumptions, including the following:

- In-state students will continue to come to us because of tradition and the comparatively low cost of in-state tuition.
- Students will continue to select us because we offer stronger programs than small private colleges or community colleges.
- Students understand that gaining acceptance to and completing college is a difficult process, and they will do whatever we ask of them.
- Adopting marketing strategies to promote our programs more effectively is inappropriate and demeaning.

The persistence of these assumptions led to a pervasive complacency within the institution. Because it was assumed the latest challenges did not apply to Oregon State, the university faculty and staff hunkered down in a tradition-based, business-as-usual mode. In staff hiring and performance review, what mattered most at the university was longevity, not the achievement of defined goals. Early attempts to address these issues were only marginally successful. The university undertook a major total quality management (TQM) initiative in the early 1990s. Teams were formed to look at various business practices and policies throughout the institution. Meaningful changes were made in key areas, resulting in more enlightened campus attitudes as well as a brief upturn in enrollment. However, with the benefit of hindsight, it would appear that the university's TQM project failed to grasp the underlying assumptions detailed above. The TQM project ended, having changed some practices, but leaving outmoded thinking largely intact. In short, Oregon State continued to operate as though it were in a seller's market with regard to its business practices generally and its admissions operations specifically.

After the brief enrollment upturn in the wake of the TQM project, enrollment declined again. In fall 1996, it had its lowest enrollment since 1980. Over those 16 years, Oregon State's enrollment fell by more than 22 percent to a low of 13,784 in 1996. This drop in enrollment, coupled with a decrease in state funding for higher education, was crippling. It finally became clear that Oregon State's core assumptions were the problem and that in order for it to reverse its declining enrollment, the university needed to revise those assumptions.

Under the leadership of a new president, the university began in 1996 to make changes designed to address its core operating assumptions and reverse the downward trend in enrollment. President Paul Risser shifted the university's focus from the past to the future. He made it clear that business-as-usual was no longer adequate, setting the clear expectation that directors throughout the university would find ways to improve their operations. He identified key strategic areas where the larger process of institutional change would begin. One of those was the Office of Admission & Orientation. President Risser initiated a review of admission practices by outside consultants, provided additional funding, and offered his own services in assisting with recruitment activities. Perhaps most importantly, the president identified increasing enrollment as the university's top priority. The president's leadership provided the necessary context for the fundamental changes undertaken within Admission & Orientation.

Project Summary

A Management Team made up of the director and four associate directors of admission and orientation initiated reengineering Oregon State's admission processes in 1996. In the wake of a reorganization of enrollment services departments, each of us was new to our position. Collectively, we had a total of four years of experience at Oregon State. Though this lack of institutional history presented some challenges, it ultimately proved to be an asset, as team members were able to bring outside perspectives and a fresh look to existing processes (see figure 8.2).

Because we were new, we recognized the importance of communicating to the staff our vision of how we wanted the Office of Admission & Orientation to operate. The result was the development of a mission statement for the office, adapted from a comparable statement developed by the Office of Admissions at the University of Minnesota. The statement reads as follows:

> The Office of Admission & Orientation supports the mission of Oregon State University by bringing to the University students who will benefit from and contribute to the OSU experience. In serving our many customers, our overriding mission will be to exceed persons' expectations in meeting their needs for information and assistance.
>
> In carrying out our mission, we will operate according to the following principles:
> - The OSU Office of Admission & Orientation will be service driven and results oriented. Our

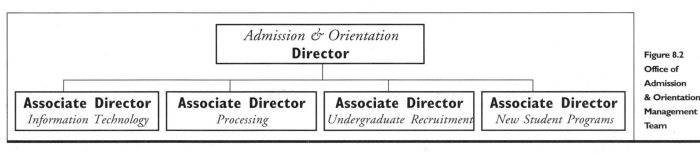

Figure 8.2
Office of
Admission
& Orientation
Management
Team

primary operating principle will be "We can and we will."

- We will work to build and maintain a sense of community that promotes open communication, mutual trust, cooperation, and respect among our staff and with other campus departments.

- By working cooperatively with every campus department, we will play a leadership role in enrolling the number and types of students which will enable the University to reach its goals.

- We will always strive to be positive about ourselves, our colleagues, our office and the University, and to translate that energy into positive behaviors and outcomes.

- Regardless of our specific responsibilities, we will be available to assist in any area where help is needed. We will be ready to do whatever it takes to meet our customers' needs and never say "That's not my job."

- We will strive for professional excellence. Individually and as a group we will seek to be the best in our field. Our goal is to make a significant contribution to our Office, our profession, and Oregon State University.

- We will actively support the University's goal to honor and enhance the diversity of the campus. In every facet of our operation we will encourage openness and sensitivity to persons of varied cultural, racial, and ethnic backgrounds.

- We will value creativity and encourage risk taking. We will learn from our mistakes and encourage constructive criticism as we seek to continuously improve everything we do.

- While holding ourselves to the highest professional standards, we will seek to be well-rounded persons. We will respect the personal dimensions of our lives and take steps to ensure that we never cease to have fun.

Establishing this mission statement was an important step for our office, which had never had a set of guiding principles. However, as we on the Management Team further assessed the office situation and began to develop strategies for more effective student recruitment and orientation, it was apparent that a number of roadblocks existed that would, if not addressed, prevent us from achieving those principles. Existing office structure, procedures, and attitudes all ran counter to what we were trying to accomplish. Our response to this realization went through a series of phases before we were ready to tackle a reengineering project.

First, we were overwhelmed. We knew we were talking about a paradigm shift, that is, a complete rethinking of office attitudes and procedures. The thought of getting into such a project was daunting. In the second phase, we attempted to limit or compartmentalize the task at hand. We wanted to make the project more manageable by breaking it into pieces and taking one thing at a time. On that point we ultimately concluded that (1) the pieces of the project were too intertwined to be handled separately and (2) by doing so we would only prolong a difficult transition process. The third phase was one of resolve. We concluded that our best approach was a comprehensive reengineering effort and quickly adopted a "let's go for it" mentality.

As we began to plan for reengineering, we reached the conclusion that the issues we faced fell into three broad categories: staff relations, office structure, and process reengineering. Staff did not share information often or well, and they tended to make decisions in isolation from one another. Staff relations in the office were best characterized by distrust and resistance to change. At the same time, it was clear to us that no matter how much we improved staff relations, the way staffing and workflow were structured was broken and needed to be fixed.

Staff Relations. Our efforts to improve staff relations were multifaceted. They began with establishing a cross-functional team to review existing practices and recommend changes. This team was formed in January 1997 and dubbed itself the Admissions 2000 Task Force. The team included members from each functional unit in the office, at every staff level, and was chaired by the director. It was clear from the beginning that the task force was to have a short life. The primary goal of its intense, short-term duration was to "work itself out of a job" by putting into place new structures, policies, and procedures that would mainstream the principles contained in the mission statement and make special, ad hoc efforts unnecessary. With this in mind, and using the mission statement as a guide, the task force proceeded to (1) set objectives, (2) identify problem areas, (3) recommend changes, (4) implement changes, and (5) evaluate changes and identify new strategies.

The task force met biweekly and tackled issues ranging from office structure (see below) to space allocation to specific office procedures. The cross-functional, multilevel composition of the group gave it great credibility in addressing these issues and "selling" solutions to other staff members.

Establishment of the Admissions 2000 Task Force itself did a great deal to assure the staff of their status within the office and ability to contribute to decision making. But this was only the first of a series of measures put in place to empower staff and improve morale. Communication problems existed both within and among the functional areas of the office. To improve internal communication, each of the functional areas was reorganized into a team structure. To address communications *among* functional areas, a monthly all staff meeting was established. Agendas include current office news, information sharing, a time to raise issues that need to be addressed, and a time for "kudos" when staff members recognize and thank each other for jobs well done. This has become an important time for the entire staff to meet together, partly for the business transacted, but even more for the team concept it engenders.

We also sought to raise the level of communication skills for all staff members. That desire led to a series of workshops involving the entire staff in learning together how to communicate better both individually and collectively. Workshops are typically a half-day in length, with half of the staff attending one day and half the next. Agendas for these sessions have focused on communication skills and goal setting.

Finally, there was a sense that to address the morale issue, we also needed to relate better in nonwork settings. With that in mind, the task force established more opportunities for the staff to interact informally. This has led to more impromptu party planning, including everything from more frequent "goody days" to monthly birthday parties to establishing annual traditions of a summer picnic and a holiday luncheon.

Office Structure. As noted above, we recognized that we needed to address two closely related issues in our reengineering effort. Improving staff relations was critical to fulfilling our mission. However, there were fundamental flaws in office structure that also needed to be addressed if we were to be successful.

Before 1993, processing functions were organized in a traditional silo manner. In 1993 we attempted to improve office processes by reorganizing the staff into multifunctional teams. Members who performed different functions were grouped into two teams to facilitate communication and understanding among staff about their different roles. Though this approach had some merit, it was done as a stand-alone initiative without concurrent efforts to address staff relations issues. Team meetings were held infrequently, meetings involving the entire staff were held only in

crisis situations, and staff members were deemed too busy to participate in staff development activities. Cross-training was virtually nonexistent. Staff parties were viewed as obligatory, were poorly attended, and were not enjoyable. Ultimately, office operations were only slightly improved after this restructuring and not nearly adequate to support a competitive admissions office.

The Admissions 2000 Task Force took a different approach to reengineering. It developed a structure that cannot be characterized entirely as silos or as cross-functional. Instead, it developed a hybrid approach. Teams returned to being more function specific, but the number of teams was reduced by combining some functions. Positions within team were restructured to be more comprehensive. The resulting "full flow" approach allowed individual staff to move students through the application process from start to finish, resulting in fewer items falling through the cracks and empowering the staff to make more decisions on their own. This in turn allowed us to raise the level of some positions, resulting in higher pay and the ability to hire more capable people to fill certain roles.

The task force established the following suggested guidelines for team functioning:

- Meet at least biweekly.
- Encourage open conversation about concerns.
- Focus on solutions, not problems.
- Seek to continuously improve the functions team members are responsible for.
- Actively brainstorm new ideas, with an emphasis on taking risks.

Along with this reorganizing, the task force recommended reducing the number of staff. This involved four data entry positions, which were at the bottom of the university's staff classification scale. Because the support staff at Oregon State is unionized, employees who were displaced from other university offices were automatically assigned to the data entry positions in our office. We were forced to accept those with limited capabilities to perform the function on which our entire recruiting operation depends: getting prospective students into our database to enable timely response. In careful consultation with the university's Human Resources Department and union representatives, we phased out the data entry positions.

Process Reengineering. One of the emphases of our mission statement was to develop a commitment to continuous improvement among the staff. We realized this would be easier said than done. The time it takes to review processes is not easy to find. If changes are identified, they are usually met with resistance. We sought to counteract those tendencies by tackling a few problem areas within the Admissions 2000 Task Force, reengineering the related processes, implementing changes, and (we hoped) creating success stories that would generate interest among the staff generally in tackling other process issues.

We were extremely fortunate that as we were engaging in process reengineering, the university was implementing major enhancements to its electronic service capabilities. Computer and other information systems were being upgraded, with significant improvements to our ability to provide services via a variety of electronic media, especially the World Wide Web. The efficiencies afforded by these enhancements were crucial to our being able to improve service delivery with a downsized staff.

Outcomes. Our reengineering effort has been extremely successful. While difficult to quantify, staff morale has improved dramatically. There is an increased sense of being a team throughout the office. Staff members are more willing to raise questions in team meetings. Risk taking is more prevalent. Social events have been increasingly well attended and enjoyable. These are clearly ongoing issues, however, with periodic lapses in our ability to identify and handle problems effectively. Those occasions become part of the overall process of improvement as we address them head-on, learn to deal with them effectively, and move on. A morale-related initiative that simply did not work was an employee-of-the-month program, which was deemed too perfunctory and was nixed by the staff.

Our structural and process changes have led to more tangible results. These include the following outcomes over the past two years:

- Reduction in the time required to respond to a request for admission information from five days to two days
- Reduction in the time required to process an admission application from two weeks to one week
- A 10 percent reduction in per-student recruiting cost
- A 22 percent increase in new freshmen

Student Services Trends

The current context of admissions work in higher education assures that virtually every admissions office in the country is involved in significant change. If enrollment numbers are not an issue for a given institution, emerging technologies alone will dictate a rethinking of processes. At the core of any of these changes is the realization that students are the center of our institutions. As obvious as this sounds, other modes of thinking and operating linger in many cases. Certainly that has been the case at Oregon State. This made the commitment to a student-centered approach the beginning point of our reengineering project.

Cross-functionality has always been advisable from the standpoint of staff communications and mutual understanding of roles. In this era of increasing expectations and downsized staffs, it becomes more imperative that staff members develop the ability to perform multiple functions and make decisions with input from all functional areas. In many cases, this is achieved by structuring teams with members from different functional areas. We used this approach to launch our reengineering project. For ongoing operations, however, we retained more function-specific teams but put measures in place to provide for information flow and decision making among teams.

In one sense, our project is isolated with the Office of Admission & Orientation, since there is no campuswide reengineering project under way. On the other hand, significant changes have occurred throughout the university that have made our project goals more achievable. The president's mandate for improving all facets of the university established a culture of change and improvement that our project benefited from. His identification of enrollment as the institution's top priority made other campus offices more receptive to our requests for assistance. In addition, the president's strategic initiatives in areas such as marketing, distance education, and athletics have elevated the profile of the university among key constituencies, making them more receptive to recruiting efforts.

Another critical factor in our success was a campuswide effort to improve the university's information services. A major expansion of electronic services provided necessary service enhancements and process efficiencies needed to implement our project successfully. These enhancements included kiosk and Web services, providing many more self-service opportunities for students in the areas of admission, registration, records, financial aid, and student accounts.

Critical Success Factors and Key Considerations

Many factors contribute to the success of an attempt to change the way 60 people work together. In our case, these are grouped into four categories: communication, managing ambiguity, adopting a comprehensive approach, and support from the top.

Communication. We are all familiar with the natural human aversion to change. While we knew resistance was inevitable, we sought to ameliorate as much as possible by creating new and numerous opportunities to share information with the staff, discuss proposed changes, and involve staff at all levels in designing our new structure. In doing so, we had to overcome time constraints, including both a real and imagined lack of time to talk, brainstorm, and plan with one another. With this in mind, the Admissions 2000 Task Force held frequent but relatively short one-hour meetings. This allowed us to be more focused and efficient during our time together. We continue to work with the staff to encourage sharing in group settings, particularly all-staff meetings.

Managing Ambiguity. By definition, a reengineering effort requires implementing changes with unknown outcomes. This is the most difficult aspect of the process. Our staff was already wary of change, particularly to the degree we were suggesting. To deal with their anxieties, they sought assurances that the changes we were proposing would be certain to work. Unfortunately, we could not give such assurances, which added to the staff's anxiety level.

There are no easy ways to deal with this issue at the outset of the reengineering process. Later, when at least some changes prove to be successful, staff members develop the energy and courage to take on new risks. In the earlier stages of our project we sought to address this issue by staying focused on our mission and goals, encouraging risk taking, and assuring staff that if a new process proved not to work we would review and adjust.

Comprehensive Approach. The list of issues and processes to be addressed in a reengineering effort is daunting. As noted earlier in this chapter, the temptation to break the task into small, more manageable pieces is strong. Such an approach, however, generally leads to two undesirable outcomes: (1) results are less positive because critical components of the change process are not addressed and (2) the difficult transition process is protracted over a longer period of time. Our comprehensive approach allowed us to achieve more change in less time.

Support From the Top. This axiom of organizational life has become rather trite. Nonetheless, it remains a prerequisite to success in implementing a reengineering project. The magnitude of change, not to mention the personnel issues related to downsizing, virtually guarantee that upper-level administrators will hear staff complaints. Senior administrators should be approached initially for their approval of the reengineering effort and must be kept well informed throughout the process. This will allow them to lend support to the effort when complaints or questions come their way.

Student Services Trends

TRENDS	IMPLEMENTATION PHASE
Student-Centered	●
Redesigned Services	N/A
One-Stop Service Center	N/A
Cross-Functional Teams	N/A
Self-Service Objectives	N/A
Department Process Improvements	●
Web-Enabled Services	●
Admissions	●
Registration	●
Advising	○
Financial Aid	●
Billing	◐
Career Services	○
Systemic Change	N/A
Replacement of Student Information Systems	●

Codes for Implementation Phase:

● Production
◐ Implementing
◑ Designed
○ Planning

Conclusion

We have recruited more students for less money with a staff that is smaller, but happier. Those obviously are excellent outcomes. Yet we remind ourselves daily that reengineering is a journey, not a destination. While proud of our successes, we are keenly aware of the processes we have not yet reengineered, of the crises that come up more often than we would like, and of the opportunities that remain unfulfilled. These are the ongoing issues we seek to address as we continue on the path of reengineering.

Part 3:

Technology as the Change Agent

9

Northern Territory University (Australia) and University of Minnesota, Twin Cities

Darlene Burnett
Christian Pantel

From In-line to Online: Transforming Student Services

Overview

How an institution manages its student services has a direct impact on its position in the academic community. Student services, from admissions to financial aid to enrollment, are essential processes for any institution. The ease with which anyone can use these services can have a profound impression on current and prospective students, parents, faculty, and staff. Colleges and universities have long understood the importance of image, and the services they offer, whether traditional (in-line) or forward-thinking (online), are essential to that identity. Many campuses maintain a traditional strategy with face-to-face in-line services; others have created a combination of both in-line and online; and some institutions today reside in cyberspace—their Web presence conveys their image. These institutions market not only their academic reputation and their ability to prepare students for life and career, but also the level of service they provide for their key customers—students.

Darlene Burnett is senior consultant with IBM Education Consulting & Services. During the past 10 years, she has helped colleges and universities solve problems and implement technology and services in administrative and academic computing. She has a bachelor's in business administration from Pittsburg State University and an MBA in organizational behavior from the University of Missouri.

Christian Pantel is project leader, user-centered design, for IBM Canada's Pacific Development Centre. He holds an M.Sc. in computing science (human-computer interaction) from Simon Fraser University. His recent research and development work focuses on the appropriate use of technology to facilitate distributed learning and the delivery of student services.

The Compelling Case for Change

Student-centered services and Web-based student services used to be considered options for institutions. Those that established such services considered them a competitive advantage in attracting prospective students. But today, students essentially require student-centered services and Web services of the institutions they attend. Regardless of whether they live in a dorm, commute to campus from home, or attend classes via the Web, students want to go from in-line to online for their student service needs. Accustomed to service on demand, they expect choice—and convenience. In the same way that they can choose to buy a book online from Amazon.com, by calling Barnes & Noble's toll-free phone number, or simply by visiting a local bookstore, students want the choice of accessing the institution's Web site for information, picking up the phone to get an answer on admission, or meeting personally with a financial aid officer. Students no longer are willing to stand in line to talk to an individual when it is not necessary. Students want face-to-face transactions to provide added value or handle exceptions. Students want the ability to access self-service when they want, just as they do at an automated bank teller. The "right" method is simply whichever meets the immediate need. Today institutions compete in both the physical and virtual worlds, and their services must be online and reflect the student-centered horizontal process.

Summary

Nearly all higher education institutions have a Web site that provides some level of information and service. A look at an institution's Web site—noting whether it includes professional-quality images, text, and designs equal to the quality of the institution's print material—should reveal very quickly whether it considers the

Web an important part of its student service, communication, and marketing strategy. In addition to the site's appearance and message, the design and services offered indicate whether the institution considers the Web a portal to the institution. Institutions that do so expect that contact by phone, written letter, personal visit, or e-mail will be handled in the same professional manner, and each avenue of contact is integrated into the process for each service provided. Staff is trained to handle e-mail requests along with other forms of communication as part of their assigned responsibilities.

The same is true for the design of the institution's Web service, which must be considered a service portal for the institution and be integrated into each process. If the institution has done process redesign for the physical processes of the institution, the Web should reflect those redesigned processes. Perhaps even more important, the Web should reflect a redesigned student-centric horizontal process. A student-centered horizontal process is the sum of all transactions a student must complete to attend an institution and enroll in classes. The process is viewed from the student's perspective, and the transactions are seamless and cross traditional boundaries. These boundaries are typically set because different functions—admissions, enrollment, financial aid, student accounts, advising, parking, meals, housing—have been designed around the needs of the institution and are in separate offices, buildings, or Web site locations. In a traditional setting, students have to make separate appointments (or wait in line) and physically go to another building or location to work with a specialist. With a student-centered horizontal process, a student can find out the status of his or her financial aid application and scheduled registration time, verify there were no holds, change his or her mailing address, and set up an appointment with an advisor at one time in one place. If the institution has not redesigned the physical process, the process is considered an institution-centric vertical process. The Web gives the institution the opportunity to create a student-centered services reputation and provide student-centered horizontal services—without making physical changes.

Creating an interactive, easy-to-understand Web site is often a challenge for an institution. Many college and university sites begin when a member of a single department posts information on the Web. For example, someone from the admissions office wants a presence on the Web. He or she might use existing text from the course catalog or another document. The information appears on the Web in the same manner it appeared in print. No changes are made to take advantage of Web technologies. Everything is linear. Then other departments decide to put up a Web page—the athletics department, the financial aid office, the housing office, parking, and so on. This approach creates "silos" on the Web, each containing isolated information and little or no integration. Very little is done to consider the marketing image of the institution, how students will use the Web site (the student-centered horizontal process), or that the Web is now a legitimate portal to the institution.

While no one would create a printed course catalog or admission brochure without ensuring it met the standards of the institution and having it reviewed to make sure it fit with the vision and mission statement, the Web is treated differently. Material is posted with little or no review, control, or standards. There is little coordination or communication between departments. Most important, no one is assigned to maintain the information, update it, or add to the site. Individuals from each department—usually a part-time student—place information on the Web for that department. Then, the student leaves or graduates. The next student assigned adds his or her own personality to the site. Eventually the site becomes a patchwork of parts.

Crucial elements to creating the Web portal for an institution and taking students from in-line to online are cost and budget. While print materials that the institution or individual departments generate usually have a set budget, a process, and skilled professionals assigned to the project, Web development often does not. The result is a mixture of images, text, formats, and communication messages that can be confusing to the viewer. As the physical silos of the institution separate the services of the campus, the Web silos now separate virtual services. If the Web is to be a portal for the institution, a budget and a process need to be defined for department, division, college, and institution participation.

Northern Territory University (NTU) in Australia and the University of Minnesota, Twin Cities are two institutions that have taken a serious approach to the design and implementation of the Web as a portal. Each in its own way has taken its students from in-line to online.

Models of the Web as an Institutional Portal

NTU (www.ntu.edu.au) has 13,500 students and is the major tertiary education institution in the Northern Territory. The university is part of the Australian National Unified System of Higher Education. NTU draws on its proximity to Asia—the nearest neighboring university is in Indonesia—and is developing important links between NTU and the countries of the Southeast Asian and Pacific regions, particularly Indonesia (General Information 1999).

NTU is the first institution in Australia to establish online enrollments. As a result, NTU, which has five campuses in the Northern Territory as well as in Malaysia and Hong Kong, can now compete directly with city-based campuses. With the installation of a new Lotus Domino-based system, the number of administrative staff has been reduced from 21 to four.

NTU started looking at solutions for streamlining and improving the enrollment process in 1996. Other types of solutions considered included voice mail and phone enrollments, but none would have changed the actual administration process (Lotus Development Pty Ltd 1997). Online enrollments began in January 1998. Students apply for enrollment directly over the Internet by filling out an online form. The self-enrollment system interfaces directly with the NTU administration system, ASCOL, to process the application. "This model is perfectly suited for an isolated campus like NTU," says Kevin Davis, pro vice-chancellor of NTU Domino's integrated Web. "Work flow and messaging technology has let us overcome our geographic remoteness. We can now compete toe to toe with the other capital city campuses for students and staff. The new Domino-based system speeds up our administration and offers students a fast and easy way of enrolling. Using the Internet, all students will have access to their enrollment details, university accounts, and course information."

In addition to enrollments and admissions, NTU will use the Web for the following:

- *A student information center.* The center will provide students with quick access to a range of services currently scattered geographically and administratively.
- *An online handbook.* Faculty, course, and staff information will be displayed in a variety of ways. For example, students will be able to see course information listed by faculty, topic, or lecturer.
- *Course development and approval.* Academic staff will instantly approve subjects for students, enter exam results directly into the database, and develop course units using Lotus Notes.
- *Human resources.* It will handle the administration process for hiring staff and processing leaves.

Northern Territory University Student LaunchPad. The student portal to NTU is called LaunchPad. Instead of Web silos for separate functions, each with a different look and feel, or asking students to navigate around the Web site, LaunchPad has enabled NTU to move students from in-line to online. According to NTU's Web site, LaunchPad provides the following services:

- Help for New Students
  1. Decide on up to 5 courses that are of interest to you.
  2. Submit an online Application for Admission to those courses.
  3. The University will notify you once a decision has been made about your application **or** you may use the On-line Admission Status Check to see if your application has been successful.
  4. If you have been successful, return to this page and submit an On-line Enrollment.
- Admission & Enrollment Information
- Courses on Offer
- Units on Offer
- On-line Admission
- Check the Status of your Admission On-line
- HECS Information —Higher Education Contribution Scheme (HECS)
- HECS Calculator

University of Minnesota. The University of Minnesota (onestop.umn.edu) has long been recognized as a leader in using technology to enable innovation. The university's primary aim is to be responsive to its students' long-term academic goals. To help accomplish this, it wanted to deliver superior-quality service to both students and staff on all four of its campuses. Minnesota also sought to reduce the overall administrative costs and leverage its new PeopleSoft® Student Administration software. The university knew that its goal wasn't about technology, it was about serving its customers—the students— better. A $750 million-a-year business, the university viewed its One Stop Web as an integral component in the management of its primary business—instructional operations. The One Stop Web fully supports and enhances every student's academic experience.

Robert Kvavik, associate vice president for academic affairs, and Michael Handberg, director of Web development, have been instrumental in creating the vision and helping develop Web services for the University of Minnesota. They note that one university survey indicated, much to their surprise, that as students moved from their freshman year to their senior year, their overall dissatisfaction increased. The survey team surmised that the students' frustration grew with bureaucracy and services each year. Handberg says, "With that in mind, the university endeavored to improve student satisfaction and create an environment that significantly improved administrative functions while at the same time deliver powerful new services to students. Like students at most other institutions, Minnesota students were spending far too much time walking from office to office to accomplish basic tasks like enrolling in classes, getting approval stamps or signatures, and changing addresses and other personal information. In most cases, students had to get a form, fill it out, take it to the correct office, hand it to a person for approval, and then move to the next office to complete the task. The process also meant that staff time was taken up with mundane tasks as they shuffled huge piles of papers."

To streamline its operation, improve student and staff satisfaction, and create a student-centered horizontal process, the university decided to integrate its existing student administration system, PeopleSoft, with a personal Web planner. The goal was to create a self-service Web-based solution that enabled students to view and search online course catalogs, register for classes, view grades, request the campus newspaper, and much more, from their desktops using any standard Web browsers. In essence, the University of Minnesota wanted its students out of the lines and online.

The University of Minnesota's One Stop Web site is unusual among institutions that provide Web access for students because it presents an integrated and seamless view to the student, based on a goal- and task-oriented approach to getting things done. Few institutional sites offer true integration of information from back end systems, and there is far from seamless interface presented to the student. On the One Stop Web site, enrollment gets back to the basics. For example, picking and scheduling classes, getting advice about correcting holds on enrollment, reviewing the tuition and fees that will be charged, signing off on the charges, and getting a printed copy of the whole transaction, from class description to meeting times to tuition, all occur through the Web browser. This new way of providing services uses a student-centric perspective that creates high levels of satisfaction for the new media generation. Once the Web site was in place, applications for admission increased 40 percent and honors applications doubled.

Minnesota's Web site is powered by an IBM WebSphere Application Server running on a scaleable, robust IBM RS/6000 SP server using Netscape Enterprise Server. The WebSphere Application Server provides a Java servlet runtime environment, where servlets access PeopleSoft Student Administration. The result is that the university's existing information is merged into new, Web-based business processes. To protect the privacy of data transmitted over the Web, Secure Sockets Layer is used.

The vision of Kvavik and Handberg to transform student services—a vision that Babson College and the University of Delaware share—can be summed up by their diagram of the old and new processes (see figure 9.1).

In the old process, specialists handled the majority of student transactions. Only a few transactions were automatically handled or available through self-service. With the One Stop Web, students manage most—75 percent to 90 percent, according to Handberg—of their transactions, allowing the staff to use their time for mission-critical tasks. If we look at the new model for delivering Web services to the students, we will see that the silo segmentation of services is no longer visible. The seamless process has been redesigned using a student-centric perspective. The student now views the process as the inverted triangle in figure 9.1.

User-Centered Design

User-centered design (UCD) is a methodology for developing products. By focusing on the users more than the technology, UCD helps to ensure that applications are easy to learn and use, intuitive, engaging, and useful. In short, UCD leads to applications that make for a delightful user experience. Because Web applications for student services are intended for use by a wide variety of people with varying skills, UCD is an appropriate method—and one that has been successfully employed—in such sites' development.

The two main tenets of UCD are that (1) the users of the application should be continually consulted and involved in its development and (2) the users, not the technology, should be the focus of the development effort.

A multidisciplinary team should be responsible for integrating the total student experience—that is, everything the student sees, hears, and touches—into the Web application. To design a Web application that will be well received, developers must know their users and understand their goals and needs, the tasks they perform, the environment in which they work, their current challenges, the tools they require, and the methods they prefer to use. User input and feedback should be sought at all stages of an application's life cycle. They should be the driving force behind each iteration of an application's development. UCD methodology incorporates user feedback–gathering techniques appropriate for all stages of application development, such as surveys, contextual inquiry, focus groups, and formal usability tests. Validating design ideas before they are developed and deployed is critical to launching a successful student service Web application.

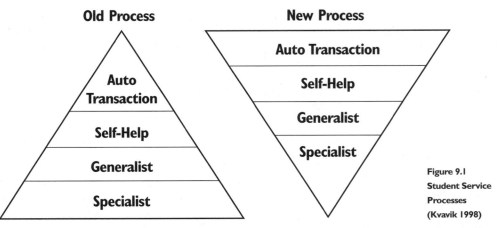

**Figure 9.1
Student Service
Processes
(Kvavik 1998)**

The team charged with designing the application should comprise a variety of skills, including leadership, user-interface design, visual design, human factors/ergonomics, marketing, training, and technical architecture. This highly skilled team has the responsibility and authority to design all aspects of the Web application that affect a student's experience. This can be seen as a broad definition of a Web's interface—the parts of the Web that students are aware

- No silos
- Integrated, seamless departmental delivery of services
- Access from any computer
- Increased accessibility by being open 24 hours a day, 7 days a week
- Electronic, no paper, easily updated format
- One source of information easily found and understood
- Control of the institution's message to students, facilitating change

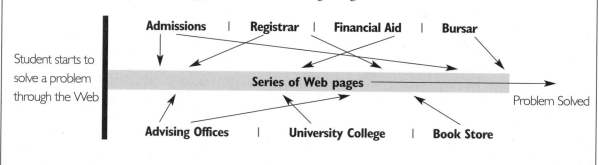

Figure 9.2
New Web-based
Student Services
(Kvavik 1998)

Reprinted with permission of Robert Kvavik.

of and that cause students to form their opinion of the Web service. For a software application, this definition includes not only the graphical user interface (such as menus, icons, and colors), but also the packaging, the accompanying documentation, the training materials, and the advertising.

Why Should User-Centered Design Be Applied? Institutions that want to use technology, including the Web, to improve their delivery of student services should adopt a UCD methodology. To a user, the product's user interface is the product. The interface must be carefully designed for the project to succeed; the likely consequence of not paying enough attention to an application's user interface is poor acceptance by users. UCD has proven to be an effective methodology in developing student service Web solutions. By concentrating on the needs of users and by empowering a multidisciplinary team of UCD practitioners, institutions can help ensure the success of their projects.

How to Develop a Web Solution. Let us assume that an institution has decided to make improving the delivery of services to its students a priority and that providing student services via the Web is one aspect of that goal. What should be done next?

First, senior administration should approve a budget and a mandate for a multidisciplinary team to apply UCD methodology to measurably improve the delivery of student services over the Web. The mandate should make it clear that where previous mechanisms for delivering student services may have been institution-centric, process-centric, or technology-centric, the new solution must be student (user)-centric. Administrators can track the progress of the UCD student services project by obtaining reports on the number of hours the multidisciplinary team spends with users and the nature and progress of the most important unresolved challenges.

The first tasks for the multidisciplinary team will include the following:

- *Understand the domain.* The domain is the subject of activity and knowledge. The UCD team should seek to understand the business of providing student services, focusing on what existing processes or technologies work particularly well or poorly. Aspects of the current delivery of student services that work well should be retained or closely paralleled in the new solution; those that work poorly are great opportunities for substantial improvement. The UCD team should spend time with the institution's student service providers to understand the domain.

- *Understand the users.* The UCD team should also spend time with the people who will use the student service Web. This cannot be stressed enough. Software developers and university personnel tend to believe they know what is best for the user. It has been shown time and time again that the best way to find out what users really need and want is to ask them directly.

- *Begin the iterative and incremental design.* The UCD team should begin prototyping design ideas. They should validate these ideas with students and staff and refine them accordingly. Additional features and functionality can be added incrementally.

Benefits of User-Centered Design. The main benefit of UCD methodology is that it leads to satisfied students, and this is clearly good for the institution. Since students are involved in the design process, having many opportunities to critique and contribute to designs, the solution is much more likely to meet their needs. Another benefit of user-centered design is that it is cost-effective. It gives administrators an additional measure of confidence that the investment they make in a student service Web will be worthwhile. They can be confident that the solution will meet their discriminating students' needs. A more traditional development methodology would have the solution built in relative isolation, with technology being the focus. This could lead to unpleasant surprises, including costly refinements and adjustments, when the system is deployed.

Critical Success Factors and Key Considerations

The two most critical success factors for applying a UCD methodology to the development of a Web student service solution are management commitment and having skilled user-centered design practitioners. Management must invest in assembling a skillful multidisciplinary team and empower them to design the solution. Managers should ensure that measurable goals are set for the solution under development and that these are met before deployment. Adequate time and resources must be allocated in the project plan to enable the UCD process. User feedback must be factored into priorities and decision making.

Other factors critical to the success of building successful Web services include the following:

- Designing the site from the student's perspective (seamless and horizontal)
- Defining Web standards and a Web image for the institution, and ensuring that the Web is managed as professionally as the institution's printed materials, to create a consistent image and message
- Cooperation among departments within the institution
- Creating an ongoing budget, process, and staff assignment for the continued enhancement and maintenance of the Web site, which will become a core part of the institution's administration

This isn't a one-time project or expense. It is an ongoing project that must be funded and staffed like other portals to the institution. It is critical that Web services become an integrated portal to the institution's existing processes.

Conclusion

A user champion is more important than a technology champion to the successful completion of a student service project. Assembling a skilled multidisciplinary team is critical to the success of a UCD project. The team members should be experienced with UCD methodology, be technically competent, work well as a team, communicate well, and truly have the users' best interests at heart. Furthermore, the team members' skills should complement each other. An empowered multidisciplinary team employing a user-centered design methodology greatly increases the likelihood of success in the development of a Web-based delivery system for student services.

Regardless of the team's talent and drive, developing a successful Web service application requires the support of the institution's leadership. The administration must recognize the project as critical to the institution's success and allocate the resources, including

Student Services Trends

TRENDS	IMPLEMENTATION PHASE	
	NTU	UMinn
Student-Centered	○ (Planning)	● (Production)
Redesigned Services	N/A	◑ (Implementing)
One-Stop Service Center	N/A	N/A
Cross-Functional Teams	N/A	◐ (Designed)
Self-Service Objectives	N/A	● (Production)
Department Process Improvements	N/A	N/A
Web-Enabled Services	●	●
Admissions	●	●
Registration	●	●
Advising	●	●
Financial Aid	●	●
Billing	●	●
Career Services	N/A	○
Systemic Change	●	●
Replacement of Student Information Systems	N/A	◑ (Implementing)

Codes for Implementation Phase:
- ● Production
- ◑ Implementing
- ◐ Designed
- ○ Planning

financial ones, necessary to make it happen. Most important, the administration should seek to end the silo structure that exists in so many institutions' Web sites and create a strong, consistent image that communicates defined key messages.

Institutions increasingly are recognizing the impact that technology—and their customers' knowledge and facility with technology—can have on even the most mundane tasks. Students today have demonstrated the desire to move to the online environment. Staff are growing more accustomed to the prospect of Web-based services, and they realize the potential benefits in terms of time and cost savings. As the projects at Northern Territory University, the University of Minnesota, and other institutions around the world have demonstrated, a student-centric Web solution, developed using the user-centered design methodology, can provide an institution with not only an efficient process for student services, but also a competitive advantage in attracting students to the institution.

REFERENCES

Kvavik, Robert. 1998. Transforming Student Services. Paper presented at Innovations in Student Services Forum, 3–5 August, at Brigham Young University.

Lotus Development Pty Ltd. November 20, 1997. News release. Sydney, Australia.

General Information. *Northern Territory University.* www.ntu.edu.au/aboutntu. (30 April 1999).

David E. Hollowell

Student Services: A Broad View

Overview

The University of Delaware began an ongoing process of improving its services to students in 1988, long before the buzzwords "reengineering" and "transformation" were applied to the change process. Delaware was among the first universities to implement a "one-stop shopping" facility for student services and has been a leader in the use of the Web and other technologies as means to provide services on and off campus. The university has been expanding the definition of student services to those that directly affect the learning process, including the library and instructional technologies. The intent of this chapter is to provide a history of this evolutionary program, the critical success factors, and lessons learned along the way.

Delaware is a privately chartered, state-assisted research university, comprised of seven colleges offering 125 undergraduate, 78 master's, and 40 doctoral programs. The university enrolls approximately 21,000 students; about 15,000 of them are undergraduates and nearly half live in campus housing. There are about 3,600 faculty and staff.

Compelling Case for Change

The university's rapid growth in the 1970s and 1980s was not accompanied by changes in procedures or administrative systems to serve the larger population adequately. A student attitude survey

---

David E. Hollowell is executive vice president at the University of Delaware. He has been instrumental in efforts to improve student services and in implementing a major campus improvement program. He is a past president of the Society for College and University Planning and a frequent presenter at professional meetings. He holds a bachelor's and a master's degree in engineering and an MBA, all from Boston University.

administered in 1987 identified many areas in which the university ranked below average both within the survey questions themselves and as compared to national norms. These areas included registration procedures, financial aid procedures, billing and payment procedures, dining services, the attitude of nonteaching staff toward students, and the general concern for students as individuals. The results of this survey made it clear that there were systemic issues as well as attitudinal issues that needed to be addressed.

In addition, the era of rapid enrollment growth was coming to an end and competition was increasing for the best students. As college costs had also risen significantly over the prior 15 years, a growing sense of consumerism was emerging on the part of parents and prospective students. It was clear that the student experience beyond the classroom was taking on an increased level of importance and perhaps those institutions that provided the best overall experience for students would be at a competitive advantage.

Vision and Objectives

The president who assumed office in 1987 took particular note of the student attitude survey results. One of his actions was to recruit me to serve as the chief administrative officer with a charge to improve administrative systems and procedures. In early 1988, a planning process was put in place to address the student service issues. This planning process had several goals, including the following:

- Improve the quality and efficiency of student services
- Develop a team orientation for management and staff
- Apply technology to its fullest advantage
- Implement a fully integrated, comprehensive, online student information system

The Planning Process

The first step in addressing these issues was to form a project team to evaluate the strengths and weaknesses of the student services functions and to develop strategies for sustained improvement. The registrar chaired that team, which included the department heads from financial aid, admissions, billing and collection, management information services, and institutional research and planning. It was quite apparent from the early meetings that these individuals were not used to working as a team. It was therefore not surprising to find that these departments were largely inward focused with little teamwork or cooperation among them. Students were run from one office to the next and often stood in long lines to accomplish the simplest of administrative tasks. Some student service units had a reputation for being uncaring, even downright unpleasant, in dealing with students.

It did not take long to determine that the noted deficiencies had two root causes. First, the administrative computing systems intended to support student services were outdated, inflexible, sometimes nonexistent, and not at all integrated. Thus, administrators and staff did not have the tools needed to get the job done. The second cause was a lack of employee training. Each job function was in its own silo with little knowledge of how that job related to others. There was a lack of training in customer service or telephone techniques, or on how their job fit into the bigger picture. Students perceived that staff did not care about providing good service. The truth was that the staff had neither adequate training nor the information system resources necessary to do their jobs in a timely and efficient manner.

The project team focused on overall goals and objectives, placing institutional issues above those of individual units. Fundamental to this was not accepting past practice without question and a willingness to change archaic policies and streamline procedures whenever necessary. The more the team worked together, the more the team members came to understand each other's issues and problems. They realized that many of the problems were held in common or caused by discontinuity of procedures from one office to another. The focus was on process and how each student service activity (e.g., registration, drop/add, fee payment) could be simplified, streamlined, and made more student-friendly. While it was stated that functional units may be reorganized if necessary, the project did not begin with an assumption that the organizational structure of the university needed to change to be successful. Several key goals emerged: (1) foster teamwork among management and staff within and across the student services units, (2) emphasize quality and efficiency of service, and (3) develop the tools necessary to get the job done. As the process evolved, several objectives were identified under each of the goals.

One objective was to apply technology to its fullest advantage. By 1988, the university had already made significant investments in computing technology and had begun to install a campuswide fiber-optic network. It was clear that any new system must be fully online and capable of being accessed by all those who need access, including the students. The system would have to be fully integrated to eliminate redundancy and to permit easy navigation from one area to another. One of the other objectives was to encourage staff to "think of themselves as a student," that is, to keep the student perspective clearly in mind when redesigning the service functions.

Leadership

The departments represented on the project team reported to four different vice presidents. For the project to move forward quickly and with the maximum cooperation of all involved, the president made it clear that this project was a top priority. He identified me as the project sponsor who would have his complete support in accomplishing the goal. The project team knew it had direct access to those who had the financial resources, who were able to change policies and procedures, and who could reorganize functions if that proved necessary. While it is possible that such a significant transformation can occur from within an organization, having leadership and support at the top greatly increases the chances of a timely success.

Implementation

In September 1988, one month ahead of schedule, the project team made its recommendation that a student information system package be acquired and installed. The project schedule and budget were developed and approved by the president in October 1988, with a two-year implementation goal. A contract was signed in December 1988, database conversion commenced in August 1990, and the system went live in October 1990. In parallel with the selection and implementation of the system, training programs aimed at improving interpersonal skills, telephone manner, and service skills were provided. As components of the system became available in test mode, staff began to receive training on their use. As an integrated system with powerful navigation tools, it would be possible for one person to answer questions that could involve retrieving information from multiple areas. For example, a person answering a billing question could review registered courses, financial aid awards, and dining plan charges to determine the basis for a billing balance.

Technology planning was also an important parallel effort. To meet the objective of providing access to all that had need, it would be necessary to have access to a campuswide computer network and to have an appropriate level of desktop technology widely available. A number of departments were selected to have access to the test versions of the system so that technology installation and training programs could be refined before campuswide deployment. Even before the system was installed, ideas for how it could be distributed more broadly were emerging. It was clear that the new system could be used to foster change as it provided tools to support new and innovative services.

Implementation of the student information system during the 1990–91 academic year was quite successful. The training programs resulted in a smooth transition, and users in the central offices quickly became comfortable and efficient in using the new system. By the fall of 1993, all colleges and departments had access to the system to assist with advising, course scheduling, drop/add, and senior checkout. Many faculty were using the system to aid in advising, taking advantage of their access to transcripts, class lists, and student schedules.

Continuous Improvement

The project team was not dismissed once the new system was selected. It was given a new charge of overseeing the implementation and looking for ways to further improve student services. In particular, the team had the goal of looking at technology and how it could be employed more extensively. It is important to remember that in the early 1990s, the Web did not exist and Internet security was not developed to the level it is today. In the beginning, access to the new system was largely limited to faculty and staff. The first applications open to student access were delivered via interactive voice applications over the telephone. Still, the ability to drop and add courses by telephone from any place, at any time was a monumental improvement in service compared to standing in long lines and not knowing if the desired choices would be available.

The Opportunity for One-Stop Shopping

One of the limitations to providing optimum service was the physical location of the various student service offices. They were scattered and not well arranged to provide efficient service even with the new system tools. In the summer of 1991, a small but centrally located building of about 11,400 square feet became available. It was a single story shop building that would need total renovation for most any other purpose. Centralizing key student service functions at this location was determined to be the highest priority for the space. A plan was developed to gut the building and design a service layout from scratch.

Given that the building was not large enough to accommodate all the offices that provide student services, the challenge was to select the functions that most needed to be there and to design a layout that would provide efficient service. The registrar and his

team were once again asked to study the issue. The team's first reaction was to bring in an architect to start laying out the space to see what could be made to fit, but this notion was rejected. The team was urged to take a step back and, again, to look at process. They were asked to consider new ways to do business and how to use the new system in ways that might even result in students' being able to satisfy their questions in a self-service mode. If that was not possible, only one person should serve the students whenever practical.

The team analyzed the kinds of questions and procedures that prompted students to visit their offices. They also looked at the functions their offices provided to determine which ones were direct services to the public and which were essentially back office functions. The team's analysis concluded that about 20 percent of the people who visited their offices did so to accomplish very simple activities, such as to request an unofficial transcript, to get a copy of their schedule, or to inquire about the status of their account. Another 60 percent had routine questions that could be answered by a person who was trained to access information residing in various components of the student information system. The remaining 20 percent required the services of a specialist in a particular area.

Using this analysis, the team developed a list of services that could be provided in a self-help mode. These included clearly signed racks for various forms and information booklets. Others would require the development of information kiosks that would allow students to access their own class schedule, financial status, and academic information on a read-only basis using their student identification number and a password for security. The inclusion of a printer allowed students to print their class schedule or unofficial transcript and be on their way.

The team envisioned the concept of a service generalist, a front counter staff person cross-trained in the various student service areas and in the use of the student information system. Specialists would ideally be located within sight of and near the generalists. As the concept took shape, it became apparent that it was much like the branch bank model. The bank lobby provides information brochures and forms along with automated teller machines; the tellers are able to provide a number of banking services; and, for those specialized questions or services, the bank officers are close by and often in clear view of the teller windows.

With the functional plan in mind, the architect was called in and the floor plan developed to meet the desired service requirements. During the construction process, training of staff and team-building activities were conducted to overcome some skepticism on the part of managers and staff. To help build enthusiasm for the project, the president met with all who would be housed in the building to offer his views on the importance of serving students

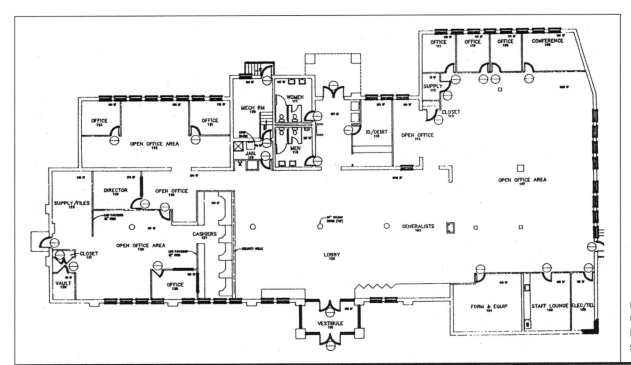

Figure 10.1
University of
Delaware Student
Services Building

well and to conduct a tour of the building during its early stages of renovation. Drawings of the layout and exterior views were displayed, as were furniture and fabric samples. The idea was to help merge the concepts with the physical realities in the minds of those who would ultimately make it all work. As construction proceeded, enthusiasm increased and the building became a frequent stop on lunchtime walks of its future occupants.

The building floor plan is shown as figure 10.1. For control and audit reasons, the cashiers are separated from other service activities. However, all staff receive the same training, so a cashier can often answer questions about the source and reason for a charge without having to refer the student to another person. The training program involved having staff spend time in various offices so they could see firsthand the work of each office and the types of information they process. A small number of people have as their primary responsibility staffing the generalist desk. Others in the facility and some students are trained to provide backup during peak service periods.

The building houses the entire billing, collection, and cashier activities; the ID office; student telephone services; and portions of the registrar's, financial assistance, and dining services offices; at peak times, staff from parking and housing have a presence in the building. The facility opened in August 1992 and has been very well received by students and others who have used it.

Since 1992, the focus has been on extending many of the services offered in the student service building through electronic means. Faculty and department staff now have access at their desktop to information needed for advising. Students can access many of their records and take advantage of many student services over the network or through the interactive voice response system from

anywhere in the world. For several years, prospective students have been able to access admissions materials and complete the admissions application on the Web. An example of more recent developments is implementation of an online degree audit function so advisors and students can assess progress toward degree completion and use it as a tool for registration planning. A few years ago, the university stopped mailing grade reports, replacing that process with e-mail to student e-mail accounts and through posting on the interactive voice response system accessible from any touch-tone phone. The latter development not only speeds up the delivery of grades to the students, but also provides a significant expense savings for the institution.

The university's accomplishments in the area of student services have been widely acknowledged. Over the six years since the student services building opened, well over 100 people from more than 50 colleges and universities have visited the campus to see the facility, to see how we employ technology, and to talk with the staff about our approach to student services. In 1994, the university received the CAUSE award for Excellence in Campus Networking, recognizing not only the extent of our networking activities but also our focus on weaving technology into the fabric of campus life. In 1996, the IBM Corporation identified the university as one of about 12 colleges and universities exhibiting best practices in student services. In 1996–97, the American Productivity & Quality Center (APQC) undertook a study of electronic student services. From 80 institutions surveyed, APQC selected six plus two alternates for in-depth study. Delaware was selected to be one of the alternates. Technology has clearly facilitated a transformation in many aspects of the university's operations.

It is worth noting once again that when Delaware started to evolve student services from the physical one-stop-shopping model to its electronic equivalent, the Web was not yet available. With its wide acceptance, easy use, and platform independence, the Web has proved to be an excellent tool for moving the student service concept to its electronic equivalent. The university has embraced use of the Web as its primary vehicle to provide electronic services.

Our migration to an electronic service center has not been without missteps. While we were very careful in planning the student service building to be process oriented and cross-functional, development of the Web services ended up organized by unit or function. In effect, while we broke down the organizational silos in implementing the student service building, we ended up creating electronic silos on our Web site. A team has been working for several months to restructure the university Web site to be more process oriented. By the time this chapter is published, the highest levels of the Web restructuring will have been implemented with work continuing on specific process areas.

The Broad View

Improving the traditional student administrative processes was the starting point for the university's focus on becoming more student-centered. However, the program has taken a much broader view. Since 1990, there has been a major program to upgrade and expand facilities, including renovation of residence and dining halls, classrooms, and student activity spaces. In addition, a new student center, a new sports/convocation center, and several new fitness facilities have been constructed. As was the case with systems and procedures, the growth of enrollment of the 1970s and 1980s was not matched by growth in facilities to serve students' academic, social, and recreational needs.

While we continue our work on our electronic student services, we are also looking at the area of academic support services. One major aspect of this effort has been library services. The Delaware library has been a leader in using technology to enhance access to traditional library holdings as well as the vast array of electronic resources more recently available. Early initiatives included making the electronic catalog accessible over the Internet and using the interactive voice response system as a means to renew books on loan. The availability of the Web has opened the door for access to a rich array of research and teaching materials, providing all members of the university community with the opportunity to take advantage of these resources from their homes, offices, and residence hall rooms.

Utilizing security features to limit access to University of Delaware students for a defined period of time has, under fair use guidelines, made possible the development of online course reserves. Under the old model, faculty would make available a copy of course-specific materials in the reserve room at the library. Students would need to go to the library to review these materials. This limited access to one student at a time only during those hours the library was open. Using electronic reserves, faculty may scan images and documents that would normally have been placed in the reserve room at the library. These materials can then be made available to all students anytime and anywhere they can access the Internet. While this is clearly a benefit for all students, it is particularly advantageous to those distance education students for whom traveling to the library may be impractical.

An emerging service is the application of electronic commerce to functions such as the bookstore. Our bookstore contractor implemented a Web site where our students can find the book adoption list for University of Delaware courses and are able to purchase textbooks and have them delivered to their home or residence hall.

As the teaching and learning process is the primary service colleges and universities offer to their students, providing the opportunity for faculty to integrate and use technology in their teaching program is also a priority for the university. Every year more students enroll in college having used and/or been taught with the assistance of computer technology. There is a growing expectation that technology will be employed and readily available for both instruction and support services. While enhancing both services and the learning process are worthy goals unto themselves, the issue of how technology affects the competition for students and how prospective students view an institution is becoming more prominent. As another example of the increased emphasis on technology, a number of the college guides now comment on the availability of technology on campuses.

Benefits

What has all this meant for the university? The results of the 1998 student satisfaction survey are a marked contrast to those of 10 years earlier. There has been significant improvement in the level of satisfaction with the services the university provides to students. This is particularly true with regard to the availability and sophistication of technology and both academic and nonacademic services provided. The 1999 edition of *The Princeton Review* (The Princeton Review 1998) reports the following:

> The University of Delaware has made a huge effort in recent years to develop an "electronic campus," connecting students, faculty, and administrative offices with each other (through an Intranet) and to the world outside (via Internet access). The results are impressive. Students here report a much lower "hassle factor" than students at similar large, state-run schools.

These results are a tribute to our investments in technology, facilities, and training coupled with the hard work of many talented and dedicated faculty and staff. We believe that some of our success in increasing the number and quality of applicants, including significant growth in our honors program, is attributable to our leading efforts in the application of technology and to becoming a more student-centered campus.

Student Services Trends

While Delaware began its student service transformation earlier than most institutions, we find that our experiences track closely with others who have used technology as a driver for change. The university is still looking at ways of using technology to provide additional self-help-oriented services and is exploring the broader view of student services, particularly academic support services. The following describes the current status of redesign activities on our campus:

- **Student-Centered Vision.** We adopted a campuswide student-centered vision early on and have applied it to more than the traditional student service areas.

- **Redesigned Services**
  - *Cross-functional Teams.* We started our first project (selection of a new student information system) using a cross-functional team and have continued to use that model.
  - *One-Stop Service Center.* We were one of the first universities to implement a one-stop service center in the summer of 1992.
  - *Self-Service Objectives.* We recognized the importance of serving students through zero or one staff contact, with zero being the ability of a student to serve him- or herself. As technology has advanced, what began at about a 20 percent self-service level is now over 60 percent and could go as high as 80 to 90 percent with further technology-assisted advancements.
  - *Department Process Improvement.* As systems were designed and technology has evolved, processes have been reviewed and modified to make them as efficient and user-friendly as possible. This area still requires work, which is ongoing.

- **Web-Enabled Services**
  - *Admissions.* Admissions materials are accessible on the Web. Both the undergraduate and graduate application processes can be completed using Web forms (www.udel.edu/eileen/welc/admissions.html).
  - *Registration.* Registration, drop/add, and many other basic registration services are possible using Web-based services (www.udel.edu/Registrar/main.html).

Student Services Trends

TRENDS	IMPLEMENTATION PHASE
Student-Centered	●
Redesigned Services	●
One-Stop Service Center	●
Cross-Functional Teams	●
Self-Service Objectives	◑
Department Process Improvements	●
Web-Enabled Services	●
Admissions	●
Registration	●
Advising	●
Financial Aid	◐
Billing	◐
Career Services	○
Systemic Change	◐
Replacement of Student Information Systems	●

Codes for Implementation Phase:
- ● Production
- ◐ Implementing
- ◑ Designed
- ○ Planning

- *Advising.* A combination of Web-based applications and online screens from the student information system are available to advisors and students to help them assess progress toward a degree and to assist in course planning (www.udel.edu/Registrar/main.html).
- *Financial Aid.* Most of the current financial aid reporting is through online functions in the student information system. However, a Web-based secure entry has been developed to assist students in accessing their financial aid and billing information. Further enhancement of Web-based access is planned (www.udel.edu/sispa1/html).
- *Billing.* See Financial Aid.
- *Career Services.* A Web site supports the Career Services Center, providing such things as information, resource references, and a calendar of events (www.udel.edu/CSC/career.html).

- **Systemic Change.** The lessons learned through the installation of a new student information system, development of the one-stop student service center, and the related process reviews in the student service area have been applied more broadly. The university has taken major steps to eliminate paper forms and to streamline procedures institution-wide. What had been a pre-audit mentality has evolved into a post-audit philosophy with empowerment and responsibilities being delegated deeper into the organization. The university is currently reviewing its human resource policies and procedures as it prepares to implement a new human resource system. A similar effort will be instituted for financial processes within a year or two. In the meantime, employing the Web as a tool to make even old technology more user-friendly has been an effective measure.

- **Replacement of Student Information Systems.** A new student information system was installed in the early 1990s and has been improved and enhanced using Web applications ever since. While it is currently our most robust system, the underlying technology is outdated and we will likely look at a replacement with client-server systems in four to five years.
- **Academic Support Services.** Enhancing academic support services is a current focus at the university. In particular, enhancing library services and the teaching-learning process are receiving much attention.

Critical Success Factors and Key Considerations

As we look back over the last 10 years and consider our success in transforming student services at Delaware, the following factors stand out as key to that success:

- Executive sponsorship (president/executive vice president)
- Use of cross-functional teams in planning and implementation
- Adequate financial resources
- Investments in technology in parallel with process redesign
- Willingness to change policies and procedures

- Open-mindedness with regard to organizational structure
- Adopting the Web as the primary delivery tool as soon as it was available
- Focusing on a "zero or one" strategy for service

Conclusion

As noted earlier, a decade of work on improving student services and more broadly the student learning and living environment has produced meaningful and satisfying results. We are attracting more and better-qualified applicants; our enrolled students are increasingly more satisfied with their overall experience at the university; and our retention and graduation rates are up. In addition, results of the periodic employee satisfaction survey indicate that employee morale is high as they now have the tools to provide quality and timely services to our students. We can hope that the increasingly positive attitudes of our students will translate into supportive alumni who will recommend attending the university and will support the institution financially. While we will continue to improve and refine our student services through innovative application of technology, we consider our efforts to have been a success and the processes employed to be a model for addressing other aspects of the university's operations.

REFERENCE

The Princeton Review. 1998. *The Best 311 Colleges. 1999 Edition.* New York: Random House.

11

Gary L. Kramer and
Erlend D. Peterson

Project 2000: A Web-Based Student Planning System

The Compelling Case for Change

Two very significant reasons brought about the need for change in the delivery of student administration services at Brigham Young University (BYU). First, BYU's three-year student system migration project simply moved the student database from one server to another, i.e., mainframe to client server environment. Although fragmentation of the student information system, among other functional problems, remained, the migration project set in motion earlier decisions about a new infrastructure. Those decisions were to create a relational database with object-oriented programming; develop a Web-based architecture; and establish an open systems architecture, i.e., systems are built to industry standards, and various systems on campus share data. The Division of Admissions and Records, including the offices of financial aid, scholarship, advisement, graduation evaluation, school relations, transfer evaluation, registration, and records, was the last to leave student systems on the mainframe. Previously, the library, student life, financial servic-

es, health services, housing, and other campus entities had committed to a client-server environment.

The second and perhaps most compelling reason for change came as a result of an intensive divisionwide self-study, which followed the rehosting project. It was determined that, although the legacy student system was driven by a sophisticated and highly customized database, it was nevertheless redundant and inefficient in its isolation of other, independent databases, such as continuing education and graduate studies. Students, parents, faculty, and the administration have not hesitated in identifying problems they have encountered. While student administration departments sought to improve services, the results were mixed: innovative approaches surfaced, yet new services or delivery approaches often were fragmented, incomplete, isolated, and inadequate. Functional but not integrated is perhaps the best summary of, and the primary reason for, change in delivering student services.

Given what we have learned from the migration project and the opportunities provided by a new database infrastructure, BYU is in the position to provide integrated student administration services from admission to graduation. This chapter unfolds this new model, to which BYU is highly committed, i.e., to develop a seamless student service or student-centered or one-stop shopping system for most routine transactions that students conduct with the university. In the past, organizational boundaries, physical plant limitations, lack of resources, and limited technology inhibited this objective. Now, with the addition of Web technology, the playing field has changed. This chapter outlines BYU's intentions to capitalize on advanced technology as it seeks to unify and connect vital student planning services.

Gary L. Kramer is the associate dean of admissions and records and professor of counseling and special education at Brigham Young University. He is widely published in various refereed journals, monographs, and books, and has delivered more than 80 professional papers. He received his Ph.D. from Oregon State University.

Erlend D. "Pete" Peterson is dean of admissions and records and assistant professor of educational leadership at Brigham Young University. As a leader in the use of technology in higher education, he has presented extensively at national conferences, published several articles, and served as a consultant to universities in the use of technology. He received his doctorate in higher education administration at BYU.

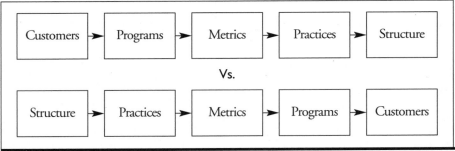

Figure 11.1
Sequence of Questions to Ask in Strategic Planning

Project Summary

This chapter discusses the processes and results of combining the twin powers of technology and human ingenuity to deliver a superior, integrated student administration system university-wide. Specifically, the primary topics presented in this chapter are (1) the process (organizing the project, establishing outcomes, collaborating with the university community) and (2) the results (the design and implementation of a Web-enabled student planning system that includes separate and unique registration methods for freshmen as well as other students and a student-centric model for delivering Web-linked academic, career, and financial planning tools).

The Student Planning System is based on an information infrastructure that is horizontal or flat rather than hierarchical or vertical. Because it is a holistic and integrative student service model, most campus units (financial services, bookstore, registration, continuing education, graduate studies, records, advisement, financial aid, honors education, career counseling) are highly supportive and collaborative. The model resembles technologically what most campuses attempt to accomplish organizationally but have difficulty in implementing: a seamless system of educational services.

The primary objective of this project focuses on cutting across traditional organizational boundaries. Reaching across campus to form partnerships and ownership of a new system of student administration services is important to the breaking down of organizational barriers. Moreover, campus collaboration places the student at the center or head of the organizational chart. This is key to the project's purposes, which are to address and meet student needs and to deliver critical educational planning information effectively.

The Process. Overall, the project asked, "If we were creating a student administration system today given our knowledge and current technology, what would it look like? More specifically, what are the systemic issues?" The following questions are examples:

1. Whom do we serve and what do they do? (Students/Customers)
2. What services do we provide them? (Respective Programs)
3. How do we know we are doing a good job? (Metrics/Standards)
4. What is the best way to provide the desired services? (Practices/Delivery)
5. What is the best way to organize? (Structure/Reengineering)

The sequence of these questions is important in strategic planning. For example, some programs are reorganized or randomly moved without giving attention first to the 3 questions or sequences given in figure 11.1.

Principles. Generally, several major principles established a foundation for the primary aim of the project: to deliver a seamless, integrated, comprehensive, and horizontal student administration system. Although, in general, the BYU student administration system is effective, a systemic review of services for preadmission to graduate training revealed that there was much work to be done to bring about a more cohesive, integrated, and efficient student administration system. Thus the following principles were defined to guide the project:

- Increase customer satisfaction with student administration services; i.e., design a system from the student's perspective.
- Synergize business processes.
- Emphasize relational or flatten hierarchical technical databases to provide ease and greater access to student administration services.
- Enable and empower students to self-direct access of key educational planning information.
- Use cross-functional teams to integrate a comprehensive system of services; i.e., create partnerships and opportunities across the campus to shape, reframe, evaluate, and own a new infrastructure.
- Establish an institution-wide perspective; i.e., involve each entity providing services along the student administration continuum.
- Clarify technology as an enabler tool, not a solution; i.e., technology provides a vital source to be competitive and to be on the leading edge, but technology itself cannot create—people create.
- Use information technology only after establishing well-defined business processes.
- Devise a rollout plan that provides for the optional involvement, training, and preparation of the university community.
- Define the vision, goals, strategies, and expected outcomes of a redesigned student administration system.

The steps outlined in table 11.1 suggest a systemic review of both the campus environment and the student administration infrastructure to advance or incorporate information technology. The table outlines the critical steps involved in assessing the relationship between business processes and the use of information technology in delivering student administration services.

Other related and important questions that guide the project include the following:

STEP 1. Purpose (Mission) of
Student Administration Services

A. Define the role; i.e., the *relational, conceptual,* and *informational* aspects of student administration services on the campus. What are the issues and unique business processes used in defining student administration services?

B. Describe the campus infrastructure for delivering student administration services; i.e., *who* delivers *what* services *when.*

C. Do faculty, students, and the academic community clearly understand the functions of student administration services; i.e., are they described in the college catalog? What are the *major student administration service issues* to be addressed?

D. Are institutional *student administration service goals/outcomes* consistent with student goals; i.e., how does the student administration service model or business process on your campus determine the alignment of these goals?

E. In what ways do student administration services *relate to/collaborate with* other campus and community services, e.g., orientation, career counseling, records, registration, admissions, and computer services?

Step 2. Planning for Technology Initiatives

A. What is the single most important or troublesome student administration service issue on your campus? In what ways will technology address the issue; i.e., how will it help? What are the major objectives (or projected outcomes) of applying technology to the delivery of academic student services; i.e., what's to be accomplished—online advising, electronic communication, kiosks, accessibility, automated academic planning?

B. Technology initiatives typically begin with needs assessment. What are the needs of students, faculty, professional advisors? To what extent have these needs been fulfilled?

C. Describe the special political/cultural milieu of the campus. What should be addressed before technology initiatives can take place?

D. What are the *obstacles* to overcome in planning for technology; i.e., what hindsight advice do you have for others?

E. How does/will the campus balance technology plans and priorities with resources (people, time, dollars, space, facilities) and the outcomes or goals of student administration services?

F. How and by whom are decisions made about technology initiatives? In what ways are campus advisors involved in defining information technology's relationship to student administration services? How do you get top-level administrative support for developing and implementing technology initiatives in student administration services?

G. What are some management strategies that can be used to achieve buy-in of information technology and overcome resistance, fear of change, fear of resource loss and territories? Who should be involved in the strategic planning process?

Step 3. Designing an
Information Technology System

A. Describe the technology infrastructure already in place to begin designing an academic student information system; i.e., hardware, networks, software, organizational structure, relationship of campus unit to computer services, remote access.

B. How would you create and foster an ongoing dialogue among faculty, advisors, students, administration, and computer personnel concerning advisement information needs; i.e., how do you build or develop a culture of mutual understanding, respect, and trust?

C. What information files are essential support systems to an integrated student administration system; e.g., integration of files for records, registration, curriculum, admissions, or advisement?

D. What is the curriculum management philosophy for your campus; i.e., how is it done?

E. What features do you deem essential to a campus-wide information system (CWIS); i.e., course scheduling, degree progress, academic record access?

F. What would students do with a CWIS, i.e., register, receive grades, check academic progress outcomes? What are the student outcomes?

G. Based on the best practices of other colleges, what features or characteristics are essential to operate your system?

continued on next page

Table 11.1
Strategic Planning:
The Student Administration Infrastructure and the Use of Information Technology

Step 4. Reengineering Student Administration Services

A. In what ways will the planning and designing technology initiatives described above balance high touch and high tech to yield high effect?

B. How do you see information technology transforming the roles in student administration services, e.g., faculty, student, professional advisor? In what ways will advising be different?

Step 5. Evaluation

A. What evaluation methods would you employ to obtain feedback on design and implementation phases, e.g., focus groups?

B. How will data be collected to enhance an integrated technology system?

Table 11.1 (continued from page 89) Strategic Planning: The Student Administration Infrastructure and the Use of Information Technology

- Which student administration services are redundant, isolated, inefficient, complex, effective, integrated, and so on, and which ones are not?

- What is the best way to blend student administration with the dynamics of technology?

- How can university student administration services be both simple and comprehensive for the student?

- What is in the best interest of students, and what is the student point of view regarding student administration services?

- Can a student administration system that is widely supported and integrated technologically assign a large percentage of routine transactions to self-directed services for one-stop shopping? What percentage of students must be assigned to a generalist versus a specialist given a sophisticated Web-enabled student planning system?

On one hand, the process of the project evolved through asking good questions; more precisely, a good question, we found, can be worth a dozen answers. On the other hand, this project is incomplete because answers do not abound regarding the questions raised. Yet, as noted below, from this process the following principles, outcomes, and strategies emerged.

Outcomes. A natural goal of a project of this magnitude,

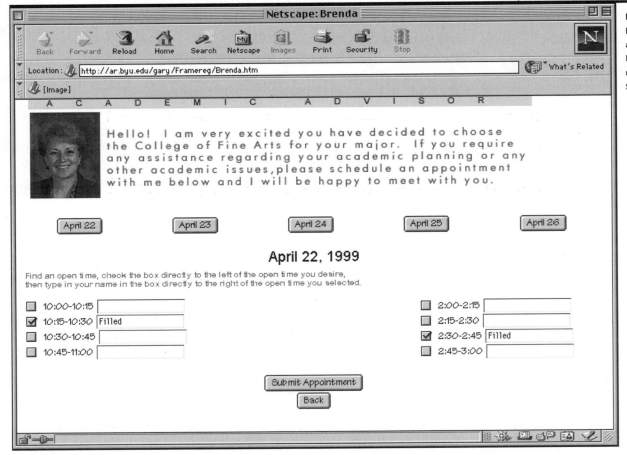

Figure 11.2 Personal Contact in a Self-Directed Learning Environment or One-Stop Shopping System

given the technological advances of the past decade, is to deploy a Web-based environment for students to conduct most, if not all, transactions with the university (e.g., registration and academic and career information). However, this project is more concerned with the way the university conducts business on behalf of its students (i.e., technology can potentially add value, but it can only enable, not create—people create). For example, for years, technology has provided a means to center advising on the student, rather than the dissemination of academic information. Yet for the most part universities and colleges go about their business as they did without the aid of technology (Kramer 1996). In other words, technology is most effective when business processes are well defined.

Today's higher education is derived from the diversity of institutions, students, and curriculum. Change in higher education, therefore, requires creating a new model for delivering instruction, information, and services. Perhaps, however, at no point in the history of higher education has there been a time like this to reconsider and recreate an environment that enhances student learning, recognizes the ways in which students learn, and creates varied forms of information delivery. A new model or focus for complementing the ways students learn and progress in the academic environment should emphasize improved faculty-student interaction, self-directed learning, and peer interaction with the use of technology (Chickering and Reisser 1993; Pascarella and Terenzini 1991; Astin 1993; Tinto 1993).

Important to this project and to a new paradigm of information delivery is the fact that students are capable and can thrive in an environment that provides self-directed learning and connection to services. Many of these services, unfortunately, reside in "functional silos," isolated from other related services. For example, we believe that students, if given the chance, are quite able to develop an individualized educational plan to graduate based on their learning pace, circumstance, and other criteria if the institution responds by providing quality planning information. A sampling of other possibilities for self-directed learning include tracking academic progress, connecting financial and registration plans, and exploring career and cocurricular alternatives related to a major or ways to become involved in the university community. Creation of opportunities for personal contact or assistance is essential to the success of a self-directed learning environment or a

one-stop shopping system in which students can complete most routine transactions with the university (see figure 11.2).

With this in mind, the specific aims or outcomes of the project are as follows:

- Design, develop, and implement an integrated and comprehensive educational planning system accessible through a Web-based architecture.
- Empower and assist students to define and plan educational goals, including financial and career goals, by allowing them to enhance the path to a timely graduation, track academic progress, and complete the registration process.

- View Class Schedules/Catalogs/MAPs
- Submit Enrollment Electronically
- Update Personal Information
- Submit Financial Aid Application
- Review Credit and Noncredit Program Information
- Connect with Advisor and Program Requirements
- View Campus Maps
- Establish Educational Plan
- Link to all campus academic services and programs

Your Personal Information
Your Academic History
Your Registration
Your Advisement
Your Graduation
Academic Calendar
Advisement Centers
Career Planning
Deferment
Financial Planning
Graduate Programs
Graduation
G.E./Honors Program
Independent Study
Majors
Map of Campus

**Figure 11.3
Student Self-Service
Functions**

- Streamline processes and procedures to create a clear and direct advisement and enrollment experience.
- Foster collaboration and integration among student administration services university-wide.
- Simplify access to educational services, and link student interests, goals, and needs to the academic and career planning process (see figure 11.3).

Strategies. The principal strategy of the project is to identify and involve stakeholders to shape, design, and evaluate the university's student administration system. This requires establishing a partnership or collaborative approach among the following campus entities: admissions, the faculty center, the bookstore, registration/records, financial services, class scheduling, co-ops/internships, career placement, general education/ honors, financial aid/scholarships, independent study, advisement centers, the counseling and career center, student life, graduate studies, student accounts, and Brigham Young University Student Association.

A customer or advisory council was established and Web-based presentations were made weekly. These events greatly assisted in detecting and resolving confusing and oftentimes conflicting policies and procedures. Also, through collaborative group effort, often around 40 administrators and student representatives of these units would attend to give the project needed clarification, delimitations, and focus. Short-range (quick success) and long-range priorities were established. For example, one team decided to provide the first Web-enabled registration and degree tracking system to all students beginning April 1999. At the same time, another team began work on a separate Web registration program just for freshman students beginning July 1999. The larger and more complex student planning system, which calls for vast linkages and continuity among campus student administration services, and a revised curriculum management system, were scheduled for completion in 2000.

The Results. This project inherited a rich and sophisticated legacy or former student system as a foundation. For example, in 1978, BYU pioneered a degree audit system. Initially, it was somewhat unsophisticated, hard-coded, and complex to read. It covered all the space on an 11-by-14-inch blue-bar sheet, yet it was nonetheless a beginning point to report student academic progress information (e.g., grades, transcript information, course scheduling, and most academic transactions) (Kramer 1994, 1996; Kramer and McCauley 1995; Spencer, Peterson, and Kramer 1982, 1983).

The touch-tone telephone system pioneered in 1984 is still in use as a registration tool by students. Over the years, these products have been reworked several times. Also, the legacy system for years provided a myriad of highly interactive, two-tone (black and green) online screens filled with student data. The advent of the client or Windows environment is the forum through which students or advisors gain access to academic information today. Nearly 30 kiosks and 700 access points are available for students throughout the campus.

The Student Planning System

Given the legacy system and recent program conversions to a client or Windows architecture, the university was positioned to convert its programs and services to a Web infrastructure; to integrate and link campus services; and to provide a comprehensive, one-stop shopping student administration system. Accompanying the sample figures on pages 93–96 is an explanation of the key transactions exemplary of the student planning system.

■ Welcome to Brigham Young University Student
   Planning System
   A—Authentication

Student Services Trends

TRENDS	IMPLEMENTATION PHASE
Student-Centered	Designed
Redesigned Services	N/A
One-Stop Service Center	Designed
Cross-Functional Teams	Designed
Self-Service Objectives	Designed
Department Process Improvements	Designed
Web-Enabled Services	Production
Admissions	Production
Registration	Production
Advising	Production
Financial Aid	Production
Billing	N/A
Career Services	Designed
Systemic Change	Designed
Replacement of Student Information Systems	Production

Codes for Implementation Phase:
- ● Production
- ◐ Implementing
- ◔ Designed
- ○ Planning

■ Student Profile and Access to Services (figure 11.4)
   A—Personalized Student Planning Components
   B—Student Profile
   C—Student Planning Resources
■ Student Resumé (figure 11.5)
   A—Student Profile
   B—Aims of a BYU Education Operationalized to
      Student Needs
   C—Student Planning Resources
■ Educational Planning (figure 11.6)
   A—Department Individualized Academic Plan
   B—Student Individualized Plan
   C—Student Planning Resources
■ Academic Progress Report (figure 11.7)
   A—Personalized Academic Plan
   B—Academic Progress Report
■ Registration (figure 11.8)
   A—Personalized Student Planning Components
   B—Registration Peripheral
   C—Student Plans
   D—Actual Registration

Student Services Trends

This project encompasses systemic change, student-centered service, self-service objectives, Web-enablement, redesigned processes, cross-functional teams, and one-stop service centers.

Critical Success Factors and Key Considerations

A primary critical success factor of this project is to obtain a unified flow of student administration services from preenrollment or entry through graduation or alumni services. This requires the cooperation, ownership, and creative work of many in the university. In other words, it takes a university community to raise a student. Next, a systemic and strategic review of campus services, especially from the perspective of a student, who tends to see university services horizontally or connected rather than in the vertical or hierarchical way in which institutions are organized, is a key consideration to the *process* of this project. Central to this project is learning, listening, and understanding student concerns, issues, and needs. Just as critical, it takes an out-of-the-box approach to challenge existing business processes, including the accompanying information technology; i.e., change means doing student administration work differently, while carefully examining the appropriate application and added value of information technology.

Yet, this project involves more than just evaluating and applying new technology support to provide student services. Clearly, it provides a vital source for institutions to be competitive on behalf of the university community. In our estimation, it is well-defined business processes that drive information technology. The two should be inextricably linked and appropriately balanced to achieve a student-centered learning environ- ment. In other words, the key consideration of this project is to design student administration processes to determine and drive related supportive technology.

Conclusion

The *results*, then, as illustrated through the prototype presented above, is a self-directed, comprehensive, and integrated student administration system that connects students to essential university resources and provides them with a single, Web-enabled system to conduct routine transactions with the university. Yet at the same time, the new student administration system must not only be navigable, accurate, and timely, it must also be personal, allowing the student to get "get off the train," as it were, and to obtain general or specific help from a personal advisor.

This *process* continues at BYU and the *results* will invariably change as we proceed with this project. While we seek to increase customer satisfaction and unify our student services, it's clear that the campus synergy must be in place to realize all of the important

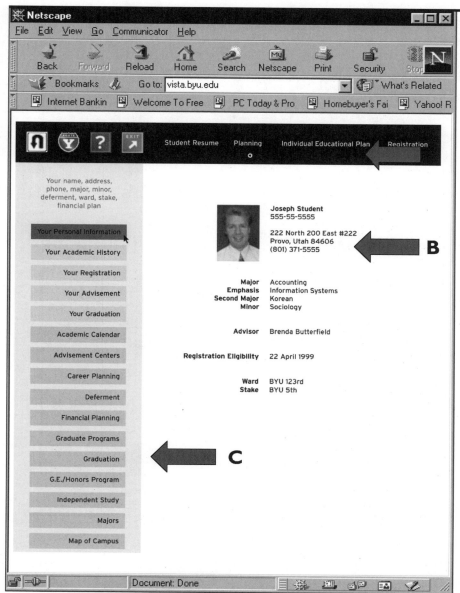

**Figure 11.4
Student Profile and
Access to Services**

things of this project: an institution-wide perspective on meeting the needs of its students.

REFERENCES

Astin, A.W. 1993. *What Matters in College.*

Chickering, A.W., and L. Reisser. 1993. *Education and Identity.*

Kramer, G.L., ed. 1996. *Transforming Academic Services Through Information Technology.* NACADA Monograph Series, 4.

———. 1996. The Human-Technology Nexus. *Transforming Academic Services Through Information Technology.* NACADA Monograph Series, 4.

———. 1994. Providing Students Critical Academic Planning Assistance Using Academic Information Management (AIM): A Remote Access Program. *College and University,* 150–57.

Kramer, G.L., and M. McCauley. 1995. Degree Progress Report (Degree Audit). In *Academic Advising As a Comprehensive Campus Process.* NACADA Monograph Series, 2.

Pascarella, E.T., and P.T. Terenzini. 1991. *How College Affects Students.*

Spencer, R., E.L. Peterson, and G.L. Kramer. 1983. Designing and Implementing a Computer-Assisted Advisement Program. *Journal of College Student Personnel* 24:513–18.

———. 1982. Advisement by Computer: A Tool for Improving Academic Advising. *College and University* 57:169–79.

Tinto, V. 1993. *Leaving College.*

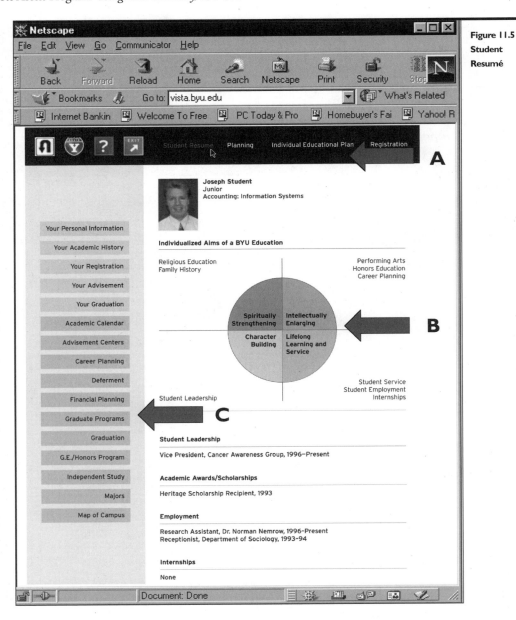

Figure 11.5
Student Resumé

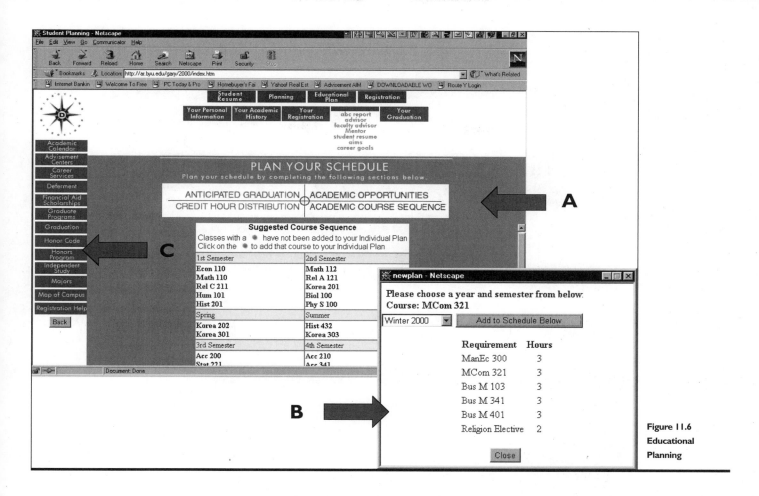

Figure 11.6
Educational
Planning

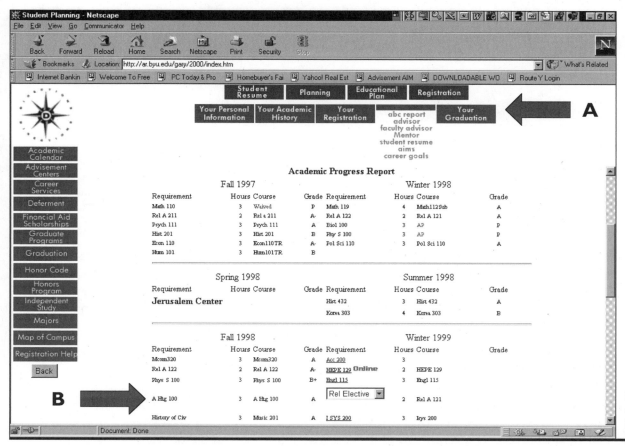

Figure 11.7
Academic
Progress Report

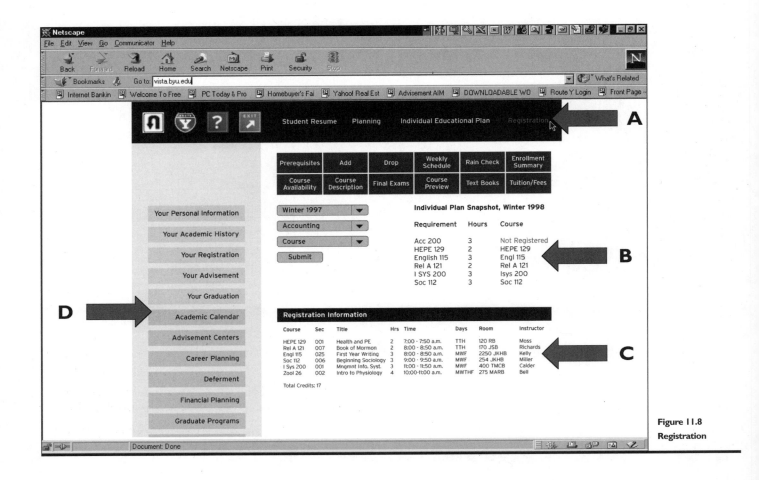

Figure 11.8
Registration

12

Mark McConahay

Virtual Access to Student Information

Overview

Indiana University[1] (IU) is a multicampus institution with a combined enrollment of approximately 90,000 students. The institution was established in 1826 in Bloomington, which remains the primary residential campus. The other locations are primarily, but not totally, commuter campuses that serve both traditional and nontraditional students. Despite the different missions and demographics of the student bodies, however, all campuses use centralized student support systems. These applications have been designed, some more successfully than others, to accommodate the service and information needs of each.

The Compelling Case for Change

In 1996, IU was in the process of reviewing its student services and the student information systems that supported them. There were many concerns, ranging from the inadequate functionality of some systems to the annual maintenance expenditure of others (e.g., federal regulations) to the perceived lack of integration at the point of information delivery. At the same time, it was recognized that the institution also possessed a wealth of electronic student information and a set of remote access services that served the institution well. This led to the creation of a project called the Student Information Systems Initiative (SIS), which was to review the delivery of student

Mark McConahay is the associate registrar, systems, at Indiana University (IU). During his tenure at IU, he has been a member of two project teams that received the Best Practice Award from CAUSE (now EDUCAUSE): one in 1995 for the Automated Course Exchange and one in 1998 for the Grade Context Record. He earned both his master's and bachelor's from Indiana University.

information to all consumers of the information (students, faculty, and staff) and recommend alternatives. A subgroup of the SIS, the Integration and Access to Student Information Subcommittee, was formed and charged with defining a set of short-term and long-term strategies for improving the delivery of student information. The Indiana Student Transaction Environment (*insite*) is the result of this group's recommendations.

Project Summary

Students desired and needed user-friendly access to all information and services that enabled them to interact with IU. However, the required information and services needed to be integrated and funneled into a common and standard portal or conduit. Students at IU had had Internet access to their current course schedule, the schedule of classes, their degree advising (audit) record, and their transcript information since the early 1990s. However, access was character-based (Telnet/TN3270) or voice/response-based, and information was delivered in isolation within each application, not integrated into an easy-to-use and understandable student information access system. At approximately the same time, IU was forced to redeploy some key processing systems (i.e., the records maintenance and transcript production systems). Remote access systems (e.g., interactive voice response and character-based applications on the network) were already in place, and the new processing (general description) systems were under development. IU leveraged both types of information systems and gathered several information providers to build and deploy the Web-based student information delivery system, *insite*.

This system delivers information from the bursar, financial assistance, and registrar support systems from a common access point and a consistent user interface. It was fully implemented in

April 1997. Information from the admissions system and a new application developed to comply with the Taxpayer Relief Act of 1997 were later added to the site. It has been well received throughout the institution and has become an integral part of our service and information delivery plans. We have received more positive feedback and comments regarding *insite* than any other information service we have provided.

Objectives of *insite*: What Was Indiana University Trying to Do? In 1996, IU was dealing with a variety of issues regarding its student information systems. The systems were built on a traditional architecture: COBOL programs running in an OS390/CICS/VSAM/DB2 environment on a large mainframe (Amdahl Millennium 535). These systems, in general, had supported the student and academic support units well. However, there were the following concerns:

- Some applications were functionally inadequate. Managers felt compelled to request replacement systems (e.g., admission contact/recruitment).

- Some applications were difficult to modify and maintain in response to both internal and external mandates (e.g., federal financial aid regulations).

- Applications required a broad range of programming tools and knowledge. Over the years, the computing organization had expanded its application base to include a variety of operating systems, platforms, and development tools. The long-term strategy for application development was to minimize development and support costs by standardizing the development tool set.

- The student information remote access systems were independent of one another. IU had many functional systems from which students could retrieve their own information. However, each had been developed separately and therefore lacked a common interface, look and feel, and entry point. Despite functional integration on the back end (i.e., the processing engines), the front ends were presented in isolation.

In response to these concerns, the IU computing organization and the administrations of several campuses began a project called the Student Systems Initiative (now the SIS). The project was charged with reviewing current operational/procedural practices and the applications that support them and developing both short-term and long-term recommendations. This group has evolved over the last two-and-a-half years into the Student Information Systems Steering Committee. The committee is responsible for all aspects of student information systems planning and for allocating resources on an annual basis.

Access to student information by students and staff members who provide academic support for students was considered paramount.

Thus, a subgroup called the Integration and Access to Student Information Subcommittee was formed and charged with the following:

- Identifying and recommending student information services that could be
  - made accessible to our primary clients (e.g., students),
  - delivered in a more user-friendly manner,
  - integrated across functional and/or operational boundaries, and
  - deployed rapidly, within four to six months.
- Identifying requirements, strategies, and/or other factors that should guide the development and deployment of student information services in the long run (a three- to seven-year period). The recommendations should include identification of
  - new or existing services that should be directly accessible,
  - new student information tools, and
  - development strategies to ensure access and integration of student information.

One of the first recommendations of this group was to develop and deploy a set of Web-based services primarily intended for students and academic advisors. The following were objectives of the project:

- Enable remote access to integrated student information and services.
- Serve all of our clients (or as many as possible).
- Implement quickly.

Development of *insite*: How Was the Service Developed and Deployed? The development of *insite* was accomplished through a combination of different tactical strategies, which included the following:

- Leveraging existing student information remote access systems
- Taking advantage of technology infrastructure modifications
- Designing new (or redeploying) student information processing systems in a manner that isolates and encapsulates business rules
- Merging new initiatives/objectives (e.g., internal mandates) with overall SIS access and integration goals

Services Available via the Internet. Since the early 1990s, IU has deployed a wide variety of remote access applications that enable students to retrieve their personal and academic information (see figure 12.1). In the late 1980s, the computing organization had nearly completed the installation of a new campus network. IU quickly capitalized on this investment and deployed the student advising application. This application placed a character-based user interface in front of our degree audit system (Degree Advising and Reporting System from Miami University in Ohio) and made it available to students. Student advising was available via the academic network and secured by using a student identification number and a unique personal identification number (PIN). The system allows students to view their course history and compare it to the course requirements of their degree program or to any other degree program (enabling students to "shop" for other programs/majors). A similar application was deployed for advisors with a separate security and authentication system. The security system allows advisors to have access to the entire student population or restrict their access by campus, school, major, or even individual students.

Following the implementation of student advising, the schedule of classes was made accessible to students via a character-based interface in 1991. The personalized schedule of classes followed in that same year. This application displays course listings after first comparing the student's academic and demographic attributes to each section's admission criteria. If the student is eligible to register for a given section and the section still has open seats, the section is listed as available and open to the student; otherwise, the section will appear as unavailable. In addition, the application identifies schedule conflicts by comparing the meeting times of the student's current class schedule (sections in which they are already enrolled) to those sections displayed. If a conflict exists, it is indicated in a display column. With this information, it was possible to provide a registration temporary schedule building tool that assisted students in constructing a conflict-free schedule before their registration appointment time.

Registration was placed on the network with a character-based interface in 1993. The automated course exchange (ACE)[2] was integrated into Internet registration in 1995. ACE takes advantage of the features of our registration system and is comprised of the following major subsystems: (1) automated waiting lists with contingent scheduling, (2) continuous schedule adjustment, and (3) rain checks for future semesters. When students encounter closed courses at registration, ACE allows them to record their needs by submitting waiting list requests at the time of registration, matches these requests with new seats as they become available, allows students to adjust their schedule as soon as the need is identified, provides enrollment managers with course demand information, and grants priority in a subsequent semester to those students whose course needs truly could not be satisfied.

In 1996, the mailing address application, which enables students to update their addresses in real time on the Internet, was introduced.

Services Available via Touch-Tone. In addition to the character-based applications, IU also deployed a set of services via interactive voice response, or touch-tone, technology. Touch-tone registration

and grade inquiry applications were implemented in 1992. In 1995, a new touch-tone registration system was developed that incorporated all of the features of the automated course exchange. In that same year, a financial assistance inquiry system was implemented. Financial aid system touch-tone allows students to hear the status of their application materials/forms, their calculated financial need, and the status and amounts of their awards. The service also allows potential students to leave their name and address information to have financial aid materials sent directly to their homes. In 1997, the bursar implemented a touch-tone application that accepts bill payments via credit

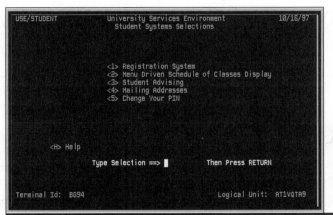

Figure 12.1
Student Services Menu Listing the Character-Based Services Available to Students via the Internet

card. All of these services use student identification numbers and PINs for authentication but are separately maintained services with separate telephone numbers.

The Integration and Access to Student Information Subcommittee, the group that was charged with the development of the Web-based service, wanted to leverage the investment that the institution had made in these information delivery services. Thus, finding a mechanism to access these information services became imperative.

External Influences: Technology Infrastructure. In the early 1990s, student populations at several higher education institutions in the state suffered an outbreak of measles. In 1995, the Indiana State Legislature created a law mandating all residential higher education institutions to collect and maintain student immunization information. In fact, students who did not provide proof of either having suffered a set of communicable diseases or having received the appropriate immunization would be denied the ability to register for courses. The Office of the Registrar was charged with implementing this system, and University Information Technology Services (UITS) was responsible for developing it. UITS wished to devote some resources to a client-server development effort that combined existing institutional data with new information. Thus, an agreement between the departments was reached: UITS would develop the new application and would use client-server development tools to retrieve, update, and display the information.

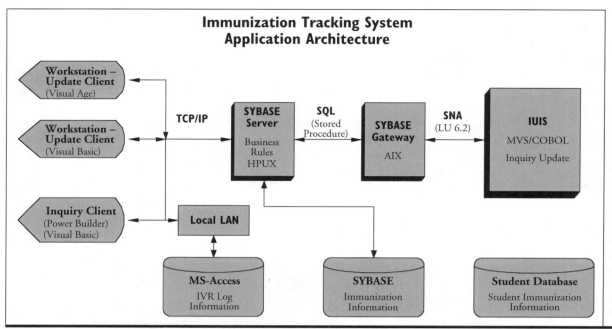

Immunization Tracking System Application Architecture

Figure 12.2 Schematic showing the architecture of the immunization tracking system. This client-server application required a real-time inquiry/update path to legacy data. The gateway enabled any client connected to the relational database server to retrieve and update data from the administrative mainframe. This gateway architecture is the backbone of *insite*.

The new application was designed to identify students and track their immunization status information. This information was updated and stored on a relational database residing on a UNIX platform. In addition, a new data element representing immunization status was needed in the registration system to comply with the provision of the law restricting enrollment in subsequent academic terms. The registration system resided on the administrative mainframe. To maintain it from the new client-server application, a path, or gateway, to the legacy system was built. The gateway performed the necessary protocol conversions between the OS/390 platform and the UNIX platform supporting the immunization application. In addition, it connected a stored procedure on the UNIX platform with a remote program call (RPC) on the mainframe. The RPC executed CICS transactions that actually updated the student data.

The immunization tracking system was implemented in 1995–96 (see figure 12.2). The gateway built to support the tracking systems became part of the computing infrastructure. It made student information that previously was available only to those directly connected to the OS/390 machine available to any number of client-server applications. This, of course, included applications that users of the Web could execute.

Isolate and Encapsulate Business Rules. In 1994, IBM announced a new release of CICS, their application and data management software. In addition, they announced that they would no longer support releases of that product before version 3.0. IU was using an older version of CICS because it was the last release that supported applications written in macro-level COBOL. Our records maintenance and transcript production systems were written in this language. Thus, by the start of the 1997 calendar year, these systems needed to be redeployed. Rather than merely rewriting the applications in a newer version of COBOL, IU decided to redesign them using an object-oriented approach. Each system was divided into

three primary components: overhead, business rules, and presentation/access (see figure 12.3). Each component was independent (i.e., encapsulated) and communicated with the other components via a standard interface. The overhead component consisted of data access and retrieval operations, data concurrency functions, and data update and logging functions. The business rule component edited or processed information before retrieving it for display or storing/archiving the data. For example, a student address update is edited to ensure the entered zip code and state match. This edit is performed each time an address is updated. These business rules were isolated and can be accessed and executed from any application. The presentation/access module was also designed separately. Presentation to the user may occur via a traditional terminal display (CICS screen), via a client-server application (e.g., immunization tracking), or via the Web. The basic idea is that programs written to display the information do not need to understand how to edit the data (business rules) or how to retrieve/store the information (overhead). Thus, services such as address updates and course history displays could easily be offered.

Merging Integration and Access Objectives with Other Institutional Goals. In 1995–96, IU began the implementation of a new initiative called GradPact, a four-year graduation guarantee. As part of that implementation, several changes were made to the degree audit and student advising systems. Specifically, modifications were made to identify GradPact students and to define Grad-Pact benchmarks (i.e., program templates with annual or semester milestones) to track student progress systematically. At approximately the same time, the Web was becoming the de facto standard for Internet access of information systems and services. The Grad-Pact project managers and the Integration and Access to Student Information Subcommittee members realized that a Web-based application that provided students and advisors access to this information would be a great tool as well as a visible component of the program. Using the same gateway constructed to support the immunization tracking system, a pilot application was built that placed the existing student advising system with GradPact benchmarks on the Web. PERL was used as the development language, and a general look and feel of the Web presence was established. The pilot application, Web advising, was deployed in time to support the first freshmen class eligible to enroll in the program. The pilot was very successful and provided the proof of concept that was necessary for further development.

Putting the Pieces Together. The following pieces required to provide students and advisors with direct access to integrated information and services on the Web were now in place:

- A technical infrastructure enabling access to legacy applications and data
- A security and access infrastructure (student identification number and PIN)
- A set of existing remote access applications
- Access to the set of enterprise business rules
- Implementation of a proof-of-concept application
- Identification of the need and the vision

Thus, in fall 1996, development of *insite* began. The review of student services and client access to information emphasized placing information and services where the consumer, the student, could gain direct access. The SIS initiative enabled the dedication of development resources to the project.

Gathering the Stakeholders and Implementing. To build *insite*, all information providers were gathered into a design and implementation team. Each of these stakeholders was engaged in and enthusiastic about the approach and the benefits of the project. The goal was to provide information and services with a single point of entry and a common look and feel. However, the group recognized that there were unique needs for each information service. IU is comprised of several campuses, and each has its own independ-

ent operating schedule, deadlines, and context into which all information must be placed. The challenge facing the implementation and design group was how to successfully leverage centralized applications (i.e., primarily those residing on the mainframe) yet give each campus the ability to place that information into the appropriate campus context (e.g., the bursar bill with deadline or the class schedule with instructions for schedule adjustment). Thus, the ability to place text, links, and other information before and after the student personal information was included. These features became known as the "headers" and "footers," and personal student information that was retrieved was sandwiched between them. This feature was a necessary component for a successful implementation at IU.

Defining the Clientele. The most visible client of the university is the student. The information and services offered in *insite* are designed for them. However, we wanted to serve the student information constituencies as well. Certainly, prospective students were in our plans, but we also wanted to assist those whose business is to assist students, primarily faculty and advisors. With impetus from the GradPact project and the success of our initial offering of *insite*, we decided to place our character-based advising system for faculty and advisors on the Web. In addition, we placed a schedule of classes inquiry application on *insite* and made it publicly available.

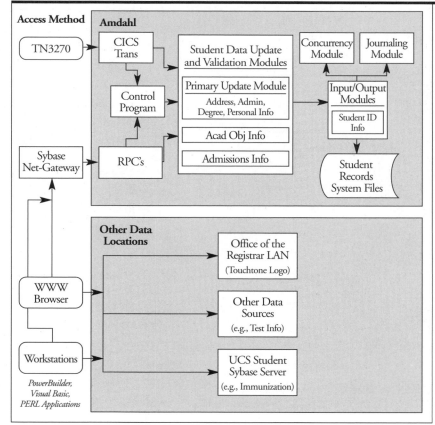

Figure 12.3 Schematic displaying the three design components of the records processing system. The overhead component is on the right, the business rules component is in the center, and the presentation layer is on the left. The design enables Web applications to access business rules using a standard interface.

Implementation. Development of *insite* began in fall 1996 and implementation occurred in April 1997 (see figure 12.4). We were able to develop and implement the system quickly for the following reasons:

- Development of the gateway
- Leveraging existing remote access applications
- Access to business rule modules on the newly deployed records maintenance/transcripts systems
- The collaboration and cooperation of the information providers
- The expertise of the development staff

Our initial offering of *insite* in April 1997 included student confidential information only. Web advising and course offerings were both added later that same year. In addition, the admissions application tracking application was added in early 1998, and the application to comply with the Taxpayer Relief Act of 1997 was added in fall 1998.

For a complete list of *insite* offerings (as of this writing), see table 12.1. In addition to these applications, we offer Web advising to faculty and advisors. For a more complete description of this application, visit wwwreg.indiana.edu/Insite/innovation_insite.html.

What Worked. The delivery of information and services via the Web was a great success. The student population has completely accepted *insite*. One of the links built into an *insite* footer is a feedback option. When users click this link they are asked to rate the *insite* services and are given the opportunity to make additional comments or suggestions. The comments are reviewed periodically and circulated to all information providers.

In general, students have provided highly complimentary comments about the service. Following are a few of the better testimonials regarding *insite*:

> THIS IS AN AWESOME WEBSITE!!! Keep up the great work!

> It is great to be able to access all of your student information online. I am hoping to graduate in Decem-

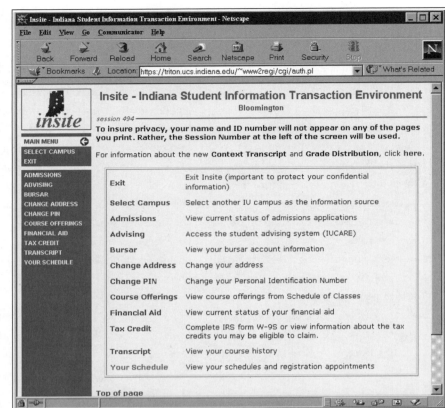

Insite - Indiana Student Information Transaction Environment
Bloomington

session 494

To insure privacy, your name and ID number will not appear on any of the pages you print. Rather, the Session Number at the left of the screen will be used.

For information about the new **Context Transcript** and **Grade Distribution**, click here.

MAIN MENU
SELECT CAMPUS
EXIT

ADMISSIONS
ADVISING
BURSAR
CHANGE ADDRESS
CHANGE PIN
COURSE OFFERINGS
FINANCIAL AID
TAX CREDIT
TRANSCRIPT
YOUR SCHEDULE

Exit	Exit Insite (important to protect your confidential information)
Select Campus	Select another IU campus as the information source
Admissions	View current status of admissions applications
Advising	Access the student advising system (IUCARE)
Bursar	View your bursar account information
Change Address	Change your address
Change PIN	Change your Personal Identification Number
Course Offerings	View course offerings from Schedule of Classes
Financial Aid	View current status of your financial aid
Tax Credit	Complete IRS form W-9S or view information about the tax credits you may be eligible to claim.
Transcript	View your course history
Your Schedule	View your schedules and registration appointments

Top of page

Figure 12.4
Indiana University's *insite* **Web site**

ber 1998 and was able to see what I needed to complete in order to be on track for graduation. Keep up the good work.

> I'm the parent of an IU freshman, and we live way out here in California. We think everything about Bloomington is fantastic and this is one of the most fantastic things of all. I didn't discover that I could access my daughter's bursar account until the last few months. Now I simply pay by phone from this each month, since I could never get Laurie to remember to forward the bursar bill. This is wonderful. Keep doing what you are doing!! Thanks again!

> It keeps getting better! Keep the change curve going. The less students need to be in some office or making calls the more efficient the university will be and the happier the students will be.

> This is the slickest thing I've seen in a long while. Someone needs a big tip of the hat.

In addition to providing material for book chapters and presentations, the students also offer excellent comments, suggestions, and complaints. By far the biggest suggestion is that we make *insite* available 24 hours a day, seven days a week. In order of frequency, the other most common suggestions/additions to *insite* include:

- Registration
- Credit card bill payment

Admissions

- Check the current status of your undergraduate admission application(s).

Advising (IUCARE)

- Produce an advising report for your current major.
- Produce an advising report for a different major.
- Produce an advising report for a special purpose program.
- Apply in-progress courses to your advising report.
- Add future courses, grades, and hours to see how they apply to your advising report.
- If you are a GradPact student, display the GradPact benchmarks and how they apply to your advising report.

Bursar Statement

- Check your bursar account status.
- Produce a summary of your recent month's activity, organized by semester/session and type of charge or payment.

Change Address

- Change your current, permanent, or bursar billing address information.

Change PIN

- Change your personal identification number.

Course Offerings

- View real-time schedule of classes information about your desired course(s), such as meeting times and place, instructor, and available seats. For some courses, a course description is also available. Course eligibility requirements are compared to your academic/demographic characteristics. Only those sections that are open and for which you are eligible appear as available.

Financial Aid

- See up-to-the-minute financial aid awards. See awards for each semester as well as annual amounts.
- See up-to-the-minute tracking of financial aid application. See which forms have been received and which are still missing.

- See the estimated cost of attendance. See how your expected family contribution is divided between you and your parents.
- See your total educational borrowing through today.

Grade Reports

- See grade reports for the four most recent semester/sessions for which you have grades.

Transcript

- See your transcript. The information provided for each semester includes campus attended, school in which you were enrolled, semester/year, course titles, school/department offering courses, course numbers, section numbers, credit hours, awarded grades, semester hours, points earned, semester grade point average, and hours passed.

Your Schedule

- Display your course schedule for a current semester. The schedule will show your enrolled courses and section numbers, meeting times and place, credit hours, audit hours, and registration status. You can also see your residency status and class level for the selected semester/session.
- If you are a GradPact student, you can see your GradPact status for the selected semester/session. (Available at Bloomington campus only.)
- If you are on a waiting list for a section, you can see your place on the list, the number of attempts made to satisfy the waiting list request, and whether or not you selected the rain check option. (Available on campuses that use Automated Course Exchange.)
- See a graphical display of your weekly class schedule (week-at-a-glance).
- See a graphical display of your final exam schedule. (Not available on all campuses.)
- See a list of the textbooks used in your courses. For each course, you will see the title, author, prices for new and used editions, and specific campus bookstore where you can buy the books. You'll also be able to tell if the book is required or optional. Finally, the total cost of the books (new or used) is given.

continued on next page

Table 12.1 Information and Services That *insite* Offers (extracted from insite.indiana .edu/about.html)

Web Advising

Web advising is a Web-based service for Indiana University faculty and advisors that provides secure Web access to the advising system. Access to information is protected by faculty/advisor network username and password followed by IUCARE advisor PIN. Information available through Web advising includes the following:

- Produce an advising report for your current major.
- Produce an advising report for a different major.
- Produce an advising report for a special purpose program.
- Produce an advising report for a program under development.
- Produce an advising report for a special purpose program under development.

- Generate a student transcript (course history).
- See how in-progress courses apply to your advising report.
- Add future courses, grades, and hours to see how they apply to your advising report.

Course Offerings

Course offerings offers individuals who do not have a student identification number and PIN an opportunity to view courses offered by Indiana University. Information available through course offerings includes the following:

- View schedule of classes information about your desired course(s), such as meeting times and place, instructor, and available seats. For some courses, a course description is also available. (Not available on all campuses.)

Table 12.1 (continued from page 103) Information and Services That *insite* Offers (extracted from insite.indiana.edu/about.html)

- Registration/scheduling planning tool
- Improved ACE/waiting list statistics
- Links to faculty homepages
- Campus maps

In general, *insite* has been one of the most well-received information systems that we have deployed at IU.

What Did Not Work. The implementation of *insite* has been a great success—almost to a fault. Use of the environment has grown at an outstanding rate, despite the fact that we have not actively advertised its existence. (We do introduce the environment to all new freshmen during their orientation session.) Despite the lack of advertising, use of the service has been remarkable. For example, during the first week of classes during the Winter 1999 semester, approximately 76,000 students logged on. On the first day of classes alone, 23,600 students logged on. It is a challenge to handle the peak demand for the services. As we have increased the performance and capacity of the server, we nevertheless have had to establish a maximum concurrent user limit. This limit is determined by establishing an acceptable response time (15 seconds); as the number of concurrent users rises so does the response time. The limit is determined by adding concurrent users until the 15-second response time is reached. Currently, the limit is 300 concurrent users[3]. However, on the first day of classes, *insite* rejected nearly 40,000 student log-on requests. Demand for the service was much heavier than expected, and when our user limit (initially 75) was exceeded, student requests for access were rejected. Student behavior is such that when they are rejected from the site, they immediately request the service again. The log-on script, termed "gatekeeper," executes a program on the server to determine the eligibility of each

log-on request, and each of these requests requires processing cycles. As students request log-on access and are rejected, the program executes even more frequently. This caused a negative feedback loop, increasing the number of log-on script executions demanding even more CPU time and crippling performance. To minimize this negative effect on performance, the gatekeeper was modified to minimize its CPU and I/O requirements.

The Future of *insite*. Although *insite* has been a great success, we recognize its weaknesses. It is at its best when delivering real-time information and tools directly to students and faculty. But the environment does not always include all the pertinent information necessary for a student or academic advisor to complete a business transaction or academic decision. One of the strengths of the University of Minnesota's offering is the placement of its real-time self-service pages in an information-rich and context-sensitive environment. The level of information integration it has achieved is striking, and it should be congratulated and emulated. IU's *insite* should and will follow that lead.

Like many higher education institutions, IU has designed and built its data processing and information delivery systems in-house. This practice has enabled the unique set of institutional policies to be implemented in a manner that closely matches the intent of the policy makers. In some cases, the uniqueness results in differentiation that can be leveraged. Because *insite* is built upon such home-grown support systems, it displays the personality and character of the university.

IU has embarked upon a new era of systems development and student services with the purchase of a new enterprise student information system. The challenge is not only to convert to the new information processing system and to maintain existing services and information delivery in the interim, but to maintain the IU personality and character. Like any other representative of the university, *insite* should continue to represent the values of the institution and respect the needs of the students and faculty whom it serves.

Insite, or something like it, will continue to serve students in the future. The success of *insite* and other such services around the country are proof that self-service applications provide significant value to both the service provider and client. Routine questions are handled though these services, allowing the more sophisticated questions to be directed to the student service specialist. Placing tools such as student advising directly into the hands of the students assists them in gathering the information they need to make knowledgeable and practical decisions about their academic futures. We recognize that the technology that has enabled us to provide *insite* will evolve over time. Likewise, the needs and expectations of the students will become more demanding and sophisticated. To be successful, we must remain vigilant to their needs and to how our tool chests will change over time.

Conclusion

Developing a set of virtual student information services can be accomplished quickly, though perhaps not easily, using legacy systems and new development tools. It may also be necessary to take advantage of local initiatives and trends and to be aware of projects and/or implementations that have created new pieces of technological infrastructure. You need to carry a vision for how the institution will deliver services and information in the future. IU was fortunate to have several of these forces converge at the key point in time leading to the creation of *insite*.

NOTES

1 Indiana University is a statewide system of eight campuses in the following Indiana cities: Bloomington (enrollment of 35,000), Fort Wayne (6,025), Gary (5,256), Indianapolis (27,036), Kokomo (2,927), New Albany (5,520), Richmond (2,345), and South Bend (7,169).

Student Services Trends	
TRENDS	**IMPLEMENTATION PHASE**
Student-Centered	○
Redesigned Services	N/A
One-Stop Service Center	N/A
Cross-Functional Teams	○
Self-Service Objectives	●
Department Process Improvements	○
Web-Enabled Services	●
Admissions	●
Registration	○
Advising	●
Financial Aid	●
Billing	●
Career Services	○
Systemic Change	○
Replacement of Student Information Systems	◑

Codes for Implementation Phase:

- ● Production
- ◑ Implementing
- ◑ Designed
- ○ Planning

2 For more information about ACE, visit www.indiana.edu/~registra and click on "ACE Information" or www.educause.edu/awards/bp/95/bp-iu.html. ACE won the 1995 CAUSE Award for Best Practice in Applications.

3 *Insite* currently runs on a DEC AlphaServer 5/533 and has three 533 MHz CPUs. It can be expanded to four CPUs, and the chip is upgradable.

The successful implementation of *insite* is really due to the talents, dedication, and hard work of the following people. Special thanks go to the analysts responsible for making *insite* happen: Gary Riggen and Nat Francis. Without their dedication and service, *insite* would still be on a white board. Thanks also to Office of the Registrar: Roland Cote, Bruce Stephenson, Mary Beth Myers, Jean Terret; University Information Technology Services: Gary Riggen, Nat Francis, Cathy Spiaggia, Larry Butcher, Bob Eckert; Office of the Bursar: Susan Cote (BL), Mike Cozmonoff (IUPUI); Office of Financial Assistance/Admissions: Steve Martino. Special thanks to Stretch and to Jerry Pugh, the registrar.

13

Ball State University

Michael E. McCauley

Enhancing Transfer Student Services Through the Web

Overview

Ball State University, located in Muncie, Indiana, supports a student population of nearly 18,000, of which approximately 15,800 are undergraduates. Associate, bachelor's, master's, and doctoral degrees are offered from 46 academic departments housed in seven colleges. Ball State subscribes to the total-intake model of academic advising, with University College being the focal point for entering and undecided students.

Our student record system was developed locally, as was our academic programs database. We use the ExCellere Associates catalog, course master, registration, grade reporting (and drop/add), and facilities management systems, and the Miami University Degree Audit Reporting System (DARS) and its transfer articulation module as advising support systems.

With declining enrollment in the undergraduate population, it becomes incumbent upon institutions of higher education to review target populations and expand existing recruitment methods to attract additional students. Among the most fluid student populations in postsecondary institutions today are transfer students. In 1996 Ball State projected a decrease in the high school graduate pool and, to counteract this projection, initiated a systems project designed to assist admissions personnel in the recruitment of transfer students, stabilize undergraduate enrollment, and improve retention.

Michael E. McCauley is director of academic systems at Ball State University, where he is a member of the Re-Engineering Task Force. He is a founding member of the National Academic Advising Association, where he has held leadership positions. He earned his bachelor's and master's from Ball State University.

It was felt that doubling the number of transfer students annually would not only stabilize enrollment, and enhance retention, but also increase state funding revenue. The system needed to be responsive to the needs of prospective transfer students, i.e., possess comprehensive, accurate academic information that was easily understood and available when the students wanted it.

Transfer students, because of their increased maturity and their experience in higher education, tend to persist at a higher rate than traditional entry-level college students. The university can be more selective in admission, taking only the students who have exhibited academic achievement and who usually have made an educational career choice. Transfer students are most likely the best retention gamble in higher education today. They need less assistance in selecting a major course of study, are more serious about their educational choices, and need less assistance from academic support services. These support services personnel, consequently, have more time to devote to high school transition students and have a better chance of making a positive impact on their retention. From a retention standpoint the transfer student can be a relative gold mine among college students in the late 1990s and early 21st century.

Vision

Ball State's vision in developing its Automated Course Transfer System (ACTS) was to enhance the recruitment of transfer students by providing comprehensive, accurate transfer course information produced in a consistent format and available in a timely manner. By realizing this vision, an overworked admissions counseling staff would find relief and the manner in which they recruited transfer students would be altered. Instead of supplying volumes of paper brochures about majors, carrying thick (usually outdated) transfer course equivalency guides, and providing degree/program booklets that might not be current, transfer admissions counselors would tote laptop computers and access the ACTS Web site for accurate, comprehensive degree/program and course equivalency data. Thus, prospective transfer students would reap the benefits incorporated in the system.

The students engaged in this computer-based exercise can produce two reports. One report (course evaluation) clearly illustrates which courses transfer and which do not, and identifies the course equivalent for each transferred course. The second report (reference degree audit) produces a report that reflects the application of the transferred courses to the student's intended academic major at the four-year institution. This Web-enabled reference audit highlights courses from the source institution (the institution from which the student plans to transfer) and illustrates course equivalents from the target institution (the institution to which the student is transferring), thereby permitting students to enroll in the courses that satisfy requirements at both schools. Thus the student maximizes course work at both institutions and more appropriately prepares for the transfer.

Objectives

The most important objectives identified for this project were the following:

- Provide assistance in the recruitment of transfer students.
- Reduce time expended in the time-consuming, labor-intensive transfer exercises by
  - delivering comprehensive and accurate transfer course equivalency data,
  - providing transfer course equivalents for thousands of courses and from hundreds of institutions,
  - providing consistency of transfer course equivalents evaluated by the appropriate campus academic unit,
  - editing data entry transactions of transfer course (transcript) information, and
  - assisting in making transfer admission decisions.
- Increase the accuracy of curricular data by
  - reducing transcript data entry errors,
  - providing course equivalency data based upon the degree/program (major) selected by each student,
  - calculating the quarter-to-semester (or semester-to-quarter) credit conversion properly,
  - translating the source institution grade point average into the target institution grade point average, and
  - properly evaluating component courses. (Component courses are those comprised of two components, e.g., lec-

ture and lab, for which separate grades are given. However, at the target institution these components are combined into one course and one grade is awarded.)
- Improve the relationship among transfer students and prospective transfer students and the university by
  - providing accurate, comprehensive curricular information in a consistent format and in a timely manner (less than 30 seconds),
  - making the data available to any student anywhere in the world via the Web,
  - fostering knowledgeable degree/program (major) decisions, and
  - increasing student satisfaction with the transfer process.

Project Organization

The project was developed in three phases: phase one, the mainframe system; phase two, the Web-based application; and phase three, maintenance of both the mainframe and Web systems. In developing the mainframe system, it was realized that the transfer process involved many different offices on campus. It was important, when creating a steering committee, to select individuals who represented each of the affected units. Following is a list of those offices that were represented on the Ball State Automated Course Transfer System Steering Committee. (These may differ from institution to institution, depending on how the transfer process is structured on individual campuses.)

- Director of academic systems (chair), the designate of the chief academic officer (provost) assisted by the coordinator of the ACTS
- Two computer center personnel (a computer center administrator and a senior programmer/analyst)
- Two or three admissions office personnel (one or two administrators and a clerical person responsible for the day-to-day execution of the transfer transactions, such as entering transcript data from the previous institutions attended and determining admissibility)
- Six to ten academic deans/department chairs (at least one person from each college plus at least three departmental administrators, those who make course equivalency decisions and apply college and/or departmental policies)
- Three to five academic advisors, those who are in direct contact with the transfer students and are frequently the "official" voice of the institution in the finalization of transfer matters
- Registrar as the official record keeper for the institution

Because the responsibilities in the development of such a system are numerous and varied, our Steering Committee was divided into four subcommittees, each addressing a specific issue. The Policy Subcommittee dealt with policy issues. Among the policies this group reviewed or initiated were (1) acceptance of substandard grades (below C but above F) for component courses; (2) a "catalog rights" policy, which permits transfer students to follow the Ball State degree/program requirements (catalog) that were in effect when they began their postsecondary studies, provided certain criteria were met; (3) determining who has the authority and responsibility to specify the acceptability of transfer courses; and (4) determining who has the authority and responsibility to identify the applicability of transfer course work (course equivalents).

The Procedures Subcommittee focused its attention on transfer processes and procedures. This group studied what occurs when an inquiry is made about transferring to Ball State, what occurs when the student has applied, what occurs when the student is admitted, and what occurs in academic advising and in academic departments after admission. Additionally they delved into the types of reports generated and when those reports were to be sent to the students, how other offices in the transfer chain were connected, and how to streamline processes to minimize irritations for transfer students.

The Transactions/Screens Subcommittee explored alterations needed to current mainframe transaction screens to make them compatible with the system and identified necessary changes to the reports that students and advisors received.

The System Execution Subcommittee was charged to provide data to identify the primary feeder schools, to review how courses had been equated in the past, and to explore proper maintenance procedures for keeping the transfer course equivalency database current and accurate.

The Steering Committee reviewed the work of each subcommittee, developed the project plan, and created the time line for implementation. It was determined that the scope of the project would include both online and batch versions, and that course equivalents would be loaded for at least the general education courses from the 123 maintenance schools. Once this was accomplished, an expansion of the institutions and equivalency tables followed. However, the only courses from these nonmaintenance institutions to be loaded would be those that had transferred in the past three years.

The time line for this initial phase was as follows:

- DARS software training: one month, included a formal DARS transfer articulation workshop
- Ball State training: one month, included understanding local transfer policies pertaining to the acceptability and applicability of transfer course work
- Identification of primary feeder institution (123): one month, included analyzing transfer data received

- Solicitation of catalogs from primary feeder institutions: four months (Although most institutions were prompt in sending catalogs, second and third contacts were necessary for several.)
- Creation of institutional master reference files and course equivalency tables for the primary feeder institutions: six months, included a review of each institution's catalog and transcript information (Often a description of the credit type, list of grades, accreditation status, and other items were found on the back side of a transcript.)
- Testing of master reference files and course equivalency tables: six months, concurrent with creation of the same files and tables, included a comparison of the manually equated transfer courses with the automated conversion of the same courses
- Validation of course equivalency tables with each academic department: four months (Approximately 10,000 course equivalents had been entered onto the tables, and each equivalent was validated by the appropriate academic unit. Professional academic advisors consulted with the departments in this process.)
- Training for admissions personnel (professional staff and clerical staff) on the altered data entry transactions, mainframe screens, and reports: one month
- Training for departmental administrators, faculty advisors, and professional advisors on mainframe screens, reports, and maintenance procedures: two months
- Writing and publishing the ACTS manual for users: two weeks

The system development costs, in terms of new monies needed, were relatively small compared with normal development costs. The Miami DARS had been in place for 11 years, and the computer center staff could be flexed sufficiently to support the project, but a full-time professional person was needed to coordinate the development. The initial request for funding totaled $50,000. These dollars were used to hire a full-time ACTS coordinator, purchase the appropriate computer hardware and office furniture, and provide for ample software training. The target increase in the number of transfer students was 100 percent (from 400 to 800), yet to recoup our development costs we estimated that only a 4 percent increase was necessary. Sixteen additional transfer students could generate additional state funding that would total more than $51,000. In short, the project was completed in 16 months (one more than projected) and slightly under budget.

Phase two, migrating the system to a Web application, was projected to take nine months, but it was completed in eight. The organization was essentially the same, except the Steering Committee played a lessor role. One admissions person, two from academic systems, and two from the computer center were responsible for the development. Our computer center Web specialist created the Web site prototype, which was then modified several times following collaboration with admissions personnel and the ACTS coordinator.

Project Development

Because Indiana does not have a community college system, per se, determining primary feeder institutions was a more involved task. By virtue of using our automated degree audit system since 1987, we had stored (individually determined and manually loaded) course equivalents on each student record. An analysis of these student records and course equivalents was conducted to determine our "primary feeder" institutions. The analysis was based upon four principles (*n* of 337 institutions): (1) the number of students from each school with transfer credit, (2) the number of transfer matriculates from each school, (3) the total number of courses transferred from each institution, and (4) the average number of credit hours per institution. From these analyses we identified 123 institutions from which we had received a minimum of five transfer students and at least 25 courses. These schools were thus identified as our maintenance institutions.

The Office of Academic Systems professional staff created the institutional master reference files, which essentially profiled each of the 123 maintenance institutions. These files contain, among other items, credit type (e.g., quarter, semester); effective date range; and a "course mask," which stipulates the coding convention of the departmental course prefix and course number. Additionally, this file identifies the grading scheme the institution employs and converts these grades into a universal grade as defined by the home institution. The table also defines other grades (withdrawal, incomplete, pass, fail, credit, and no credit) according to the standards established by the Standardization of Postsecondary Education Electronic Data Exchange Committee of the American Association of Collegiate Registrars and Admissions Officers.

The articulation tables for each school were created concurrently with the institutional master reference files. Initially the courses loaded to these tables were those that had been previously equated manually for use on the automated degree audit system. Since that information was stored on the student record, it was easily retrievable. However, only about 60 percent of the courses had been determined to be one-to-one matches, with the other courses falling into one of the following categories: one course to multiple courses, multiple courses to one course, or multiple courses to multiple courses.

Additionally, some source courses carry more credit hours than the equivalent target course, making it necessary to limit credit hours passed from the source course to the target course and requiring the creation of a generic course to accommodate the additional credit. Often, more than one source course equates to the same target course, necessitating the selection of one source course to be the equivalent and giving the other source course a generic course equivalent.

A frequent occurrence was that a source course could have a different course equivalent, depending upon the degree/program (major) a student selected. For these situations a degree/program mask was created to permit one source course to have a different equivalent, based upon the major a student identified.

Many other conditions occur that make an automated course transfer system difficult to establish and maintain. For instance, a department may establish a course equivalency only when the grade earned is an A or B. The course would have another equivalent when the grade is below B. The DARS transfer articulation module can, in an automated fashion, equate the course properly based upon the grade earned. Another fairly routine condition occurred when two source institution courses equated to one target institution course but the grades earned differed. In this situation, it became necessary to combine the grades and calculate a weighted average to ensure that the minimum acceptable grade was achieved. These and other conditions require a thorough knowledge and understanding of target institution policies as well as the intricacies of the system algorithm.

Target institution policies associated with the transfer process must be reviewed concurrent to the development of the files and tables. As mentioned previously, determining under what conditions, if any, substandard grades will be accepted and/or which target institution catalog (degree/program) requirements are in force for the transfer student (equitability being the focal point) are policies that, if altered, usually must proceed through regular university governance channels. This exercise frequently takes months to accomplish when passage through undergraduate/graduate policy councils and faculty senates becomes necessary. Similarly, planning for the flow of students and receipt of hard copy reports to ensure the proper results is time consuming. And finally, the establishment of course equivalency and maintenance procedures to ensure absolute academic integrity of the transfer data for each and all source institutions requires much cooperation, negotiation, and patience to accomplish.

Maintaining accurate course equivalency tables requires constant and careful attention. At Ball State, a full-time professional position has been allocated to this responsibility. The maintenance process has been divided into two categories—maintenance of data for our maintenance institutions and for our nonmaintenance institutions.

In each of the 123 maintenance institutions, we have identified one or two individuals, called maintenance contact persons, with whom we communicate regularly. At least once annually we send a report to each contact person detailing the courses from their institution we have on our equivalency tables and asking for any changes to be marked and returned to us. The report is sent in mid-April and returned by mid-July. From mid-July through September we update our tables with the changes, so by the time prospective transfer students apply to Ball State (usually beginning in October) the tables reflect comprehensive and accurate data.

We update the tables of our nonmaintenance schools as we receive courses that are not on our equivalency tables. Because the automated process labels each with a special generic course prefix, they are easily identified. Once a new course has been identified, a course equivalency approval form is sent to the appropriate academic unit for evaluation. Following the evaluation by departmental administrators, the forms are returned to the ACTS coordinator and the course equivalent is added to the equivalency tables.

When the admissions office receives a transfer inquiry from a student whose institution is not in our database, the Office of Academic Systems is notified. The ACTS coordinator contacts the institution and requests a catalog and other pertinent information and builds a master reference file and a generic equivalency table. The admissions office can then enter transcript data, and the system reports that no course equivalents exist on the table. Upon receipt of the institution catalog the course descriptions are forwarded through academic advising to the appropriate department for evaluation. The evaluations are returned to academic systems and added to the table, and then a report is generated and mailed to the student. Our ACTS Web site (www.bsu.edu/bsu/acts) is equipped with an e-mail connection to facilitate the student whose institution is not in the database. This contact is made directly to academic systems, and the ACTS coordinator responds immediately. A request for a catalog (if one is not available on the Web) is made, and the aforementioned process of evaluating the course is pursued.

These processes have been daily activities since the ACTS was placed into production. The number of institutions in our transfer database has increased from the original 123 to more than 1,400, and our equivalency tables today support nearly 30,000 course equivalents.

The ACTS has not only enhanced Ball State's transfer student recruitment (and subsequent enrollment); our native students can use it to attend an institution in their home communities during the summer to augment their campus studies. Since the reference audit illustrates Ball State course equivalents for the source institution courses, our students have found it to be a vital source for accurate curricular information.

Although other initiatives have been added to support the recruitment of transfer students, since the ACTS was placed into pro-

duction status in May 1997, the number of transfer students has increased from approximately 400 to more than 700. It is anticipated that our transfer student population will increase more in the future and will include students with transfer credit from foreign countries.

Currently the ACTS is being expanded to include international institutions. We anticipate adding approximately 65 institutions from Europe, the Far East, and the Middle East in the near future. Student records at international colleges and universities are often kept differently from the U.S. models. It has become necessary to match course equivalents on course titles, rather than on course numbers, and convert grades differently. However, our software has the capacity to accommodate these differences, and we have received student inquiries, via our Web site, from Japan, the United Kingdom, China, Guam, and Puerto Rico.

The relative success of the ACTS can be attributed to a number of factors. Included in these are support from executive-level administration and cooperation among admissions, colleges/departments, academic advising, and computing services. The centralization of system maintenance responsibility in the Office of Academic Systems has contributed greatly to the effort, as has the support from individual faculty and our maintenance contacts at the source institutions. Prospective transfer students use the system because it provides the appropriate information in a relatively short period of time. Our goal is to return to applicants and admitted students a Course Evaluation Report in next-day mail. For the prospective students using our Web site, we have produced the Course Evaluation and the Reference Audit, once all course work has been entered, in less than 30 seconds. Before the ACTS, the determination of course equivalents and how the equivalents applied to an intended major could take anywhere from three weeks to three months to accomplish. The ACTS produces accurate, comprehensive reports in a consistent format very quickly, which expedites the transfer process and gives the data academic integrity.

The ACTS is only one of several projects currently under development to establish a "web-stop-shopping" environment for our students. Even though we have placed most of our student services in one physical location on campus, we recognize the need to respond to the expectations of our student and prospective student clientele and provide many of these same student-centered services on the Web. The admissions Web site is complete with a Web-based admissions application, and a telephone registration system will become Web-enabled in late 1999. However, we have discovered some limitations to our registration system and are exploring other telephone systems.

Although we currently have our automated degree audit and our course planner (schedule of classes) on the Web, our advising support systems will not be complete until our catalog is "Webified" late in 1999. The Financial Aid Office provides some Web-enabled support, but a need for an improved financial aid system is apparent. Discussion and exploration of the proper alternatives is taking place, but no target date for acquisition of a new financial aid system has been determined. We have installed a new billing system, and transporting this application to the Web is under development. Our career services office was one of our first Web-based systems created and has been in production for several years.

Upon the recommendation of a consultant, Ball State is implementing a new structure for its Web development office, which will include the addition of a full-time programmer and a content developer. Each academic unit and all offices engaged in student support services are supporting this campuswide initiative. Each unit/office has designated a Web-proficient individual who will assist in the continuing development of our Web-stop-shopping efforts.

In the summer of 1998, we considered the need to replace our student information system. Our Reengineering Committee, upon the advice of our computing services administrators, decided to postpone any active pursuit of acquiring an integrated student information system until we can discuss implementation strategies with those institutions currently engaged in the development processes. However, some institutions were targeted for visitations.

Student Services Trends

TRENDS	IMPLEMENTATION PHASE
Student-Centered	●
Redesigned Services	N/A
One-Stop Service Center	●
Cross-Functional Teams	N/A
Self-Service Objectives	●
Department Process Improvements	N/A
Web-Enabled Services	●
Admissions	●
Registration	●
Advising	●
Financial Aid	◑
Billing	◑
Career Services	●
Systemic Change	◑
Replacement of Student Information Systems	N/A

Codes for Implementation Phase:
● Production
◑ Implementing
◑ Designed
○ Planning

14

Buddy Ramos
Dick Vallandingham

Student Development Model as the Core to Student Success

Overview

Johnson County Community College (JCCC), is a single-campus, suburban community college located in Overland Park, Kansas. JCCC is the largest of the 19 community colleges in Kansas, serving more than 16,000 credit students and 17,000 noncredit students per semester. An overview of the JCCC Fall 1998 Enrollment Report provides the following description of the student body characteristics: While most students continue to attend JCCC part-time (70 percent), full-time students account for more than half the credit hours (53 percent). Approximately 35 percent of students are attending JCCC with the intention of transferring to another college or university. Nearly 57 percent of students preparing to enter the job market, change careers, or improve skills for their present jobs are enrolled in six or fewer credit hours.

The JCCC Student Services Division has a strong tradition of providing services that are based on a student-centered philosophy, with the belief that student services are an integral part of the total learning experience at JCCC. Student service staffs view themselves as being in the business of helping students develop personally, academically, socially, culturally, physically, and emotionally. The student service professionals view their office as a classroom for applied learning. This has been especially true for the JCCC counselors who perform academic advising for all students at the college.

Consistent with the IBM best practice model of having academic advising as the core of student support services, JCCC counselors play a pivotal role in a student's educational experience. This provides an advising experience that is based on a developmental advising philosophy (Habley 1981; Winston, Ender, and Miller 1982). Within the developmental framework, JCCC advisors assist students in the clarification of their life/career goals and the development of educational plans for the realization of these goals. Advising is a process that focuses the students' interaction with the higher education enterprise, not simply on their course of study (Frost 1991). This approach is in direct contrast to the more traditional prescriptive approach, where the advisor acts in a more authoritarian manner with a focus of helping students select classes for the following term's registration.

The Compelling Case for Change

As the 1990s progressed, the college found itself in an increasing growth mode. Enrollments had grown from 8,000 credit students in 1985 to a current enrollment in excess of 16,000 credit students. While the college built classrooms to accommodate this growth, the Student Development Division acquired very little additional space. With this growth in enrollment, the demands and expectations on student services also increased. Along with an increase in students, new career programs were added to the curriculum and

Manuel "Buddy" Ramos is a higher education consultant for IBM Education Consulting & Services. He previously was director of the Counseling Center and the Student Access Center at Johnson County Community College. An active member of the National Academic Advising Association, he received his doctorate in higher education from the University of Kansas.

Dick Vallandingham is the director of the Counseling Center and the Student Access Center at Johnson County Community College. A frequent presenter at national conferences, he is also an active member of the National Academic Advising Association. He did undergraduate work at Oklahoma State University and graduate work at the University of Tulsa. He completed his doctoral work at the University of Arizona.

existing programs underwent extensive modifications. This meant a tremendous increase in the amount of information counselors were responsible for in their academic advising role.

Just as significant, changes were made in admission and retention policies and procedures. Assessment testing was required of all new students to evaluate their writing, reading, and math levels. Students scoring into developmental reading or writing courses were identified as underprepared and were required to meet with a counselor before enrollment. An academic progress policy was implemented with criteria for identifying students who were not making satisfactory academic progress. Those students identified were placed on academic probation and required to meet with counselors before enrollment.

While these events resulted in an increase in demand for services, including processing and support services, there was a decrease in our ability to provide staff to meet this increasing demand. The number of new positions was limited as the governing board undertook a very conservative approach to the fiscal management of the college. It was necessary to look for innovative ways to deliver additional services and maintain the quality of services with the same staff serving more students.

Similar to the changing requirements of career programs, there was a change in the diversity and specialized needs of the student body. As at all institutions, the number of students with documented disabilities requiring accommodations increased. The number of students entering selective admission programs, certificate programs, and cooperative programs, with their inherent additional staffing needs, also increased.

Student feedback obtained as part of an ongoing program evaluation suggested that our processes were becoming increasingly fragmented, sending students from one office to another for signatures or facing long waits in lines. Counselors were voicing frustration that, in many instances, they were working with students who had waited a long time to see a counselor when all they needed was a form signed or a simple question answered. In other cases, counselors voiced frustration because they were spending time with students explaining routine, redundant information, e.g., what a credit hour was or when and how to register for courses. It became necessary to develop innovative approaches to delivering a high quality of service for a diversity of needs.

There is a body of common knowledge or assumptions regarding student success among colleges and universities. For example, we know, or believe we know, that students with clear educational/career goals are more motivated toward success within the academic environment. We believe that students who make some sort of personal connection to the institution are more persist-

ent in their educational efforts. We think that students who become truly engaged in the educational process, including career/life planning, are more likely to succeed. When these assumptions are applied to the community college, developmental advising that is based on student involvement in an educational/career/life planning process becomes a key component toward creating an environment for student success.

Developmental advising implies meaningful connections and relationships between students and advisors. Use of technology allows for a new level of student involvement in the planning process. Academic advisors who use a combination of high-tech/high-touch advising strategies can meet the challenges of a diverse student body within a changing world of work. The use of technology within the developmental advising model empowers students by giving them access to a variety of tools to use in their exploration, planning, and decision-making processes. Additionally, integrated student data technology requires an active involvement of academic advising with student services and instruction. Thus, the use of technology within a developmental advising model allows for the development of a highly interactive educational partnership with students, advisors, faculty, and student services.

Project Summary

JCCC has been involved for the last three years in developing and transitioning to a new student service model based on student development and relying heavily on developmental academic advising. A look at how JCCC recognized the need for change, developed a plan for change, and implemented that plan may give insight into the application of a developmental model. Several factors converged to bring about an awareness of the need for an optimal driving philosophy for the college and student services in relation to student success. One of those factors was the proposal of a new building to allow for unification of student service offices. In addition, several administrative positions went through changes, allowing for a new administrative focus. A new student data system was implemented and, academically, competencies and outcomes were becoming the measures for student success. These factors in combination created an opportunity for innovation.

The first step in the process was to identify what was driving student services and the advising process and determine if, in fact, student success was being addressed. It appeared that enrollment was the driving factor that determined subsequent involvement with a student. The first question for potential students was: "Do you want to enroll in classes?" The appearance of the semester schedule of classes initiated involvement in the advising process. Assessment, financial aid, child care, and other aspects of student services all followed from

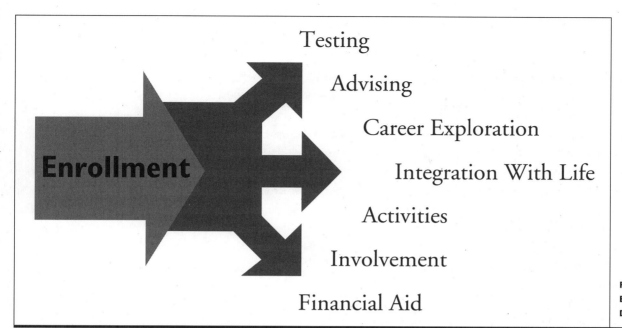

Testing

Advising

Career Exploration

Integration With Life

Activities

Involvement

Financial Aid

Figure 14.1
Enrollment-
Driven Model

the enrollment involvement. Although fairly effective, at least from an institutional view, and typical, the model did not seem to actively promote student development and success. The enrollment model was backward. It provided for advising after the fact and didn't help students prepare for their academic lives (see figure 14.1).

A model that maintained institutional effectiveness but focused on student development needed to be created. The model could then serve as the design template for planning the new building and for modifying and implementing processes and procedures. A systematic planning process was implemented to develop a model that addressed student development and success. Cross-functional teams from across student services and with faculty and student representation were established (13 teams with a total of 150 people involved). These teams addressed three questions:

1. What do we value in student services at JCCC?
2. What processes or procedures do we need to change to ensure our values are met?
3. What does our space need to look like to facilitate the processes and functions we have developed to reflect our values?

The information these teams generated resulted in several products, one of which was the following JCCC Student Services Statement of Values:

- JCCC Student Services is student centered.
- We believe in the dignity and growth of each individual, the uniqueness of each individual, and the fundamental right of each person to realize his or her fullest potential.
- We believe Student Services is an integral part of the total learning experience at JCCC. The quality and completeness of education at this institution is our top priority.
- We believe in providing friendly, easily accessible, trustworthy, and efficient services in an environment that is caring, confidential, and secure.

- We believe in an internal environment that will nurture our values: people, respect, openness, ongoing staff development, and care for ourselves and each other as staff members.

In addition, the team identified the following processes and procedures that would allow for these values:

- Front-line basic information for all enrollment processes should be in one easy-to-access location.
- Second-level, more detailed information for enrollment processes should be consolidated into a central location.
- Cross-training will be needed for frontline information staff to be able to answer the myriad of questions they will be expected to answer.
- Increased use of technology and the World Wide Web and Interactive Voice Response will be needed; therefore, students must have access to computers and the Internet.
- Students must be able to move easily between offices; therefore, offices need to be in close proximity to each other.
- Study and social areas are vitally important to insure student comfort levels and must be available.
- A phone answering process must be implemented to facilitate a maximum of two transfers.
- Student development offices will provide the front door to the campus.
- Cross-trained generalists will meet first-level needs.
- Materials, services, and resources will be easily accessible.
- Well-trained and available professionals will work within the developmental model with individuals.

One of the basic assumptions of the JCCC student services model is that the student development component of student services should be the "front door" to the college for potential students, new students, and current students (see figure 14.2). This approach acknowledges the importance of student involvement in their own educational and career planning and the necessity for early connection of students and the student development model. To achieve this, the concept of a Success Center was developed.

The Success Center, staffed by trained, knowledgeable, and accessible generalists, is the natural first stop for new and prospective students. It contains easily accessible information available to students. The goals of the Success Center are to assist students with the first- and second-level questions they typically bring on their first visit, to assist them in gathering the information needed as part of their planning process, and to direct them to the appropriate specialist for individual assistance. The generalist in the Success Center is not only able to guide students through the sometimes-confusing process of college enrollment, but is trained to anticipate the unasked questions, provide answers, and make appropriate referrals.

Resources and technology in the adjacent Career and Academic Resource Library and Lab are readily available for students, allowing them to engage the student information system. This fosters the student's ability to be an active participant in the educational planning process. For example, the technology allows for printing individual schedules that assist with time management or researching educational and career options for different focus areas.

In this model, technology is used to take information to students rather than force them to stand in line, function within restricted times, or compete for processing functions. Workstations in the Success Center and the Career and Academic Resource Library and Lab allow students to access and input their own admission, financial aid, and registration via the Web and/or touch-tone telephone. The Success Center allows using technology for access to financial aid processing.

Ongoing preadvisement information sessions are part of the model's resources and are available for groups or individuals. Ongoing computerized ASSET testing allows students to complete requirements quickly and easily for enrollment and gain information about appropriate starting places for educational plans. These preparatory steps allow the advisor to focus on the developmental aspects of advising. The initial question throughout student services has now changed from "Are you enrolling in a class?" to "Where are you heading and how can we help you get started toward that goal?"

Another foundational key to the JCCC student services model is the belief in the "dignity and growth of each individual, the uniqueness of each individual, and the fundamental right of each person to realize his or her fullest potential." In this way, the JCCC model moves beyond the traditional concept of "one-stop shopping," which views enrollment as the end product. Rather, it focuses on the facilitation of each student's growth and development, encouraging learning and promoting achievement of individual goals. Chickering (1969) points out the following:

> By looking at individual "identity," we are reminded that there is more to development in college than acquiring information and developing intellectual competence. Colleges and universities will be educationally effective only if they reach students "where they live," and only if they connect significantly with those concerns of central importance to their students.

The JCCC student services model is committed to the philosophy of promoting the growth of the whole student. Educational, career, and personal issues must all be addressed. Academic/career counselors are available for quick questions in the Success Center or for extended consultations in private offices on a walk-in or appointment basis to assist students in the process of goal setting, problem solving, and goal attainment. Student activities professionals work within the model to promote leadership and social growth. Cocurricular programming, wellness programs, and athletics are also promoted within the scope of the whole-person developmental principle of the model.

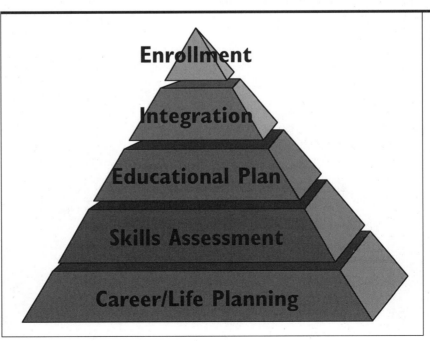

**Figure 14.2
Development-
Driven Model**

The implementation of this model has clarified the function of several areas. The Career Center now functions as a source for connections (with business and career programs, for example) and resources (including Web-based job search information). The Counseling Center is the area responsible for the one-on-one developmental advising that involves educational, career, and personal counseling. The Success Center functions as the interactive activity area where students access career and transfer information and prepare for individual developmental advising sessions. Technology is a vital tool for this model. Not only is technology necessary for the retrieval of student information, but it also becomes the students' avenue for a greater level of involvement in their own educational and career planning. It is that involvement, along with the information accessed, that encourages student success. This use of technology allows for implementation of this student-centered approach.

The implementation of this model has affected all of student services. One of the major challenges to emerge has been the need for cross-functional training coupled with ongoing professional development. An internal conference was conducted to allow for all student service staff to participate in workshops focusing on the redesigned services. Additional professional development activities have been initiated in the Counseling Center on an ongoing basis. These include professional roundtables as a regular part of the weekly staff meeting, specialized workshops on career assessment interpretation, and an annual Master Counselor Workshop. Challenges still remaining for the complete integration of the model include some technology challenges related to admissions and billing. Online application and billing is currently in the implementation phase. JCCC is also implementing distance advising using e-mail advising, video advising, and interactive Web sites.

Even with the challenges, several measure of success have already been noted. The number of students using Web-based enrollment has increased and become so common that only Web-based enrollment will be offered for walk-in enrollment. In fact, student use of Web-based information (grades, transcripts, and class schedules, for example) increased tremendously. While the number of students using technology for information and enrollment increased, the number of students using counseling/advising services stayed constant. However, the flow of students is beginning to be affected. Students are visiting the Counseling Center throughout the Web-enrollment period—a rather large "window"—rather than visiting en masse during a walk-in period immediately before the beginning of classes.

Students have also begun to use the Success Center in a much more comprehensive way. On a daily basis throughout the year, you may find students in the Success Center enrolling, checking on their records, involved in career/life planning activities, doing job searches,

Student Services Trends

TRENDS	IMPLEMENTATION PHASE
Student-Centered	◑
Redesigned Services	◑
One-Stop Service Center	◑
Cross-Functional Teams	◑
Self-Service Objectives	◑
Department Process Improvements	◑
Web-Enabled Services	●
Admissions	◑
Registration	●
Advising	●
Financial Aid	●
Billing	◔
Career Services	●
Systemic Change	◑
Replacement of Student Information Systems	●

Codes for Implementation Phase:
- ● Production
- ◑ Implementing
- ◔ Designed
- ○ Planning

gathering information before an advising session on transferring—in short, actively involved in their own educational planning.

Critical Success Factors and Key Considerations

The success to date of the model is possible for several reasons. First, the model has a strong philosophical/theoretical base. The philosophy states that in a student-centered learning environment, all aspects of student services must work together in a developmental manner as partners with the student and the teaching faculty in discovering, analyzing, and implementing obtainable and relevant career/life plans. This change in philosophy from an enrollment-driven model to a student development/career/life planning model affects all aspects of student services, from the initial questions asked of potential students to the manner in which enrollment takes place.

The second major factor affecting success relates to the fact that the model was developed as a collaborative effort involving all parts of student services as well as teaching faculty and students. This not only insured ownership and involvement of all parties in the implementation of the model, it also allowed for group consensus on what the model should address and how. The successful implementation of the model required appropriate use of technology as an interactive tool for students and staff. Web enrollment, e-mail advising, Internet and Intranet information sources, and computer-based assessments all are important components of the working model.

Finally, timing was a factor in the successful development and implementation of the model. The time was right for a new approach to be explored. The factors mentioned above allowed for a window of opportunity for exploration and implementation.

Conclusion

The JCCC student services model has allowed for the coordinated activities of the Student Services branch to be driven by a student development–based philosophy. The initial question for prospective students has changed from "Did you want to enroll in a class?" to "Where are you heading and how can we help you get there?"

The model allowed for new processes and procedures to be developed with one basic criterion in mind: "Is it good for students?" These, in turn, allowed for the design of the physical space to provide the most efficient services. In this way, the new Student Services Center at JCCC will be more than a one-stop shop for students—it will be the initial step in a highly interactive educational/career/life planning process.

REFERENCES

Chickering, Arthur W. 1969. *Education and Identity.* Books on Demand.

Frost, S.H. 1991. *Academic Advising for Student Success: A System of Shared Responsibility.* ASHE-ERIC Higher Education Report No. 3. Washington, D.C: George Washington University School of Education and Human Development.

Habley, W.R. 1981. Academic Advisement: The Critical Link in Student Retention. *NASPA Journal* 18 (4): 35–37.

Winston, R.B., S.C. Ender, and T.K. Miller, eds. 1982. *Developmental Approaches to Academic Advising.* New Directions for Student Services No. 17. San Francisco: Jossey-Bass.

Vicky Seehusen

Student Services × 13:
A Consortial Approach

Overview

The community college system in Colorado is comprised of 16 community colleges. Of that number, 13 colleges belong to the Colorado Community College and Occupational Education System (CCCOES or the system). One of these 13 colleges is Colorado Electronic Community College, established in 1995 to manage distance degrees for the CCCOES colleges. CCCOES is the largest system of higher education in Colorado, enrolling six of 10 freshmen and sophomores enrolled in public higher education. The system serves 90,000 credit students annually at one of 12 main campuses and 26 physical delivery sites throughout the state.

The Compelling Case for Change

By 1997, it was obvious that many businesses and industries strongly believed in, and supported, the concept of anywhere, anytime delivery of products and services. The system, ever conscious of the pulse of the communities it serves, was already leading the charge by providing students with alternative learning options through telecourses, self-paced courses, and satellite training. In the late summer of 1997, three community colleges within the system also offered an additional anywhere, anytime learning option—using the Internet and e-mail to deliver course materials and communicate with students. These three colleges are all located in large urban areas of Colorado

Vicky Seehusen, vice president of instruction for Colorado Electronic Community College, is a frequent speaker and consultant on distance education programs for college consortia. She holds a Ph.D. in educational innovations from the University of Colorado at Denver, an MBA from Regis University, a bachelor's from the National University in Denver, and a bachelor's from New Mexico State University at Alamogordo.

and serve urban students who, for a variety of reasons, seek courses outside the traditional classroom environment.

The system observed the unbalanced learning options for rural and urban students. In rural areas, students were limited in course and degree choices because the colleges there could not find enough students interested in the same courses to make their creation economically viable. Also, because of the limited choice of Internet providers in many rural areas, community colleges did not want to invest large sums of money in creating Internet courses. The concern was that these courses might have limited appeal because the infrastructure to deliver them was so poor. Economics always plays a large part in the decisions about course offerings. Courses that do not show promise of large enrollments will probably not be offered. The result was that students in rural areas were underserved. While there was a need and desire for certain courses, it was not great enough for the colleges to sustain the courses economically. A partnership of rural and urban community colleges would minimize, if not eliminate, the problem of economic sustainability. By sharing courses across the community colleges, a course would never have to be cancelled. Colleges could jointly enroll enough students to make the courses viable. By sharing course development across the community colleges, new courses could be developed at a fraction of the cost for each institution. The sharing of courses and the costs associated with them would allow the colleges to be responsive to current training needs within their communities and the state.

The system saw a collaborative effort as a positive way to respond to its twofold mission to "contribute to Colorado's economic growth and vitality" and to "develop Colorado's human resource potential." Using the Internet is one way students and faculty anywhere in the state can continually learn and simultaneously refine their technological skills. A plan was developed for the 13 community colleges to pool their financial and instructional resources to capitalize on the Internet technology. This meant that instead of delivering a few scattered online courses through three or four colleges, all 13 colleges banding together could deliver complete degrees and certificates to the entire community college population of Colorado, both rural and urban.

The challenge was to provide high-quality instruction and support services at a reasonable cost to encourage Colorado community college students to stay enrolled in Colorado colleges. It was obvious that students wanted Internet courses: urban colleges offering Internet-delivered courses were seeing an increase in course enrollment every semester. In addition, surveys indicated that distance education students were seeking more and varied courses delivered via the Internet and that students wanted more interaction with their instructors with more student services available electronically.

CCCOnline was a response to student needs for additional learning and student services opportunities, and college desires to meet the system mission. The presidents of individual community colleges designed CCCOnline as a new learning-teaching model that centralized instructional design, faculty management, and student enrollment. Other services such as advising, career counseling, transcript evaluation, and tuition payments were decentralized, thus allowing individual colleges to provide support services to their local students who chose to take all of their courses online or mix them with traditional classroom offerings.

Project Summary

Vision. In developing a vision for CCCOnline, the presidents, administrators, and faculty within the system reviewed the services offered to students, employers, and taxpayers. Traditional services included providing the following:

- The first two years of college education to students wanting transfer to baccalaureate degree–granting institutions
- Technical education to students seeking new or updated job skills
- Education to strengthen the academic background of students and prepare them to pursue educational and career goals
- Diverse educational experiences for community members desiring to enhance their occupational, intellectual, cultural, social, or personal development
- Assistance to students in selecting, entering, continuing, and completing their course of study by providing effective student support services

It was determined that these traditional student services should be available to students regardless of how they chose to have their courses delivered. The vision, though not clearly described in a written statement, could be summed up as follows: "Students will be able to access all of the services offered by our colleges, both on-campus and online, at their choice."

Goals. CCCOnline created a number of goals that, when met, would lead toward successful implementation of the vision. The goals are to provide the following:

- Learning when and where the student wants to take advantage of it
- Up-to-date curriculum that is responsive to the needs of a constantly changing and mobile workforce
- Curriculum that serves the needs of employers who desire to give employees professional development opportunities while on the job
- A core transfer curriculum with consistent learning objectives and outcomes for all online students regardless of their home colleges
- A single enrollment Web site to simplify the application and registration process for online courses
- Multiple start dates in any given semester, thus allowing students some latitude in how and when they receive their instruction
- All student services, including advising, payment, and library services online

Structure. A local vendor who had experience creating online college sites was involved in the process from the very first meeting of the presidents. The vendor acted as a consultant and an educator about online educational opportunities and the use of vendors such as itself to provide the online college site. So once the presidents reached an agreement to create a shared online college site, things began to move very quickly. In September, the vendor made a proposal to provide the college site, complete with online registration and enrollment management and instructional design support for faculty. The college presidents accepted the proposal and agreed to split the initial start-up costs 13 ways. They also selected the Colorado Electronic Community College (CECC) to manage the creation of CCCOnline. The CECC, the 1999 Winner of the Bellwether Award: Planning, Governance and Finance, was the clear choice to plan and implement the consortial delivery of degrees because it was not a competitor of any one of the system colleges and already had experience managing a degree at a distance for one of its sister colleges.

The goal was to have a degree online by January 20, 1998. In simple terms, the program design specified that all students who wished to take classes offered on CCCOnline would register and enroll for these online classes at CCCOnline's Web site. Then, on a nightly basis, this student information would be uploaded to the system computer department. Once the data were uploaded, software, written specifically for this purpose, would separate the data by college and upload the data to the individual college databases. This would allow the student to be enrolled in an online class such as College Algebra (prefixed as MATH 105 in college catalogs) with students from other colleges but still be listed as a student at his or her home college. Of course, this meant that every course at the online site would need to be listed in the schedule of every college. So that the courses would not be confused with the traditional college classroom offerings, they were to be given a special suffix, beginning with the letter C. Therefore, MATH 105 on campus might be MATH 105-001 in the college schedule, while its online version would be designated MATH 105-C11.

After initial conversations with various colleges' staffs, it was also determined that students who wanted to take advantage of online classes would have to enroll and register online, even if they were taking other classes at their home school. The vendor and the CECC management team reasoned that students had to have some level of Internet expertise if they were to be successful in their online course of study. They believed that one way to ascertain the student's level of expertise was to require him or her enroll online.

While efforts were made to provide a logical sequence of implementation, this is not necessarily what happened. There were too many questions, concerns, and fears on the part of the individual colleges. Those urban schools that had strong Internet programs were concerned that CCCOnline, at its worst, was going to take away their students; they also feared that CCCOnline, at its best, would cause undue confusion for students along with advising and financial aid nightmares. CECC took on the challenging task of educating the various college constituencies about the program and framing their support roles.

Initially, the five overarching challenges were to determine the following:

- Tuition costs
- The number of start dates to have in any given semester
- Consistent faculty pay
- CECC program management fees
- The initial degree that would be offered

It is interesting to note that the presidents did not envision that providing student services such as advising online would be an overarching challenge because a number of technology enhancements had been put in place for students and staff in the preceding few years. At the time of CCCOnline's inception, students could register and receive grades by phone and the colleges' personnel had e-mail access. The presidents believed that the underpinnings were in place to provide additional student support services such as online advising.

By late fall of 1998, the colleges realized that advising was also a challenge, particularly as it related to career assessments and basic skills. While the students were getting responses from the advisors, they were requesting additional services such as online assessments. Online assessment is an area that all of the colleges are now seriously considering.

Approach. In an effort to respond to the overarching challenges, representatives from the instruction, business services, advising, financial aid, registration, and cashiering departments at the colleges gathered in a series of meetings around the state. These meetings were their opportunity to share their concerns and ideas about implementing such an ambitious program. The first meeting was a multisite videoconference to which representatives from all of the departments were invited, although not every college had a representative from each department at its college. At this time, the colleges were informed of the decision to create a collaborative online degree. Most of those in attendance had many questions and concerns. The ideas of using a third-party vendor and having multiple start dates in any given semester seemed to cause particular angst. Thus, from this first meeting, it was decided that the business officers and financial aid officers would meet next to determine course pricing and review the financial aid issues that students would face.

Recall that one of the goals was to provide multiple start dates in any given semester, thus allowing students some latitude in how and when they received their instruction. To provide this latitude, the program was organized so that all courses would be offered in three separate 15-week sessions with three different start dates in the fall and spring semesters and two sessions with two start dates in the summer semester. The sessions would start five weeks apart. A student choosing to take a course in the spring in session three would not begin the course work until the end of March. This meant that the student wouldn't complete the course until mid-July. There was a great deal of concern that the financial aid students would loose their eligibility if they didn't have recorded grades at the end of the typical semesters. The president of CECC contacted the U.S. Department of Education (DOE) to explain the unique start date concept and assure that the financial aid students would continue to be eligible for benefits. The response was enthusiastic and we believe that this program will be instrumental in changing financial aid rules. In fact, the DOE announced a pilot program that will allow colleges to try special financial aid models for distance education students.

Other ad hoc committees were organized to deal with issues as they arose, and the e-mails back and forth amongst committee members were numerous. One of the big issues was to identify the staff at the individual colleges who would be the points of contact for online students who needed help with financial aid, academic advising, career counseling, payments, and library resources. After many discussions, it was determined that e-mail links would be provided for these services for each individual college. Each link was designed to generate an e-mail message to at least one staff person and his or her backup in the advising, financial aid, admission, and cashier departments at each college. Sending e-mail to multiple staff at each college was a way to ensure that the student would receive a response within 24 hours from someone in the department. Most of the colleges rose to the occasion and did a fine job of responding quickly. When students did not receive quick responses, they would tend to e-mail the online help desk, which would notify staff at the CECC. We would provide responses and simultaneously use the opportunity to provide training to campus staff at the home schools. We realized that the home college staffs weren't uncaring, just ignorant of the many issues revolving around distance delivery in a consortial model.

What Worked/What Didn't. The students reported that the instruction they received was very high quality. The site provided for chat rooms, online lectures incorporating multimedia, ongoing threaded discussions with their instructors and other students, and online testing. The students commented that they liked the threaded discussions that "forced" them to be online at least once a week; they liked the ability to participate in classroom (threaded) discussions; and they felt confident that their instructors would take their responses seriously. Students liked the ability to interact one-on-one with the teacher through e-mail. They also appreciated the online tests and the immediate feedback provided on those tests, which were comprised of objective (true/false, multiple choice) questions. Essays and open-answer tests still required instructor intervention. Also, the online student services, such as advising and career counseling, were minor credits to the program: the key college contacts responded to student e-mail inquiries in a timely manner and with accurate information. Comments were generally favorable from students and advisors, but a comment that came up repeatedly was that we needed to provide online assessments and career interest inventory tests. Federal financial aid forms were available online, and the students expressed appreciation for the convenience. Following is a sampling of what students have said thus far regarding the quality:

I think this course is really excellent. The professor has made it very easy to follow and understand, and she is very accessible when I have problems.

I have been very surprised how easy it has been to follow. I think a person may learn more since they have to study more.

It is a great way to learn and get credit while you work.

Following are some comments from students about the advantages of taking the online courses:

The advantages for me are being able to be home for my children, able to take them to/from after-school activities, saving money and valuable time by not having to commute (which for me is 25 minutes one way to campus), and the quality of life for my entire family and myself. Even though it is more costly to take courses online, I'm thankful that I'm not away two to three nights per week and then having to spend the weekends working on homework and studying.

Flexibility—you can do the assignments at any time and at your own pace.

I can do it all at home, and I don't have to miss any work or make up work to take a few classes.

I can take these classes at home, which is perfect for me. I have a small child, I work full time, and I have a spouse in the military. Without online courses I would not be able to attend college.

The breakdown in student services occurred when students visited the actual campus offices and talked to other staff who were not designated key contacts. The program had moved so quickly from idea to inception that not everyone in any given department was trained to talk about it intelligently with students at the beginning. Although CECC moved quickly to get staff members up to speed by mailing program information to the colleges and providing on-campus training, it was still many months before all the staff members at the colleges were even aware of the existence of the program.

A larger problem occurred when students enrolled online but chose to visit their campus cashier department to pay. In some cases, the student would enroll online late in the evening or in the morning and then visit the college in the afternoon to pay. Their enrollment data had not yet been uploaded into the individual college databases, so there was no registration record on file requiring payment. This delay in records updating concerned students who were used to immediate updates of registration data. The site did not tell the students that it would take 24 to 48 hours to complete the transaction. (Subsequently, we took steps to provide this information on the Web site.) They were afraid that they might not have enrolled correctly online and that they might "lose their seat" due to course limits. In some cases, even when students waited a couple of days after online registration to pay, the data were not in the college database because the translation program designed to move the data from the vendor database to the college database had failed. The data translation failure occurred quite a few times in the fall of 1998 when the vendor upgraded the site with new software and added fields that the translation program was not written to accept. After a number of communications between the system computer services staff and vendor programming staff, the problem areas were uncovered and repaired.

A smaller, but nonetheless annoying, problem was that financial aid students could not use vouchers to purchase their books from the online bookstore. The student would request his or her home college bookstore to provide the book and if it was not in stock there, the student would have to wait one to two weeks while the book was placed on order. While the issue of providing books in a timely manner to students who wish to use vouchers is not completely resolved, we have listed all the books and ISBN numbers online so that students may order the books from their home college bookstore. There is generally a delay of a week or so if students choose to use their home college bookstores, but most students are happy to accept the delay if they can use their financial aid vouchers.

Student Services Trends

One of the major benefits of CCCOnline is that it has made the system colleges aware of the opportunities that exist to improve student services for all students, whether they take courses online or at a campus. As recently as early 1999, representatives from the 13 colleges gathered to discuss a collaborative initiative to upgrade student services through the use of technology. This discussion might not have been possible before CCCOnline. Change is always painful and sometimes risky, but the colleges recognize that while improvement may come at a cost, it is bearable and the colleges and the students can survive it. The system has made major changes in how and what it provides to students in terms of support services.

Student-Centered Vision: Implemented. From its inception, CCCOnline has had a student-centered vision. Not only was the learning designed to be anywhere, anytime, but student service functions were also designed to provide maximum convenience and consideration to students. Other distance education programs stressed the instructional component, but CCCOnline moved the system forward by insisting that all services for students were equally important.

Self-Service Objectives: Planning. The consensus is that we can provide additional options for students who feel confident and comfortable enough to proceed in their learning without much human intervention. We are now discussing creating online degree-planning forms. Students will fill in the classes they have taken, and a program will generate a list of additional classes that the student will need to take to complete the degree. The colleges also want to create databases of frequently asked questions that will be searchable using one to two key words.

Department Process Improvement: Implemented. The CCCOnline program was initially designed to centralize instruction and decentralize student service functions. As the program came online, it was apparent that some student service functions would have to be centralized also. When CCCOnline first started classes in January 1998, a 33-page document outlined the various grading options at the individual colleges. Some colleges did not allow an F, some did not allow an administrative withdrawal. Some colleges required 75 percent of a student's work to be done to receive an incomplete, some required 80 percent, and some required 90 percent. Recently, the colleges agreed upon a uniform grading policy, reducing the 33-page document to one page. The colleges also agreed on uniform grade change forms, withdrawal forms, and applications. These uniform grading policies and forms, while aimed specifically at online students, will eventually permeate to the student service departments and positively affect students in traditional classrooms as well.

Web-Enabled Services: Implemented. Admissions, registration, advising, financial aid, and billing are all possible on the CCCOnline Web site. There is agreement that improvements can and should be made, especially regarding financial aid. The consortium of colleges has recently applied to the U.S. Department of Education to be a pilot site to design a new set of financial aid rules for students taking courses on CCCOnline. In fact, CCCOnline is proud to say it has been instrumental in pushing the federal agency to rethink its policies. Billing also needs some improvement; the data flow from the vendor database to the individual college databases is not always seamless and clean, but system programmers, working with vendor programmers, are confident that these issues can be worked out in the near future.

One Web service that CCCOnline does not offer is career advising. However, the colleges all agree that this service is an important offering. Current discussions have centered on providing online assessments with electronic feedback from career counselors, interest inventory tests, and career information about the best locations for different jobs, salary ranges, and education required.

Systemic Change: Planning. CCCOnline can be credited as a driving force for change in our community college system. It has forced the individual colleges to think differently about the services they offer and when they offer them. It has laid the groundwork for other collaborative efforts amongst the colleges. As state funding becomes tighter and the colleges continue to deal with workforce development needs, they have begun to think in terms of creating shared statewide and regional offerings. Individual colleges have operated within their own service area lines for many years, but these lines are getting fuzzy as students begin to access colleges that are not in close geographic proximity to their homes.

Critical Success Factors and Key Considerations

As many colleges begin to look at forming consortia to provide high-quality student services and instruction, some key pieces should be examined before proceeding. College partners should ask themselves the following questions:

- Do we have a series of courses with the same course numbers, descriptions, credit hours, and outcomes and objectives that we will share and accept at our individual colleges?
- Do we have a uniform degree or certificate?
- Do we use or can we agree upon uniform
  - grading policies,
  - incomplete forms and guidelines for their use,
  - grade change forms,
  - withdrawal forms and guidelines for their use,
  - applications,
  - payment options, and
  - drop dates?
- Do we have a staff development plan in place to train campus staff to deal with online students?

Conclusion

Clearly, the implementation of CCCOnline taught us many lessons. Delivery of seamless student services online is difficult to manage. Even if CCCOnline were a single college, we would need to study processes we have used for many years to provide services to traditional campus students. Our campus-delivered services often do not translate well to an online environment. Students expect rapid responses to requests for academic and career advising, grades, assessments, transcript evaluations, and transcripts. In an online environment, student services staff cannot see the students to determine if they understand the information they receive. Everything is in print, and there is little margin for error: our student services staff must present clear, concise, and correct information so there is little or no room for student interpretation. For a

Student Services Trends

TRENDS	IMPLEMENTATION PHASE
Student-Centered	◑
Redesigned Services	N/A
One-Stop Service Center	N/A
Cross-Functional Teams	N/A
Self-Service Objectives	○
Department Process Improvements	◑
Web-Enabled Services	◑
Admissions	◑
Registration	◑
Advising	◑
Financial Aid	◑
Billing	◑
Career Services	○
Systemic Change	○
Replacement of Student Information Systems	N/A

Codes for Implementation Phase:

- ● Production
- ◑ Implementing
- ◐ Designed
- ○ Planning

consortium of colleges such as ours, these issues of service are multiplied by the number of schools in the consortium.

Every semester, enrollment is increasing in our online program, indicating that more students will take advantage of Internet course delivery. Students who have participated in online classes and choose to continue with online classes will become more technically savvy. Younger students will come to us with a high level of technical skills. It is of paramount importance to work toward solutions to online student service issues. Online students, dissatisfied with the student or instructional services they receive, can simply enroll in another college by logging onto its Web site. We want to prevent our students from choosing to enroll in another college and attract the students who have been less than happy with the services they have received from other online colleges.

Part 4:

Planning for Success: Key Considerations for Successful Transformation

16

Stephen W. Klenk

Customer-Based Transformation

Transform the Institution? Why?

For centuries, students have enrolled in institutions to explore new theories, discover new concepts, and gain new skills—and they will continue that same quest for learning for centuries to come. There are, of course, some significant differences between yesterday and today. The global economy, global technology, and global transportation now provide students with easy, fast, and affordable opportunities to quench their thirst for knowledge when they want it, anywhere in the world. Virtually thousands of excellent worldwide educational institutions, apprenticeships, corporate training programs, and distance learning opportunities are readily available to those students heretofore viewed as a captive market by institutions. Students are liberated by these choices, consumerism has gained a strong foothold in the industry, and the term "customer" has become the new moniker for students. The new students of the *Consumer Reports* generation make prefatory assessments of return on investment (ROI) before investing their time and money. ROI is measured according to the outcomes we produce, the prestige of our diplomas, and the perceived value of the overall learning experience.

How do we as educational institutions respond? We must transform ourselves from teaching captive students to understanding, responding to, and exceeding the needs of our student customers. We will evolve from viewing ourselves as regional or national monopolies

Stephen W. Klenk is a management consultant with IBM Global Education, helping colleges and universities design customer-focused student services. His 23 years in higher education include student services and information systems management at the University of Connecticut, Brandeis University, and Coopers and Lybrand. He holds a master's degree in college student personnel administration from Indiana University.

of intellectual capital to vigorous competitors for customers in the global marketplace. We will win in the marketplace when our programs and services are no longer invented solely by internal committees, but rather are planned in response to market forces and designed in collaboration with our student customers. This chapter illustrates how we can transform our institutions from traditional teaching institutions fighting for students to customer-based service organizations that offer the marketplace highly perceived ROI—and, consequently, long-term viability for our institutions.

Transformation: From What to What?

Transformation, redesign, reengineering, evolutionary change—whatever the term, the idea is to rethink the way we do everything on our campuses from the perspective of our students. It's about moving from teaching to learning, from seeing students as a captive audience to collaborative partners, and from selling programs and services to responding to market demand. Transformation is about the following:

- Rethinking what we want our institutions to become
- Identifying who our student customers should be
- Determining which programs and services they will buy from someone
- Deciding which of those programs and services we will offer
- Redesigning (or creating) those programs and services based on our student customers' definitions of quality
- Ensuring that our employees have the right skills to implement and deliver the new customer-based programs and services
- Building the appropriate technology infrastructure to support the new "anytime, anywhere" information needs of today's consumers

- Gathering appropriate ongoing feedback to measure progress and continue to improve in the eyes of our student customers

Why Customer-Based?

From campus to campus, the term "customer" refers to everything from our raison d'etre to a dirty word that interferes with all that has been so good for so long. In this book, "customer" refers to the recipient and ultimate evaluator of all of the goods we produce and the services we deliver. The customers who assess ROI are normally external to our campuses. They include prospects, students, feeder schools, businesses that send us students and/or hire our graduates, schools at which our students enroll once they leave our institutions, accrediting and licensing bodies, agencies from which we receive funding, and the board to which we report our status. As we consider transforming our campuses to become world-class customer service organizations, we must also consider the needs of our internal customers, those employees who design and deliver our curriculum and support services. This chapter assumes that our key customer is the student and, as such, the term "customer-based" should be considered synonymous with "student-based," "student-focused," and "student-defined."

The movie *Field of Dreams* suggests that "If we build it, they will come." This may be the case, but our student customers won't stay with us or return to us unless they believe that they are receiving better quality and service for the investment than they can receive elsewhere. Do not make the mistake of factoring student loyalty into your formula for retention—if your competitor offers better quality or service for the price, your student customers will leave to join the competitor. "In today's marketplace, it's no longer a question of *caveat emptor*, but of *caveat factor*" (Champy 1995, 17). We earn loyalty from our student customers by demonstrating our commitment to understanding and meeting their needs as consumers. If we are able to provide them with the choices they expect from our institution, they will not only come, they will stay and return as lifelong learners. And as our best recruiters, they will convince others of the benefits of attending our institutions.

After All These Years, Don't We Know What Our Student Customers Want?

So often we hear, "We don't have to conduct all those surveys and run those focus groups to find out what our student customers want. We know what they want." Or, "It isn't about what they want. It's about what they need, and we know what they need. After all that's why they come to us." Or, "Why change? The number of complaints has gone down, so we must be doing something right."

Becoming complacent—and losing in the marketplace—is the risk we take when we don't reconcile everything we do to what our student customers expect us to do. Believing that our campus, unchanged, will continue to thrive as it has over the past century brings an inordinate level of risk to the institution. Tuition and fees have escalated well beyond the ability of many consumers to pay, the Internet is bringing opportunistic competitors into our backyard via distance learning, and deferred maintenance on our campuses is claiming an ever-increasing portion of our budget. As a result we are forced to make tough budgetary choices that will allow us to invest our available funds in those programs and services that yield the greatest ROI for our institution.

How do we effectively prioritize our investments? We ask our student customers what is important to them, what services they expect to receive from us, and how well we are doing in their eyes. As the ultimate evaluators of all that we do, our student customers come to us to fulfill their dreams. They expect us to help them gain the knowledge and skills they will need in order to pursue future career opportunities and/or graduate study. They want to learn from our faculty, not to stand in lines. They expect to take advantage of our learning opportunities, lab facilities, and library resources, not to be placed on hold when they call, to encounter a closed registration office while evening classes are still in session, or to be referred to a supervisor by an employee who is not authorized to make decisions. If we ask our student customers what is important to them and determine what is not being performed to their satisfaction, we will quickly arrive at the list of programs and services that warrant careful consideration for investment. It's not "If we build it, they will come"; rather, it's "If we ask them, and then build what they asked us to build, they will come!"

How Do We Determine What Kind of Customer Service Organization We Should Become?

Before heading down the path of hiring new employees, building training plans, rethinking processes, or buying software, it is paramount that we clearly communicate our vision for customer service. A well-conceived vision, coupled with specific goals for delivering service to our student customers, will serve as the guidepost for all of the institution's transformation strategies. It will focus the activities on improving the institution in the eyes of our student customers, help the institution reconcile all strategic and tactical initiatives to their impact on meeting students' expectations, and help the institution choose between competing priorities for investment.

A broad spectrum of the institution's managers, service providers, and student customers should build the customer service vision and goals statement. They should develop it during a facilitated workshop that allows uninhibited expression of opinions by all participants. Techniques to gather anonymous opinions of institutional strengths and problems should be employed. The workshop might include small group breakout sessions and a healthy challenge for each group to define the attributes of world-class customer service (with a prize for the winning group as agreed upon by all of the participants). The point here is not to "tow the company line," but rather to create an opportunity to break free of the cultural ties that bind us to the old ways of doing business. The best components of each group's work can then be merged into the institution's customer service vision and goals.

Participants should explore a good balance of customer service examples from higher education as well as from outside our industry. We have a lot to learn about customer service from our corporate cousins. For example, the Nordstrom company structure is represented by an inverted triangle that places customers on top and the board of directors on the bottom ("We all work for the customers"). The company's employee handbook consists of a single five-by-eight-inch card that reads in its entirety as follows:

> Welcome to Nordstrom. We're glad to have you with our Company. Our number one goal is to provide outstanding customer service. Set both your personal and professional goals high. We have great confidence in your ability to achieve them.

> **Nordstrom Rules:**
> Rule #1: Use your good judgment in all situations. There will be no additional rules.

> Please feel free to ask your department manager, store manager or division general manager any question at any time.

Nordstrom encourages its employees:

> "You get a lot of operational freedom here; no one will be directing your every move, and you're only limited by your ability to perform (within the bounds of the Nordstrom way, of course). But if you're not willing to do whatever it takes to make a customer happy—to personally deliver a suit to his room, get down on your knees to fit a shoe, force yourself to smile when a customer is a real jerk—then you just don't belong here, period. Nobody *tells* you to be a customer service hero; it's just sort of expected." (Levering and Moskowitz 1993, 327–332)

The institution's final customer service vision should be short, compelling, clearly understood, widely communicated, and contin-

uously preached. It should become part of the institution's published literature; its Web page; and all communications with future, current, and past students. It should become the new mantra for all of the institution's stakeholders, a key tenet of the new culture. The five to 10 customer service goals, while more specific than the vision, nonetheless should also be widely publicized and communicated. If the authors of the customer service vision and goals feel ownership for their creation, they will champion the benefits of customer service to the campus community, and they will ensure that all future activities and plans reconcile to the values set forth by that vision and those goals.

Great, We Have the Customer Service Vision and Goals. Where Does Transformation Begin?

Using the newly crafted vision and goals as a starting point, a team of customer service disciples should brainstorm all of the possible services that each student customer might want or expect. Such services might include providing (1) the choice for updating student information via the Web (self help) or receiving personalized attention to solve problems, (2) a single campus location for students to receive answers to most of their questions, and/or (3) online library resources and services for anywhere, anytime research and study. The goal should be to refine the list down to 20 to 30 possible services so that a survey or focus session guide can be built and used to gather student customer input.

During the survey or focus session, the student customers should indicate *how important* each of the services is to them for each set of services (e.g., 4 = critical, 3 = important, 2 = unimportant, 1 = irrelevant). Also, they should indicate how well the institution is currently performing each of the services (e.g., 4 = excellent, 3 = good, 2 = fair, 1 = unacceptable, N/A = not *currently performing* the service). It is important to also ask the student customers to prioritize their top five ("If we could only deliver five of these services to you, which five should those be?"). This addresses our inability to prioritize among the services if the respondents rank every service a "4" (critical), which they so often do!

The results can then be plotted for each service on a graph, with *Importance* on the Y-axis from low to high and *Performance* on the X-axis from low (and N/A) to high. The transformation priority projects become those services that our student customers rank as very high in importance and low (or N/A) in performance. Services identified as highly important *and* performing well are usually included among our niches and become our opportunities to market the great news about our institution. All services ranked as unimportant by our student customers should become possible candidates for automation, elimination, or outsourcing. If our student customers don't care if they receive those services, why should we continue to invest in those areas? One important note—we should look at those service areas ranked unimportant and well performing. After they have been automated, eliminated, or outsourced, we should consider reassigning the managers and operators of those areas to our priority project transformation teams. After all, if they have "made a silk purse out of a sow's ear" (i.e., while working with irrelevant or unappreciated services), imagine what they will be able to accomplish when charged with improving an area of service that is highly regarded and sought by our student customers!

How Do We Start to Transform Any of the Priority Service Areas?

Assign a transformation team, comprised of creative free thinkers unencumbered by historical norms and analytical people who will be able to help bring the design to implementation. Be sure to include a cross section of your institution's stakeholders on the team—managers, front liners, advisors, faculty, students, and business partners. Don't forget to involve all unions early in the planning process; they will want to be part of the planning and will contribute positively if invited to participate up front. Obtain assurance from everyone prior to joining the team that they will be willing to set aside current politics, policies, and cultural barriers to change in order to build the institution's new customer service organization.

The team should *not* spend an inordinate amount of time mapping and analyzing current processes. You are not there to focus on the current but rather to envision the future. The team should quickly define the current processes at a medium level, identify the external and internal customers of each subprocess within the major process, and identify the outputs from each subprocess. This is to ensure that as you redesign the process (1) you do not forget to consider critical subprocesses and (2) you have a full menu of outputs from which you can prioritize those outputs truly valued and sought by your student customers.

The team, working with critical outputs as a starting point, should be challenged to create the best process it can in order to deliver the needed outputs. "Best" might well be defined after a discussion of best practices both within higher education and outside of the higher education industry. Do not overlook pockets of excellence that already exist on your campus; there are areas where best practices have quietly been in place for years. Hint: Check out the continuing/extended education and branch campus service providers in your institution. They have likely been wearing multiple hats and providing one-stop services to students for many years. Perhaps their tried-and-true processes are worthy of being replicated campuswide.

Redesigning your key processes is a time for creativity, fun, and healthy competition. As done during the customer service vision process, split the team into breakout groups and challenge them to design (at a high level) the world's greatest registration (or admission or financial planning) process. The design work might be segmented to organize and focus the analysis. For example, the criteria for redesign might include the following:

- *Process management (customer service delivery):* how the customer service processes will be designed and managed to exceed student customer requirements and continuously improve quality and operational performance
- *High performance work systems:* how the work, job design, and compensation/recognition structure will encourage all employees to contribute effectively to exceeding student customers' expectations
- *Employee education, training, and development:* how the education and training programs will enhance the institution's capabilities and contribute to employee motivation, progression, and development
- *Employee well-being and satisfaction:* how the institution will maintain a work environment conducive to the well-being of all employees

Campuswide buy-in to the new customer-based organization will only come about through nonstop leadership, communication, training, and employee recognition. Invite all campus stakeholders to attend regularly scheduled focus sessions and campus "town meetings" to provide feedback on the design, to ask questions, to raise any fears about the change being undertaken, and to stimulate unplanned innovation. Strive to answer the questions and to address the fears during those meetings. Publicly acknowledge the high value of all campus stakeholders suggesting new ways to improve customer service ("There are no bad ideas!"), and reward, rather than criticize or judge, all suggestions for innovation. Post the feedback, suggestions, questions, and answers on the Web, and publish them in a monthly newsletter. Do this right and you're on your way to effectively managing the toughest part of transformation—the people part.

After Redesigning the Process, What's Next?

Now that we have designed a set of processes that meet or exceed student customer expectations—fast and easy processes that provide accessible, accurate, complete, and consistent information—we need to create the organization that is up to the task of delivering world-class service to those student customers. Roles and responsibilities associated with each process must be identified, required skills must be defined, available skills must be assessed, skill gaps must be identified, and new skills must be acquired through retraining and/or hiring.

If our best practice customer service organization includes one-stop shopping and single-point-of-contact information, some of the skill-building considerations include cross-training of employees, mentoring and coaching, customer service training, technology training, team building, and team evaluation procedures.

It is during the skills assessment, team building, and retraining of employees that time and compassion must come into play. Plan to phase in changes to your employees' roles and responsibilities. Build a plan over 12 to 18 months during which your employees are provided opportunities to integrate into the new customer service organization at their own pace. For example, you might want to prototype the changes with a controlled cohort of students (e.g., one academic department) and a few excited employees during the first six months, testing out and refining the new processes and practices. The second six months may be an opportunity for more employees to receive training and participate in the new service center, one-stop shop, or welcome center. Finally, you should plan to have all employees adequately trained and integrated during months 13 through 18.

How Do We Optimize Our Chances for Success?

Customer-based transformation requires a clearly communicated need for change, a customer service vision for the institution, and a willingness by all campus stakeholders to forgo power and individual perks for the good of the institution and its students. The critical success factors for customer-based transformation are as follows:

- Verifying (and/or redefining if appropriate) the institution's *mission, vision, values, and goals for customer service.*
- Building a *strategic plan* to clarify the institution's direction, prioritize and focus institutional investments, provide a highly specific road map for achieving the institution's vision and goals for customer service, and define measurable outcomes for each strategy.
- Developing *formative measures* for monitoring each strategy's activities during implementation and progress toward the completion of project milestones. Formative measures help keep the project focused on "in-scope" activities, managed within budget and completed on time.
- Developing *summative measures* for evaluating performance and accountability by operating units and individuals after the new processes have been implemented. Summative measures help ensure that the implemented processes continue to meet and/or exceed customers' expectations, that employees'

behaviors contribute optimally to the success of the operating unit and the institution at large, and that customers continue to view the institution as a customer-based organization.

- Establishing *cross-functional redesign and implementation teams* comprised of representatives from all service areas and processes affected by the redesign. The teams should be comprised of student service employees, faculty and professional advisors, other service providers, business partners, and, of course, student customers. The team members should bring a variety of creative, technical, and analytical skills, and a collaborative spirit; be assigned on a full-time basis for the duration of the project; and be empowered by the project's sponsors to identify issues, evaluate alternatives, and make decisions on behalf of the institution. Part-time subject matter experts should also be identified and scheduled for participation on an ad hoc and/or activity-by-activity basis. All members of the team should be introduced and recognized for their planned contribution during the project's kickoff in a town meeting setting.
- Preparing *change management plans* that help ensure ongoing communication of project activities via a variety of media to support stakeholders' diverse learning styles; solicit feedback and suggestions from all stakeholders; and provide training opportunities for employees and students to learn new processes, responsibilities and required skills.
- Engaging *change consultants* independent of the institution who can facilitate the transformation process without institutional bias, identify and help overcome cultural and/or political barriers to change, and bring a time-tested approach for planning and conducting the transformation project. The institution is typically best served by using experienced consultants to facilitate the institution's definition of the vision, goals, and strategies; help the project team redesign its processes, organization, use of facilities, and technology enablers; develop an implementation plan that minimizes risk to the institution; help ensure a smooth, phased implementation of the changes through effective project management and change management; and train employees and help ensure that required planning, design, implementation, and operating skills are successfully transferred from the consultant to the institution's employees.
- Ensuring that *committed executive leaders* publicly "champion" the vision and mission-criticality of the desired changes, allocate the necessary financial support, and guarantee the availability of required resources throughout the project and after the changes have been implemented.

Design your new customer service environment based on your student customers' expectations, pay careful attention to the change-related needs of your employees, ensure that you continue to exceed student customers' expectations, measure your ongoing success (if you only measure one thing, make it student customer satisfaction), and continuously improve your process performance. The result will be an institution transformed to that of world-class stature—a truly best practice competitor in a truly competitive world.

REFERENCES

Champy, James. 1995. *Reengineering Management: The Mandate for New Leadership.* New York: Harper Business.

Collins, James C., and Jerry I. Porras. 1994. *Built to Last— Successful Habits of Visionary Companies.* New York: Harper Collins.

Levering, Robert, and Milton Moskowitz. 1993. *The 100 Best Companies to Work for in America.* New York: Doubleday Currency.

17

Earl H. Potter III

Change Management

The Case for Change Management

Of the higher education leaders I have worked with over the last few years, some have been familiar with the idea of change management and some have not. Those unfamiliar with the concept have often asked about the difference between project management and change management. Many of those who have been successful throughout their careers—without change management—have also asked why they need change management now.

"Change management" is the term for the act of attending to the human processes involved in bringing about change. "Project management," on the other hand, is the management of the tasks that must be accomplished to bring about change. The difference is a matter of perspective or focus. For example, people in the middle of change are most in focus when they resist change. The challenge of change management is to understand enough about the way people behave during change to anticipate and plan for that behavior. If you do this well, people become a transparent element of the change process. If you do not do this well, resistance to change may be all that you can see.

Most leaders who are successful at change management have successfully led complicated projects before. However, they might not be able to tell you what they did in order to be effective. In addition, in large change projects it is not enough to have a few skilled people in leadership positions. The ability to manage change must be distributed widely throughout the organization. Leaders

who have led change successfully but who cannot teach others how to do the same may find that the project as a whole suffers for lack of widely distributed leadership and change management skills.

One way to provide for project and change management leadership throughout the organization is to develop change management skills and commitment among line managers in the organization. Another way to support distributed leadership is to train and commission "change agents" who are experts in change management to serve as a resource for line leaders. Human resource managers often fill this role in organizations. But it is important not to confuse the roles of leading and supporting change. Neither consultants nor human resource staff can successfully lead a major institutional change project. This is not because they don't know how to lead such a project; it is because they don't have the formal authority or the right to lead it. In the end, both skill and authority are necessary to bring about change.

A significant investment in change management is not necessary in every change project. For example, if you have the power to compel change successfully, it might not make sense to invest time or money in surveys to understand employee attitudes. Likewise, if a project is very costly but has wide support and does not require that employees learn new skills, human behavior may not play a part in the success of the project. For example, building and staffing the new campuses of state systems in Arizona, California, and Washington did not require change management.

However, change management can represent a significant component of the budget for change in an organization. And it is often possible to compel change only in emergencies when people cede their right to participate in decisions to leaders who can act decisively. Following the earthquake at California State University,

Earl H. Potter III is dean of the School of Management at Lesley College and the former director of organizational development and employment services at Cornell University. He received his Ph.D. in organizational psychology from the University of Washington in 1978.

Northridge, President Blenda Wilson had this freedom. But it is a rare example. Thus, an investment in change management makes sense any time (1) the results of the project are of essential importance to the future of the organization and (2) people's failure to change can derail the project.

This investment in change management has occurred at most of the colleges and universities whose projects are described in this book. But when the IBM Best Practice Partner group first met, most partners were focused on the technical aspects of their projects. However, after four years of work together, nearly every partner identified issues of human behavior as the most persistent challenges. To some degree this is the result of a natural change in focus over time, as projects have moved from design phases to implementation phases. Yet in every case in which human behavior has become an issue in the success of a project, the project leader has acknowledged that earlier attention to these issues could have made a difference.

In short, each of the projects described in this book is among the best in North America. The leaders of these projects include functional specialists, vice presidents of finance and administration, information technology specialists, and systems analysts. They are the best, and they agree that effective leadership, appropriate training, shared understanding, sustained energy, positive attitudes toward change, and a commitment to excellent student service are critical success factors in the projects that they lead. All of these require effective change management.

Before You Start

Some colleges and universities face more difficult challenges than others in implementing 21st century student service practices. Some institutions, in fact, should not undertake a major change initiative at all until leaders have created a culture that is ready for change. However, even an institution that is not fully ready for change has a higher probability of success with effective change management. Therefore, when an institution must change, it might be best to begin even under conditions that most would consider risky.

Most institutions thinking about major change start from positions that are similar to those of the three following types of institutions. Thinking about these three types might help you to assess the challenges that you face.

- *Leading institution.* Employees in a leading institution have had successful experiences with large-scale change. Managers lead and employees work with a focus on results. Leaders support substantial, ongoing investments in staff development, and these investments are both targeted and evaluated by referring to widely understood and accepted personal evaluation and development processes. The philosophy of

the organization could be described as market oriented, and systems are in place to identify and adopt best practices. Information flows easily throughout the organization, and governance systems are strong and proactive. Knowledge and expertise are valued wherever they are found in the organization, and boundaries between units are permeable. Flexibility and speed are understood as giving the organization a competitive advantage. The budget is balanced, and resources are available to invest in new initiatives.

- *Model institution.* This institution has a healthy position in its market. Solid program evaluation processes are in place, and the organization has the resources to support change. Governance systems are functional and responsive. Leaders are competent, and employees are effective when assessed against familiar standards of excellence. The goals of the institution include being among the best. Units perform specialized functions, but managers and employees are willing to collaborate when required to do so. Employees have the information they need to do their jobs. This organization watches and learns from its peers, which include the best colleges and universities.

- *Following institution.* This institution operates in a catch-up mode. It has marginal financial flexibility and is likely to have numerous instances of "deferred human resource maintenance." Shared governance systems are weak, and relationships across institutional boundaries can be contentious. Employees and managers tend to be inwardly focused. Routine work takes most of the available energy, and change leaves everyone exhausted. Information is hard to get, and more silos exist than on a dairy farm. This institution is, however, fully accredited and possibly has a long history.

Few institutions fall neatly into just one of these categories. In fact, in large institutions different units might fall into different categories. Nevertheless, the more your institution looks like a leading institution, the greater your chances of success in bringing about change. The more your institution looks like a following institution, the more active change management will be essential. The model institution is the most puzzling case. Such an institution has all of the hallmarks of strength yet may not be ready for change. If you find yourself in a model institution, you should carefully assess your institution's readiness for change before deciding how large an investment you will need to make in change management.

Know Where You Are Going

Readiness for change begins with a clear definition of the goals of change. People's inclination to resist change and, in particular, change that threatens their control over their environment cannot be evaluated in the abstract. People have to know what changes they are being asked to make before leaders can determine how much resistance there will be. This task poses one of the greatest challenges for planners. In most student service reengineering projects, specific targets cannot be set until analysis and design phases have been completed. Therefore, at the beginning of a project it is much easier to say, for example, that the goal is to reduce costs than to say that the goal is to cut costs by 20 percent and eliminate 50 jobs.

Thus, it seems that it may be impossible to do what should be done. However, we know that the longer employees know that change is coming without knowing what the change will be, the higher their anxiety. That is why Boston College (chapter 5) promised that it would not lay off employees as it worked to cut costs. That is also the reason Babson College (chapter 4) created a broad competency model early in the project to which selection, training, performance management, and compensation strategies were tied. With strategies like this, it is possible to define goals for change that leave room for the processes that will further define those goals. To do this, however, human resource managers must be involved in the earliest stages of planning the project. The goals of the project will then include financial goals, customer service goals, goals for process improvements, *and* goals that define the changes people need to make to be successful in the organization that will emerge as the project moves forward.

Initial goal statements will not answer all employee questions. Therefore, some anxiety will always be associated with a project. However, proactive commitments to people at the beginning of a project can be combined with broad financial goals in ways that enable leaders to assess the magnitude of change that the organization and its people must accomplish. If goals can be stated, measurements can be created for those goals. It will be these measurements that define success, focus attention, and shape behavior during the project.

Don't Confuse Support for Change With Agreement on What Must Change

One of the best tools available to bring different kinds of measurements together is from Kaplan and Norton's *The Balanced Scorecard: Translating Strategy into Action* (1996). The balanced scorecard integrates measures that assess financial performance, customer satisfaction, work processes, and employee growth and learning. The last two measures focus on developing capacity that ensures future performance, while financial performance and customer satisfaction measures give information about past performance. Oregon State University's change project is an excellent example of a project

with goals that require this kind of measurement (chapter 8). The university's fundamental goal was to increase enrollment, in part by increasing customer satisfaction with services. To do this, staff relations and business processes had to be changed. These four areas of focus correspond to every quadrant of the balanced scorecard. Enrollment and customer satisfaction tracked past success. And, while change was ongoing, improved staff relations and decreases in cycle times documented changes that predicted future successes.

The more clearly leaders state their objectives, the more clearly they can document success. And an early, documented indication of success is one of the most powerful forces for building support for change. Moreover, a strong measurement strategy is the best protection against the judgment that "if you don't know where you are going, any way will get you there." It may seem obvious, then, that agreement on the objectives of a change project is the most important first step and that measuring progress toward those objectives is the obvious next step. However, many projects begin with only the most general agreement on the objectives of the project.

Consider the possibility that you might discover the need for policy changes in order to make changes in systems that support student services. At Cornell University, major project delays resulted when emerging designs required a reconsideration of policies that controlled access to student information. The ensuing debate could have been avoided if an early conversation about project goals had addressed goals for access to information. Of course, the conversation would have had to include representatives of the faculty, who later blocked change until faculty issues were addressed. Their inclusion in earlier conversations would have made those conversations more difficult. Nevertheless, when agreement was reached, the project could have proceeded without delay and the goodwill created by the early inclusion of the faculty might have made other potentially difficult conversations easier. The choice to open debate and raise the potential for conflict is one that project leaders sometimes avoid. (See chapter 5 for Boston College's description of the strategy project leaders chose to avoid a contentious debate.) Avoidance of confrontation may work on some campuses, but it may be the kiss of death on others.

An institution that uses the balanced scorecard as the framework for discussing goals will be forced, early in the project, to gain consensus on the purposes of the project. These purposes will include goals that easily win support and those that reveal underlying disagreements about the way the institution should be run. The foundation of any successful change project is a compelling case for change. However, as Babson College's experience shows, general support for improving efficiency and reducing costs may not indicate support for the major cultural transformation that project leaders envision. It may be difficult to reach consensus concerning the specific, desired outcomes of a change project. However, failure to obtain agreement on key objectives at the outset will only raise project costs in the long run. Disagreement concerning goals that erupts in the middle of a project can even destroy the project entirely.

Understand the Process of Change in a Major Change Effort

Readiness for change also requires that leaders have realistic and appropriate expectations about what it means to navigate change successfully. Even the most successful best practice partners note that employees were at times fearful or angry. The reactions of leaders to these feelings were not the same, however. At Seton Hall University (chapter 3), leaders trying to avoid layoffs experienced this pain directly. At Babson College, on the other hand, project leaders who knew what to expect reacted calmly to employee anxiety. Both were successful, but the costs to individuals and the organization at Seton Hall University was probably higher than at Babson College. Moreover, if you read closely, you will notice that the expectations of Babson College leaders pushed them to create a leadership and communication plan in anticipation of the stresses of change that enabled the organization to ride through the storm of change with somewhat greater confidence.

The change leader who knows what to expect of people during change first understands the process of change. The following outlines what we know about the way individuals deal with organizational change:

- ■ Change is a process in which people leave the present and move over time into the future.
  - • Personal change can involve learning new skills, seeing familiar challenges in new ways, developing new relationships, finding the way around new spaces, and meeting new performance expectations.
- ■ Change is always happening.
  - • We are not always aware of change as it happens.
- ■ Every change has real personal costs.
  - • All change requires adjustment, and adjustment takes energy.
  - • Just how much energy any one change takes depends on how threatening the change is to the individual who is required to change.
  - • Change that doesn't take place at work still makes demands on employees.
- ■ Given the cost of change, it is natural for people to resist change.
- ■ Resistance is greatest when change means that a person will lose control, influence, and/or status.
- ■ Resistance also occurs when a change is positive.

- • With every change there is uncertainty.
- • Positive change requires an investment before the returns come in.
- ■ Our experience with change shapes our attitude toward change.
  - • Our energy is not unlimited. It is possible for organizations to undertake so much change that available energies are exhausted.
  - • Change that succeeds for the organization at the expense of individual employees may create attitudes that make the next change more difficult.
  - • Positive experience with change creates an expectation of success that increases the energy available for the next change.
  - • Positive feelings about change result from being successful even when the process of changing has involved fear, anxiety, and anger.
- ■ The true cost of change to an organization cannot be evaluated without good performance measures.
  - • Some organizations cannot "go out of business." It is possible for these organizations to permanently fail without leaders losing their jobs or even being aware that their organizations are not effective.
  - • Organizations with underutilized staff cannot track time spent at the water cooler.
- ■ Effectively managed change adds value to an organization.
  - • Results are achieved faster with lower costs.
  - • The organization will be better prepared for the next change.

A careful consideration of the list suggests several conclusions: (1) complex organizational change is likely to be messy and difficult, (2) it is not possible to keep everyone happy while you negotiate a long and complicated path toward change, (3) leaders are responsible for accomplishing the objectives of change while at the same time making the best use of the organization's resources, including human resources, and (4) leaders are more likely to be able to accomplish #3 if they can clearly define and measure success.

With a clear understanding of how change happens in organizations, leaders can define objectives for an organization's human resource systems that support and track change management effectiveness. Then, whether an organization is leading or following, project leaders have some chance of bringing employees through the change successfully. Without both a clear understanding of how change happens and clear objectives for the effective management of human resources during change, some level of success may still be possible. However, each of our best practice partners would now predict that under these conditions, unpleasant surprises will occur, the costs of change will be higher, and project timelines will be extended. Some organizations—those who define success as meeting project goals on time and within budget—would no longer call such a project successful. And some academic institutions could not afford to continue to pursue the original objectives of the project.

Critical Success Factors for Successful Change Management

Managing Ambiguity. Project leaders who have written chapters for this book have identified critical success factors for their projects. Not all of these factors are related to the human processes that have to be managed during change, but many are. In fact, one critical success factor Oregon State University identified could nearly substitute as a definition of change management. The "management of ambiguity" addresses the fundamental need that people have to imagine themselves as successful in the new organization. It is not enough to convince employees that the organization must change. Employees must see how they are going to get from where they are to where you want them to go. If you are successful in defining a compelling vision of the future, some employees will find their own way there, others will need a guide, and still others will decide not to go. Successful change leaders reward those who make the journey on their own, provide support for those who need help, and say goodbye to those who choose not to go. The effective management of ambiguity leaves no doubt in anyone's mind concerning how leaders will respond to employees in any of these three situations.

Sustained Leadership. For change to occur, leaders must lead change, not just support it. Presidents who are engaged in leading change are visible and present. Successful leaders in the midst of creating new organizations do not spend all of their time on big picture and strategic issues. They pay attention to the details of making change work by showing up at staff meetings and demanding results from managers who enact plans. For example, Dave Hollowell, the executive vice president at the University of Delaware (chapter 10), and Keith Pedersen, vice president for administration at the Southern Alberta Institute of Technology (SAIT) (chapter 7), act as if their own jobs depend on the success of the project.

It is not difficult to get this level of commitment at the beginning of most projects. The greater challenge is gaining sustained commitment for the life of a project, which may last three to five years. Sustained leadership is most apparent at Boston College, the University of Delaware, SAIT, and Oregon State University. These institutions are also further along in the change process, so sustained leadership is more visible. In all of these cases, student service projects were set in the context of university-wide presidential initiatives. The presidential initiative in each case pushed the infor-

mation system and human resource management changes that the student service projects needed to be successful. In each of these cases, presidents believed that the success of the initiative was essential for the university to succeed in the future.

In support of their initiatives, they selected and prepared other leaders who would assist in leading change. In fact, the ability to lead change was the primary reason those leaders were selected. Furthermore, the following two themes are consistent across all of the best practice projects:

- To sustain change leadership, leadership must be widely shared.
- It is easier to select new leaders than to keep satisfied, entrenched leaders.

This strategy is subject to one common pitfall, however. The leaders who are chosen must have the authority to lead. It does not help to put the associate director on the design team while leaving the "old" director in place to implement the change.

What if you are one of those leaders in the middle and you recognize that there is an absence of leadership from the top? All of us who have been engaged in the best practice project have been asked what middle managers can do about this situation. The simple answer is to choose one of three alternatives: (1) persuade the boss that the project will fail without his or her engagement, (2) recognize the limits of what is possible with limited leadership commitment and make that work, or (3) find a new job.

Communication. Every successful project has created effective strategies for communicating project objectives, progress during the project, and information that employees need to find their place in the new organization. The most effective strategies provide for face-to-face, two-way communication. Newsletters, Web pages, and presentations all have their place, but substantive exchange (e.g., town meetings) between leaders and followers marks successful organizations.

This work is too important to be delegated to professional communication staffs. First, the most important information that leaders can receive is freely given by employees in the process of resisting change. However, many organizations try to "manage" resistance out of existence. If the case for change is truly compelling (and sometimes it really is not compelling), objections to change carry information about potential problems or needs for assistance that managers need to know. The fact that leaders care enough to listen wins a certain amount of sympathetic support. Real action on what leaders hear wins even more. Second, it is difficult for even the most honest communication professional to resist putting a positive spin on the news. Employees who are worried about what change means to them can spot a less-than-candid response to their questions. Finally, building trust within an organization that you hope to lead through change is too important a task to delegate.

A different aspect of communication is involved in making sure that information flows freely across all the boundaries within the organization. Every unit engaged in planning for and implementing change will need more and better information about what others do than they have ever had before. Any cultural barriers to the sharing of information can be deadly. Creating a collaborative culture where one did not exist before is the task of leaders who are laying the groundwork for change. Some of the problem-solving strategies that change leaders use in reengineering projects actually do this quite well. You will notice that Boston College and the University of Delaware chose to map existing work processes as a way of educating employees and discovered along the way that employees liked understanding their jobs in a larger context and solving problems with more complete information. The resulting sense of shared success increased the commitment to further collaboration. SAIT and Seton Hall University, on the other hand, achieved the same sense of synergy in the process of reinvention. In fact, both institutions avoided mapping existing processes for fear that a focus on the past would slow the project. In the process of doing the work that must be done, people learn the skills they need to work effectively in the new culture.

Involvement. The projects described in this book took a variety of approaches to the involvement of stakeholders. SAIT included students (learners) in its redesign team. Babson College began by organizing a team of executive team members and later added staff members and a faculty member when it realized that the executives did not know enough about how the work was done. Boston College avoided the use of consultants whenever possible and instead relied on the insight and experience of employees. For Boston College, this choice was a calculated statement of confidence that enhanced the usual benefits of employee involvement.

The choice to work with the institution's current resources or bypass the leaders and staff is one of the most difficult puzzles leaders have to face early in the life of a change project. A number of best practice partners determined that the leaders in place could not lead change. On the other hand, the University of Delaware chose to work with leaders in place even though it was apparent that they were not used to working as a team. Poor teamwork was attributed to poor systems and lack of training. Oregon State University also made the choice to work with the leaders in place. Leaders there believed that an awkward structure and inefficient work process were the cause of poor staff relations. In both cases, active involvement in planning for change revealed employees who cared a great deal about their work and who were frustrated at their own inability to do a good job due to systems they could not control. Reengineered jobs freed them from routine tasks and enabled them to do more demanding tasks more effectively.

These lessons pose tough questions for project leaders. Every manager can recite the benefits of employee involvement; the chief benefit is that involved employees will buy into decisions that they have helped make. On the other hand, how many managers will allow employees to plan for change when they perceive those employees as part of what needs to be changed? It is true that some employees prefer familiar, less-effective old processes to threatening, more-effective new processes. But good leadership can help even the most change-resistant employees understand the need for change. Involvement will enable more employees to move forward with the organization. How much involvement can the organization afford? And what will be lost if the investment is not made? Any college or university will be able to answer those questions if it already has a proactive approach to the management of human resources.

A Proactive Human Resource Management Strategy. Every best practice partner has realized that employees need a different kind of competence to work successfully in the organizations that are emerging from change. The development of competency models for organizations of the future is itself a key institutional competence for organizations that can manage change effectively. These models allow employees to assess whether they have what it will take to be successful in the new organization. They also allow organizations to evaluate the match between the staffing requirements of the new organization and the strength of the human assets they have in place. The most effective organizations have a human resource management capability that is ahead of the organization's need for change leadership. It is unfortunate that many human resource units in higher education are more suited to the task of managing routines than of leading change.

In 1998, the best practice partners asked for help in taking stock of the human resource management strategy that supported their change efforts. Some, like Babson College, Boston College, and Carnegie Mellon University (chapter 6), had close partnerships with human resource leaders from the start of their projects. At Boston College and Oregon State University, university-wide change initiatives led to stronger, integrated human resource management strategies and practices. This was not the case for all.

In organizations with strong and proactive human resource management strategies, the culture is more likely to fit the description of a leading institution than a model or following institution. Assessing the effectiveness of an institutional human resource management strategy includes a list of best practices. It also includes the results of those practices, characteristics of cultures that manage change effectively. The following list was created to help best practice partners take stock. It includes both characteristics of change-friendly cultures and the human resource management practices that support such cultures. This list can also serve as a useful guide for planning the steps that will lead to more effective change management.

- If you answer "yes," or if you don't know the answer, to the following questions, you need a strong, proactive human resource management capability in place to manage change effectively.
  - Will the changes in job roles that will result from this project require major changes in the skill sets that student service staff members need to do their jobs?
  - Will anyone lose a job as a result of this project?
  - Will employees lose some things, other than their jobs, that are important to them as a result of this project?

- The degree to which the following statements characterize your institution indicate how well suited your human resource management strategies and practices are to the kind of change you are trying to make. Practices or aspects of the culture that do not describe your organization should be addressed in your plans for change.
  - The human resource vice president or director has been directly involved in this project from the outset.
  - The institution has a record of keeping its promises to staff.
  - We have done a "gap analysis" that identifies the difference between current skills and skills needed after the transition.
  - The training plan that is in place (with an appropriate budget) will enable employees to learn the new skills that are required.
  - We have a performance appraisal system that works to identify the developmental needs of staff.
  - Our personnel classification system supports flexibility.
  - We reward performance and merit.
  - We are hiring staff whose competencies will suit our future needs.
  - We are willing to fire people who are unable or unwilling to meet our standards.
  - Our employees are able to assess their own ability to meet job expectations.
  - Our employees take responsibility for their own learning and development.
  - The human resource transition strategy that is in place provides for retraining, reassignment, job security, and layoff/placement support during reengineering.
  - We have made plans that allow enough time between now and the implementation date to prepare employees for their new roles.

- The sponsor understands the costs of preparing employees to be successful after the transition and will make sure that the costs are budgeted.
- There has been full communication about the changes associated with this project—employees know what to expect.
- Unit leaders are prepared to support their employees during the transition.
- We notice and celebrate small wins and changes.
- We have paced ourselves so that we are not attempting to change too much at once.
- We are going as fast as we can without jeopardizing the success of the changes we are attempting to make.
- Human resource leaders and staff feel personally responsible for the success of all employees during this transition.

Conclusion

The University of Delaware and Brigham Young University (see chapter 11) started their change processes before most of the rest of us realized the need for change. They had the luxury of learning at their own pace before the Web changed everything. Now, when these institutions consider next steps, they do so with a staff that is prepared for successful change. They are leading institutions.

For an institution that is just beginning to change today, the challenges are enormous. Few institutions of higher education are ready to undertake major change initiatives without some soul searching and preparation. At the same time, for-profit institutions of higher education that are rich with capital, corporate universities, and distance education providers threaten all but the most powerful brand name institutions. Time is not on the side of traditional institutions that need to change.

Under these conditions it is tempting to narrow your focus to the essentials and hurry to get the job done. Don't! If your review of the questions above suggests that you have work to do to get ready for change, do that work first. With a committed team of employees who are ready for change and trust that you will not forget their interests as you transform the institution, you will go far. It is not too late to be a leader.

REFERENCE

Kaplan, Robert S., and David P. Norton. 1996. *The Balanced Scorecard: Translating Strategy into Action.* Boston: The Harvard Business School Press.

Index

A

Academic
  advising 15, 22, 39, 40, 113, 114
  planning 30
  records 31, 33, 34
  registration 31, 33, 34
  services 53

Academic Progress 14
  policy 114
  report 92, 95

Access to Services 34, 88, 91, 92, 93

Accrediting Associations 14

Action Plan 30

Activity Value Analysis 38, 45

Add/Drop 23

Administrative
  processes 21, 26, 31
  services 29, 53
  software 24

Admissions 8, 10, 21, 23, 24, 26, 30, 31, 33, 34, 35, 39, 40, 44, 51, 53, 56, 57, 60, 61, 62, 63, 66, 68, 69, 70, 73, 74, 75, 78, 80, 82, 84, 87, 91, 92, 98, 102, 105, 107, 108, 109, 110, 111, 112, 117, 123, 124
  online 74, 75
  practices 66
  processes 8, 50

Advising 10, 14, 15, 16, 17, 22, 26, 33, 34, 35, 40, 44, 49, 53, 56, 60, 63, 70, 74, 78, 81, 82, 84, 91, 92, 98, 99, 100, 101, 105, 107, 109, 111, 112, 113, 114, 115, 116, 117, 120, 121, 122, 123, 124

Advocacy 31, 33, 34, 35

Ambiguity 137

American Assembly of Collegiate Schools of Business 29

American Productivity & Quality Center (APQC) 82

Application Server 76

ASCOL 75

"As is" review 38

Australian National Unified System of Higher Education 74

Automated 26
  degree audit system 110, 111
  needs analysis 52
  teller machine (ATM) 42, 43

Automated Course Exchange (ACE) 99

Automated Course Transfer System (ACTS) 8, 107, 108, 110

B

Babson College 6, Chapter 4, 135, 136, 138
  Reengineering Design Team 30, 31

Baby Boom Generation 65

Balanced Scorecard 135

Ball State University 7, 8, Chapter 13
  Automated Course Transfer System (ACTS) 8, 107, 108, 110
  objectives of transfer student program 108

Benchmark 39, 56, 100

Best Practices 7, 22, 25, 27, 113, 130, 137
  examples 48
  research 30

Billing 10, 21, 26, 30, 34, 35, 43, 44, 48, 49, 53, 63, 70, 78, 79, 80, 82, 84, 92, 99, 101, 102, 105, 112, 117, 123, 124

Bookstore Services 15

Boston College 6, Chapter 5, 48, 135, 137, 138
  AGORA 42, 43, 44
  Project Delta 6, 37, 38, 39, 40, 41, 42, 45

Branch Bank Model 81

Brigham Young University 10, Chapter 11, 139

Bureaucracy 31

■ ■ ■ ■ **B** *(continued)*

Bursar 22, 24, 26

Business
  case 23
  processes 21, 30, 32, 33, 34, 36
  rules 98, 100, 101

Buy-In 23, 32, 44, 60, 62, 63, 130

■ ■ ■ ■ **C**

Cable Television 15

California State University, Northridge 133

Canada 55

Career 55, 56, 57, 58, 60, 61, 63
  advising/counseling 15, 16, 40
  placement 34, 40
  services 10, 25, 26, 30, 31, 34, 35, 39, 44, 53,
    56, 63, 70, 78, 84, 88, 91, 92, 105, 112, 113,
    114, 116, 117, 120, 124

Career Services Center 84

Carnegie Mellon University 6, 9, Chapter 6, 138
  Enrollment Group 48, 51
  Enrollment Process Reengineering Team 48
  The HUB 9, 49, 50, 51

Cashier 48, 49, 50, 51, 52

CAUSE award for Excellence 82

CCCOnline 120, 121, 123
  goals 120

Centralization 34

Change Chapter 16
  agents 36, 133
  budget for 133
  case for 21, 29, 37, 47, 48, 52, 55, 65, 73, 79,
    87, 97, 113, 119, 135
  fear of 52, 59, 89
  initiative 32, 33
  investment in 134
  management 6, 25, 27, 31, 32, 35, 50, 60,
    131, Chapter 17
  process of 136, 137

readiness for 134, 136
  support for 135

Civil Rights Movement 65

Classification and Compensation 44

Clerical Work 24

Client-Server Environment 87

Collaboration 88, 91, 127

Colorado Community College and Occupational Education System 119

Colorado Electronic Community College
  (CECC) 7, Chapter 15

Commitment 134

Communication 6, 8, 22, 23, 25, 32, 33, 35, 36,
  38, 39, 41, 44, 45, 49, 50, 51, 52, 56, 57, 58, 59,
  60, 61, 62, 67, 68, 69, 137

Competencies 42, 44

Competency-Based Model 32

Competition 14, 28, 29

Competitive Environment 66

Component Courses 108, 109

Consultants 15, 21, 22, 24, 25, 31, 38, 44, 56,
  62, 66, 131

Consumerist Approach 28

Cornell University 135

Cost 29, 30, 37, 45
  analysis 38, 39
  increased 22, 28
  operating 30, 31, 32, 37
  recruiting 69
  reduction 21, 37
  savings 23

Council, customer or advisory 92

Counseling 117

Course Equivalency
  approval form 111

guides   108

Course Evaluation Report   108, 111

Course Selection   36, 102

Credential Review and Outcome   39

Critical Success Factors   6, 16, 27, 35, 44, 56, 62, 63, 69, 78, 79, 85, 93, 117, 124, 131, 134, 137

Cross-Functional   24, 52, 67, 68, 69
  departments   26, 67
  team   7, 8, 9, 10, 24, 26, 31, 33, 35, 38, 40, 41, 44, 50, 56, 61, 62, 63, 67, 70, 78, 84, 85, 88, 92, 105, 112, 115, 117, 124
    See also *Multidisciplinary Team*

Cross-Training   9, 22, 24, 26, 27, 28, 43, 57, 59, 62, 68, 115, 116, 131

Culture   37, 44, 48, 50, 51, 52, 56, 57, 62
  changes   34, 134, 137, 138

Curricular Innovation   29

Customer   6, 7, 8, 9, 22, 23, 24, 25, 26, 27, 28, 30, 32, 34, 35, 36, 56, 57, 58, 59, 60, 62, 127, 128, 129, 130
  services   16, 22, 23, 30, 31, 32, 42, 55, 56, 57, 58, 59, 60, 61, 62, 63, 127, 128, 129, 131
    See also *Student Services*

Customized Programs and Courses   55

■ ■ ■ ■ **D**

Decision Support Tools   49

Degree Advising (Audit) Record   97

Degree Audit Reporting System (DARS)   98, 107, 109, 110

Degree Audits   15, 16, 41, 43

Degree Audit System   98, 100

Degree/Program Booklets   108

Demographics   3, 23

Department Process Improvements   10, 26, 35, 44, 53, 63, 70, 78, 84, 92, 105, 112, 117, 123, 124

Design Team   38, 40, 41

Developmental Advising   113, 114, 117

Diagnostic Review   21

Direction Statement   6, 37, 38, 39, 41

Distance Advising   117

Distance Education/Learning   Chapter 2, 15, 83

Domain   77

Duplication of Effort/
  Redundant Work   21, 22, 34, 41, 49, 57

E ■ ■ ■ ■

Educational Planning   39, 88, 91, 92, 95

Electronic
  campus   83
  communication services   39
  resources   83
  services   14, 69, 83

E-Mail Links   121

Employees   25

Employers   55

Energy   134

Enhanced Services   21

Enrollment   21, 22, 23, 24, 25, 26, 65, 66, 69
  decline   7, 66, 107
  model   115, 117
  online   74, 75
  process   48, 49, 50, 51, 52, 74
  services   9, 21, 22, 24, 25, 26, 27, 47, 49, 50, 51, 52, 53
  statement   7
  student   17

Enterprise Resource Planning   11

Enterprise-Wide Systems   11

Evaluation   87, 90

Executive Sponsorship   6, 61, 62

■■■■ F

Facilitation 24

Facilities
management 38
space reconfiguration 43

Faculty Recruiting 37

Faculty/Staff Support 38, 42

Field-Based Learning
administration 30, 31, 34

Financial 21
counseling 49
investment 37
planning 39, 49
services 8, 31, 34, 35

Financial Aid 10, 24, 26, 30, 34, 35, 38, 39, 40, 41, 43, 44, 48, 49, 50, 52, 53, 56, 60, 61, 62, 63, 69, 70, 73, 74, 78, 79, 80, 84, 87, 88, 91, 92, 98, 99, 105, 112, 114, 116, 121, 122, 123, 124
assistance 15
enhancements 41
funding 22
investment 37
processes 22, 39, 50, 57

Floor Plan 81, 82

Focus Groups 6, 8, 22, 30, 35, 37, 43, 48, 50, 57, 58, 61, 62, 128, 129

Footers 101

Formative Measures 131

Front-Line
basic information 115
customer service 62

Funding 66

■■■■ G

Gateway 100, 101, 102

Generalist 8, 9, 24, 27, 34, 40, 52, 81, 82

GI Bill 65

Globalization 3, 13

Goals 120, 135

Grades 23, 52, 110

GradPact 100, 101

Graduation Audits 15

H ■■■■

Headers 101

Help Desk 17

High School Graduates
See *Figure 8.1, page 65*

Higher Education 13, 21, 25, 26, 28, 29, 30, 65, 66, 69

Hiring Decisions 25

Holds 23

Holistic Student Service Model 22, 26, 27, 32, 33, 62, 88

Horizontal Process 73, 74, 75, 88

Human Behavior 134

Human Resources 6, 11, 31, 32, 40, 41, 42, 43
classification and compensation 42, 44
information system 38
learning and development 42, 43
management 138, 139

Hybrid 68

I ■■■■

IBM
Best Practice Partners 5, 7, 134, 138
Best Practice Study 5, 113
Innovation in Student Services Forum 5, 56
WebSphere 76

Implementation 23, 24, 26, 27, 29, 30, 31, 35, 131

Indiana University 10, Chapter 12
automated course exchange (ACE) 99
Indiana Student Transaction Environment (*insite*) 10, 97
Student Information Systems Initiative 97, 98, 101

Information Age 3

Information Delivery 91

Information Infrastructure
  hierarchical or vertical 88
  horizontal or flat 88

Information Technology 30, 31, 32, 34, 38, 40, 41, 42, 43
  designing 88, 89
  strategic plan 26

Institution
  following 134
  leading 134, 139
  model 134

Institutional Vision 11

Instructional Technologies 17

Integrated Student Administration Services 79, 87

Integrated System 80

Integration and Access to Student Information Subcommittee 97, 98, 99, 100

Interactive Video 15, 17

Interviews 57, 61

Intranet Site 42, 58

Involvement 138

J

Job Outplacement Services 25

Jobs 27

Johnson County Community College Chapter 14
  student services model 115, 116, 118
  Student Services Statement of Values 115

K

Kiosks 4, 9, 10, 40, 69, 81, 89, 92

L

Labor Costs 23

LaunchPad 75

Leadership 6, 24, 25, 26, 27, 35, 41, 43, 44, 47, 49, 50, 51, 52, 53, 56, 62, 66, 67, 131, 133, 134, 136, 137, 138
  executive sponsor 61

Learner-Centered 14, 56

Learners 55, 56, 57, 58, 60, 61, 62
  prospective 58

Learning and Development 42, 43

Legacy Student System 87

Library
  holdings 83
  services 15, 16

Loans and Collections 39

Local Service Centers 38

Long-Range Priorities 92

M

Maintenance Institutions 110

Market 127, 128

Marketing Image 74

Massachusetts Institute of Technology 48

Measurement 135

Methodology 22, 25, 56, 57, 60, 61

Mission 48, 51, 53, 89

Multidisciplinary Team 76, 77, 78
  See also Cross-Functional team

N

National Center for Education Statistics 3

Netscape Enterprise Server 76

Network Computers 43

New England Association of Schools and Colleges 29

■ ■ ■ ■ **N** *(continued)*

New Service Model 32, 34

Newsletter 33, 57, 58, 59, 62

Nontraditional Students 3, 65

Nordstrom 129

Northern Territory University
  (Australia) 7, 73, 74, 75
    Launch Pad 75

■ ■ ■ ■ **O**

Objectives 108

Object-Oriented Programming 87

Office Structure 68

"One or none" philosophy 9

One-Stop 8, 58
    service center 7, 8, 9, 10, 22, 23, 24, 26, 27,
      35, 44, 50, 53, 60, 63, 70, 84, 92, 105, 112,
      117, 118, 124
    shopping 14, 17, 33, 34, 35, 49, 59, 60, 79, 81,
      83, 87, 91, 116, 131
    Web 75, 76, 77

Online
    application 117
    billing 117
    library 129
    registration 14, 23, 52

Open Systems Architecture 87

Operating Budgets 30

Oregon State University 8, Chapter 8, 135,
  137, 138
    Office of Admission & Orientation 66, 69

Organizational
    boundaries 87, 88
    changes 5, 38, 44
    design 30, 32, 38, 41
    goals 42
    hierarchy 22

Orientation 15

Outcomes 88, 90, 91, 127

P ■ ■ ■ ■

Paradigm Shift 67

People, Process, and Technology 6, 7, 8, 56

Performance Measures 32, 57, 59

Personal
    assistance 23, 58, 59
    communication services 39
    counseling 15
    scheduler 41
    services account 39, 41
    Web planner 75

Phases 108

Physical Plant 23
    limitations 87

Polytechnical Institute 55, 63

Positive Energy 134

Preenrollment 15

Presentation/Access 100

Presentations 61

"Primary Feeder" Institutions 109, 110

Principles 67, 88, 90

Problem Solving 47, 48, 50, 52

Process 5, 21, 22, 25, 26, 27, 79, 80, 88, 93, 130
    changes 38
    cross-functional 24
    design 41, 45
    flows 57, 60, 61
    high-level 38
    horizontal 73, 74, 75
    improvement 27, 32, 33, 36, 39, 47, 48, 61,
      68, 69, 77, 84, 123
    mapping 21, 22, 23, 33, 138
    policies and procedures 30
    redesign 5, 22
    reinvent 22, 23, 28

Process-Centered Organization 25, 26, 27

Professional Academic Advisors 109

Project Management 24, 26, 38, 133

Project Team 80, 81

Prototype 24, 25, 26, 30, 31, 32, 33, 34

■■■■ Q

Quality 47, 48, 66

■■■■ R

Records 69

Records/Learning Tracking 57, 60, 61

Recruitment and Retention 8, 65

Redesign 22, 23, 24, 25, 26, 29, 30, 31, 33, 36,
38, 39, 44, 56, 57, 58, 127, 130, 131
as a change agent 5, 6
learner-based 55
organization 38
teams 23, 62

Redesigned
processes 8, 24
services 7, 8, 10, 16, 26, 35, 44, 53, 63, 70, 78,
84, 92, 105, 112, 117, 124

Reengineering 21, 22, 23, 24, 25, 26, 27, 29, 30,
31, 32, 34, 35, 47, 48, 49, 50, 53, 67, 68, 69, 70,
79, 88, 90, 127, 138
admission 65, 66, 68
business process 38, 65

Reference Degree Report 108

Registrar 22, 24, 26, 30, 35, 39

Registration 3, 7, 8, 10, 15, 16, 24, 26, 30, 34,
35, 40, 41, 42, 44, 48, 49, 53, 56, 57, 60, 62, 63,
69, 70, 74, 78, 79, 80, 84, 87, 88, 91, 92, 96, 99,
100, 102, 104, 105, 107, 112, 113, 116, 117,
120, 123, 124, 128
audits 16

Reinvent 22, 23, 60, 61

Relational Database 87

Renovation 27

Replacement of Student Information
Systems 7, 10, 11, 26, 35, 44, 53, 63, 70, 78,
84, 85, 92, 105, 112, 117, 124

Resources and Technology 116

Results 92, 93

Retention 7, 14, 17

Return on Investment 127, 128

Review, Systemic and Strategic 93

Routine Transactions 9

S ■■■■

Second-Level Information 115

Self-Assessment 17

Self-Directed
learning 91
teams 31, 51

Self-Help 58, 59, 129
mode 81

Self-Service 8, 9, 10, 22, 23, 26, 36, 41, 42, 43,
44, 69, 81
objectives 7, 9, 10, 26, 35, 44, 53, 63, 70, 78,
84, 92, 105, 112, 117, 123, 124
options 37
technology 24, 26
transactions 40
Web-based solution 75

Self-Study 87

Service 8, 29, 30, 34, 37
orientation 26, 28
unit 40

Seton Hall University 9, Chapter 3, 136, 138
Enrollment Services 9, 22, 24, 25, 26, 27
Enrollment Services Redesign Team 22
implementation team 24, 25
student enrollment advisor (SEA) 9, 24

Silos 9, 10, 11, 25, 56, 58, 59, 60, 68, 74, 75, 77,
83, 91, 134

■■■■ **S** *(continued)*

Single Point of Contact/Service   22, 33, 34, 35, 58, 129, 131
   See also *"One or none" philosophy and One-Stop*

Skills   62, 130, 131, 133

Social Support   15, 16

Southern Alberta Institute of Technology   6, Chapter 7, 137, 138
   Customer Service Redesign Team   57, 60, 61, 62
   Implementation Team   59, 61, 62, 63

Space   43, 44

Specialist   8, 9, 24, 32, 34, 40, 49, 50, 52, 81

Staffing Levels   30, 32

Staff Relations   67, 68

Stakeholders   31, 32, 101

Standardization of Postsecondary Education Electronic Data Exchange (SPEEDE) Committee   110

Standards   74, 78, 87, 88

Strategic Planning   29, 30, 88, 131
   unit   40

Strategies   88, 90, 91

Streamlined Processes   22, 25, 27, 41, 60

Student Access Statistics   24

Student Accounts   39, 69

Student Advising   98, 105

Student-Centered   6, 7, 8, 10, 25, 26, 35, 44, 53, 63, 69, 70, 73, 78, 84, 87, 92, 105, 112, 113, 117, 123, 124

Student Development-based Philosophy   113, 116, 117, 118

Student Development/Career/Life Planning Model   117

Student Information Systems Initiative (SIS)   97, 98, 101

Student Information Systems Steering Committee   98

Student Life Model   38, 42

Student Loans Administration   30

Student Market Analysis/Development   39

Student Planning Services   87

Student Planning System   88, 90, 92

Student Profile   92

Student-Related Business Processes   34

Student Resumé   92, 94

Student Satisfaction   38, 39

Student Services   15, 38, 42, 43, 44
   model   9, 37, 38, 114, 115, 116
   support unit   40
   trends   7, 10, 26, 34, 35, 44, 53, 63, 69, 70, 78, 84, 92, 105, 112, 117, 123, 124

Subject Matter Specialists   24, 26, 32, 56, 60, 131

Summative Measures   131

Support   70

Support Services Personnel   107

Surveys   5, 6, 8, 32, 39, 52, 57, 58, 61, 128, 129

Systemic
   change   7, 10, 11, 26, 35, 44, 52, 53, 63, 70, 78, 84, 92, 105, 112, 117, 123, 124
   issues   88

T ■■■■

Tactical Strategies   98

Team   24, 38, 39, 40, 41, 42, 44, 45
   leader   27, 41
   work   42

Technical
   assistance   15
   skills   15, 17

Technology   5, 6, 7, 8, 9, 10, 11, 13, 14, 17, 21, 22, 23, 24, 27, 37, 38, 39, 44, 56, 57, 59, 60, 62

as a change agent 5, 6
as an enabler 56, 57, 60, 62
back-end 40
changes 38
design 41
enabling 31
front-end 40
infrastructure 38, 55
initiatives 89
planning 80
requirements 38, 39, 40, 41, 43

Threaded Discussions 122

Time Measurements 48

Touch-Tone Technology 9, 10, 92
bill payments 99, 102
financial aid system touch-tone 99
grade inquiry 99
Interactive Voice Response 99
registration 10, 99

Town Hall 33, 57, 58, 59, 62, 130, 131

Traditional Services 3, 73, 74, 77, 120

Training 6, 22, 24, 27, 32, 33, 42, 43, 44, 55, 56,
57, 58, 60, 61, 62, 63, 134

Transcript Evaluation 15

Transfer of Skills 24

Transfer Students 107, 108, 109, 110
recruitment of 107, 108, 111

Transformation 6, 21, 26, 28, 37, 56, 62, 63, 79,
80, 82, 84, 127, 129, 130, 131

Trends 13, 28
"good practice" 16
student services
See *Student Services trends*

Tuition 29, 30, 37

University Information Technology Services
(UITS) 99

University of Delaware 9, 22, 48, Chapter 10,
137, 138, 139

University of Minnesota 7, 74, 75, 104
One-Stop Web 75, 76

University of Pennsylvania 48

U.S. Department of Education 13, 121, 123
Fund for the Improvement of Postsecondary
Education (FIPSE) 15

User-Centered Design 11, 76, 77, 78

U.S. News & World Report 29

Values 48, 51, 53

Videotapes 15

Virtual Student Information Services 105

Vision 48, 51, 53
and goals 6
statement 48, 57

Visioning Workshop 57, 61

Voice Response 40, 42, 99, 115

U

Understanding 134

Union 24, 130

W

Waiting Lists 41

Web (Internet) 7, 9, 10, 11, 15, 17, 23, 28, 37,
40, 41, 43, 45, 55, 56, 59, 60, 69, 79, 81, 82, 83,
84, 85, 115, 116, 117, 128
access 41, 58, 97, 100
advising 101, 102
design 7, 11
development office 112
front-end 24, 62
infrastructure 61
interface 25, 55
navigation 41
portal 74, 75, 78

 **W** *(continued)*

site   73, 74, 75, 78, 83, 84

technology   37, 39

Web-Based (Internet)

application   108

architecture   87, 91

course delivery   124

enrollment   117

information   117

service delivery   38, 40, 69

student services   16, 42, 73

technology   26, 28

Web-Enabled   36

applications   32

reference audit   108

services   7, 9, 10, 26, 34, 35, 44, 52, 53, 63, 70, 78, 84, 92, 105, 112, 117, 123, 124

software package   27

"Web-Stop-Shopping"   111, 112

Western Cooperative for Educational Telecommunications   14

Western Interstate Commission on Higher Education (WICHE)   14

Work flow   27, 75

Z ■ ■ ■ ■

"Zero or One" Strategy   84, 85

Editors

MARTHA BEEDE, a senior consultant for IBM Global Education, has worked with organizations in the public, private, and not-for-profit sectors for the past 15 years. During the past 10 years, she has worked primarily with higher education institutions, assisting in improving service and efficiency through organizational, process, and technology changes. She specializes in helping institutions redesign their student service operations to meet the demands of today's environment. She has been involved in a number of studies on best practices in student services and has focused her efforts on working with the best practice leaders to move the student services agenda forward. She is also responsible for planning, coordinating, and hosting the annual Innovation in Student Services Forum. She has published articles and delivered numerous presentations on best practices in student services.

DARLENE BURNETT is senior consultant with IBM Education Consulting & Services and has more than 25 years' experience working with technology and services. During the past 10 years, she has helped colleges and universities solve problems and implement technology and services in administrative and academic computing. Her focus is on helping institutions move toward student-, staff-, and faculty-centered services with an emphasis on productivity, effectiveness, accountability, and improved access and quality. In 1994, she began research on student-centered services and studies on best practices in student services. At IBM she has been recognized for her achievement in improving and integrating existing processes to improve effectiveness, quality, and customer satisfaction. She frequently speaks about student services and has published a number of articles on the topic.

About SCUP

The mission of the Society for College and University Planning is to promote the advancement and application of effective planning in higher education. SCUP members span multiple planning disciplines—from facilities, academic, and information technology planning to fiscal and resource allocation. All types of institutions, systems, governing boards, and commercial firms share the philosophy that cross-boundary planning is integral to the health and vitality of higher education.

SCUP was founded in 1965 and has 4,300 institutional and individual members worldwide.

PHONE: (734) 998-7832

FAX: (734) 998-6532

E-MAIL: scup@scup.org

WEB: www.scup.org